TALES FROM
The Top Table

TALES FROM
The Top Table

How boxing's superstars took over a town

CRAIG BIRCH

First published by Pitch Publishing, 2019

Pitch Publishing
A2 Yeoman Gate
Yeoman Way
Worthing
Sussex
BN13 3QZ
www.pitchpublishing.co.uk
info@pitchpublishing.co.uk

ISBN 978 1 78531 537 4

Typesetting and origination by Pitch Publishing
Printed and bound in India by Replika Press Pvt. Ltd.

CONTENTS

The oracle – foreword by Richie Woodhall 7

Your author – Craig Birch 18

1. When pretty boy met pretty woman – Floyd Mayweather . 25

2. Made a scapegoat for what went wrong – Ray Mancini . . . 40

3. When the tables were well and truly turned – Vinny Paz. . . .61

4. This could have been different – Barry McGuigan 87

5. It's undisputed he's a tartan legend – Ken Buchanan 105

6. Building an empire, building a legacy – Anthony Joshua
   and Carl Frampton .127

7. From the Dark Destroyer came light – Nigel Benn 151

8. An enigma wrapped in a riddle – Chris Eubank 179

9. You only get out what you put in – Steve Collins 207

10. Unbeatable to the last – Joe Calzaghe 229

11. The cobra may be no saint – Carl Froch and George Groves 261

12. Back from the brink – Tyson Fury 296

THE ORACLE – FOREWORD BY RICHIE WOODHALL

BOXING has been a huge part of my life. It was the same for my father, Len, who is sadly no longer with us. We had some great times together.

Dad was from West Bromwich, that's why I'm an Albion football fan, but I was born in Polesworth, a part of Warwickshire. We lived there for a couple of years.

Dad was a bricklayer, so he went where there was lots of work for him and that took us to Telford in 1970, when I was two years old.

My mother is actually Dutch. Everyone knows her as Vicky but her actual name is Wilhelmina. She came over to England after the Second World War.

Mum settled in Birmingham, where she met my dad, and they got married. When we got to Telford, we moved to Woodside, which was one of the new estates that had been built.

There wasn't a lot to do apart from go to the community club, which became a boxing gym in the evening. Dad became a coach there, because he'd done a bit himself as an amateur.

My elder brother, Lawrence, started boxing before me. I first went along when I was about seven and you can't have a proper bout until you're 11.

I learned my trade. I went because it was something to do and I just became good at it. That said, I lost my first fight.

I never won a national title as an amateur. I got to the semi-finals twice as a schoolboy, at 12 and 16. One of those years, I had to box eight times to get that far. It was tough back then.

I made my England debut when I was 18 and my career really took off from there. I represented my country 35 times and only lost five of those.

It was obvious my style was more suited to international boxing and, mainly because of that, I got picked to go to the 1988 Olympic Games in South Korea.

I lost, in the semis, but no one had really heard of my opponent, Roy Jones Jr, before then. In fact, at 19, he was the youngest boxer on the US team.

It was there where I believe Roy was born as a fighter. He got to the final and won it, for me, but didn't get the decision. I got a bronze medal, so it was a good Olympics for me.

It took the best boxer in the tournament, who didn't have it all his own way, to beat me. I won the second round of the three, remember. I could see the positives.

I was always very confident in my ability and, two years later, I had another great experience at the Commonwealth Games in New Zealand. That time, I got the gold.

I had a good think about what to do next. It was another two years until the next Olympics and I was getting loads of offers to go pro. I decided that was the time.

I turned over with Mickey Duff and won the Commonwealth title in my ninth pro fight, then became European champion.

I knew I'd do well, because my style was to hit and not get hit. I was disappointed not to get a shot at the British title, but I went up to world level after that.

I only ever lost three times as a pro, and they were all for world titles. Joe Calzaghe was the best I've ever been in with, but Markus Beyer and Keith Holmes were also excellent.

My contract expired after I went over to America to take on Holmes. Mickey lost his television deal with the BBC, so I signed with Frank Warren. Some said that I jumped ship, but I didn't.

It was my night to become a world champion against Thulani Malinga and I didn't want to do it anywhere else than Telford, in front of my own supporters. It was a dream come true.

Beyer boxed really well to beat me in Telford for the belt a year later, so there was no shame in it. He was very good. It was Calzaghe and then retirement for me.

When my career came to an end, I hadn't really planned ahead, so I was lucky that the BBC gave me a call about becoming a pundit and commentator, which I'm still doing now.

This is my second stint as a coach for Team GB. My first spell didn't work out but I went back in 2009, when there were a few changes in the air.

I can't work there full time, because of my commitments to television, so I'm only there two days a week. It's great to work with the best amateur boxers, on all new methods of training.

I came to be involved with Bar Sport through the owner, Scott Murray, who is an old friend. I remember him boxing as an amateur himself.

He asked me to come down and do the interviewing for one of his events. I can't remember who the first one was but it was good. I've been coming from Telford to Cannock ever since.

Floyd Mayweather may have been the biggest name they've had there, but I wouldn't say it was the most enjoyable interview. It was fantastic to have him there, though.

It went OK. I was told beforehand I'd only get 20 minutes but I managed to get more. I didn't speak to Mayweather before or after the speech; he just came in and we took it from there.

It was no problem. I knew all about his career and it turned out to be a good interview. It wasn't as if he was bored; he was quite happy to talk with me.

Some of his people were telling me I needed to wrap it up and, if they hadn't, I think he would have chatted to me for longer. He seemed to be enjoying the questions.

What he has done in the sport is unbelievable, to amass that winning record and win all of those world titles is remarkable. He was a brilliant fighter and a very clever man, too.

It's difficult to compare people from different eras and weights, but many people talk of Mayweather as one of the pound-for-pound greats.

What was so good about him was how he handled any style of boxer put in front of him. No matter whether it was a front-foot fighter or how strong they were, he just dealt with it.

He built up that record having taken on the best that was out there and beat them convincingly, having never looked troubled.

You've got to give him credit, although there are people who are not fans of his because of the way he fights. He boxes to his strengths and doesn't let his opponent do the same.

There are not many who can go through 12 rounds and you can count the times they've been hit with clean punches on one hand. He came out, sometimes, without a mark on him.

Ray Mancini was another nice interview for me to do. He's a lovely bloke and I always looked upon him as a great world champion. Had he been boxing today, he'd have been a superstar of the sport. It was really interesting to hear his story and he's become a very successful man.

When Vinny Paz came, the first thing he said to me was, 'I've always wanted to meet you, I was getting ready to fight you.' We'd lined it up, but he wanted too much money.

I told him that and we had a little joke. He thought he would have beaten me, until we met and he couldn't believe how tall I was. We had another good laugh about that!

Ken Buchanan deserves to be talked about as one of the best British boxers of all time. When I was asking him questions, I wanted to know the answers as a fan myself.

Dad always used to talk about him when I was a kid, so I learned about Ken from a young age. His career was incredible. Again, if he'd been fighting today, he'd earn millions.

It was such an entertaining night with Barry McGuigan. I could have talked to him until the cows came home about boxing. He was brilliant.

I've known Barry for a long time anyway and I've always admired him. I thought his left hook to the body was the best in the business, at that time.

Barry was a great fighter. I'm a massive fan of his and I was still a teenager when he won his world title. He's someone I've looked up to since I was an amateur.

When I watched him become a world champion, I was camping with a bunch of mates. We had a little portable TV, which we rigged up to the car battery.

I first started to concentrate on Carl Frampton after he'd turned pro, but I remember him as an amateur for Ireland. He always said boxing for his country meant a lot to him.

I thought he was very explosive and sharp, even back then, I liked his technique and he had some fast combinations. Years later, I interviewed him at Bar Sport, which was ironic.

I've been to Belfast to watch him and the atmosphere was unbelievable. Protestants and Catholics come together to support him. He's got a special relationship with both of them.

Almost all of us get beat and you lick your wounds when that happens. I've been there. You go home, spend time with your family, have a few days to recover and then go again.

I know Anthony Joshua very well. He was obviously part of the Olympic cycle for 2012, so I trained him quite a lot. I've taken him on the pads many times. I still see him frequently.

He's got one of the most incredible stories out of them all, to be honest, because four years before that he wasn't even boxing.

To be an Olympic champion and then become the superstar he has is sensational. He's used to speaking in public now, but he hadn't done a lot when he came to Cannock.

'Josh' is a great talker anyway, so he wasn't nervous at all. I just told him to act like it was a chat between me and him. It went well, on both occasions.

I came into the super middleweight division just after Chris Eubank, Nigel Benn and Steve Collins, but I looked up to the three of them.

Nigel was a fearless fighter, who could knock you out with either hand. He had some skill, as well, but his main strength was his power. I admire him, so to interview him was fantastic.

Eubank is a strange character. He doesn't actually do many after-dinner events, so I was a bit surprised to be interviewing him. He demands that you listen to him when he speaks.

He made it easy, actually. I kept my mouth shut and butted in occasionally! I'd ask him a question, he'd go off on one and we'd have four or five other topics to talk about next.

He thanked me for the interview afterwards, but he also said that these shows are not really his thing. It was just as well Bar Sport got him when they did.

I love Collins, he was one of my heroes. The thing with him is that he learned his craft the hard way in America, losing two world title shots there before he got it right.

I was always guided by my dad and he always said Collins was a proper fighting man, because of his pedigree and how tough he had it coming through the ranks.

He persevered and became a two-weight world champion, which showed what a class act he was. He was a brilliant fighter. I've spoken to him many times and he's a great lad.

I didn't win my world title until 1998, so I was young and up and coming and he was much more experienced than me. We didn't meet at all before he retired. Going up against people like Collins would have been massive fights financially, but the man at the top when I was trying to get there was Malinga.

Equally, when I was at middleweight, the world champion I went up against was Keith Holmes. That's the way it is; you get in there and fight whoever you get the chance to fight.

What would have happened if Mike Tyson had boxed Lennox Lewis at his peak? Lewis knocked him out but had Tyson been at his very best, then you just don't know.

Super middle has always been a competitive weight, but it was definitely stronger when Benn, Eubank and Collins were there, compared to when I was a world champion.

Calzaghe brought the division on after that and he had it all, as I can attest. I don't understand how he has *any* critics.

He never avoided anyone and you box who is out there at the time. To debate whether he would beat anyone before him, at their peak, is a hypothetical question.

He came out on top against who was out there. The only other thing he could have done would have been to beat Rocky Marciano's record of 49-0 and get there before Mayweather.

One of those wins was against me. It was weird; we were good friends but we had to box each other, because we were managed by the same promoter (Warren).

We had to show our professionalism, put that to one side and get on with it. The fight was offered to us and neither one was going to back down.

It just had that little bit of extra spice to it and everyone wanted to see it happen. It was a good all-British world title fight.

I had no complaints about the stoppage (in the tenth), but I think it was always close and competitive. I had spells and moments in the contest where I think I did OK.

I came forward and hit him with some really good shots that just bounced off him and, in the end, he came through it.

As an opponent, Joe just had all of the answers for me. He's an underestimated fighter technically, too. He was exceptional.

He had a great chin, he was powerful, he could fight on the inside or at range and he put me up against it. He was that little bit too sharp for me.

You only know that when you are in there with him, but it still took him ten rounds to stop me. He was a good 12-round fighter, though; he finished as strong as he started.

I was still a name, to some degree, so it was a good win for Joe and he got a lot of credit for it. I was a genuine contender.

It was my last chance to become a two-time champion and I already considered him, at the time, to be the best out there at the weight.

I wanted to test myself and, if you're a true fighter, you go after the top names, but I was coming to the end of my career anyway.

When you've had enough mentally, that's probably a bigger question mark on your career than the physical side of it. That's when you know it's time to call it a day.

Once he'd beat me, I'd had enough. There's no turning back after that. You can try and have a go again but, deep down, you know it's over. I was clever enough to see that clearly.

People love the British world title fights; you had me and Joe and then the really big nights like Eubank–Benn. Carl Froch versus George Groves, I'd say, was up there with that.

They genuinely didn't like each other. They kept a lid on it to a certain degree but you could see it was the real deal. It was fierce between them.

Froch may have won both contests, but I thought George was competitive in both of them despite the manner in which he lost.

You have to respect how he carried on after that, battling and battling until he eventually became a world champion. I was proud of him.

George is a good all-rounder with an underestimated jab, in my eyes, and he's powerful. Unfortunately for him, Froch was one of the toughest I've seen in the ring.

Froch deserves to be remembered as one of the best. In his time, I can't name another British boxer who went on a run like him. He was the perfect role model for young fighters.

Tyson Fury is a natural for this sport, but I think the most of him for what he has become as a person. He's taken everything that has happened to him and come back.

He's a true fighting man, like he says he is, and he's probably got more fans now than he's ever had. I hope he gets the credit he deserves. He'll always be a huge draw.

I remember being in the minority when he beat Wladimir Klitschko; in fact I think I was the only pundit who had him down to win from the start.

It wasn't just that Klitschko boxed badly, it was a good display from Fury. I just knew he had the height and reach to do a job, if his performance was good enough.

He was an up-and-coming kid and Klitschko was nearly a 40-year-old bloke. For me, there was no doubt he was going to win and I couldn't see why other people thought differently.

You speak to these guys and, when you learn how they got to the top, they are amazing stories and that's why they are special people.

These are not normal everyday fighters; most of the people I have interviewed in Cannock are among the elite. They are like the kings of the Premier League!

I must be doing something right, because Bar Sport keep asking me to come back. I'm more than happy for that to continue.

YOUR AUTHOR – CRAIG BIRCH

THERE'S something magical about rubbing shoulders with the boxing heroes who seem to be larger than life on our television screens and devices.

Because, make no bones about it, that's as close as most of us get to today's world champions and yesterday's superstars.

The majority of fans don't have the money to jet around the globe, following their fortunes as they do battle in the ring. It's not a cheap hobby. But, even if they did, they probably wouldn't be afforded the sort of access an intimate behind-closed-doors date with their idols can offer.

How many people have gone abroad to watch boxing and not got within ten feet of those they are following? Like football, you're talking about most of those making the trip.

It's not the fighter's fault; they go where they are told and, for the most part, pay little attention to what's going on around them. Above all, they have a job to do.

If they see you, almost all of them have no problem posing for a selfie and the like, but you can nigh on guarantee that any meeting will be short-lived.

Much like the beautiful game, there's that ever-increasing danger that pugilists are becoming more and more detached from their audience. That debate rages and is ongoing.

The major difference is that most boxers don't usually make the vast amounts of cash that footballers do and, therefore, are always open to ways to supplement their income.

Sponsorship and endorsements help, but a few grand on the hip to go out and talk about your passion to like-minded people is hardly hod carrying.

That's where the after-dinner circuit comes into play and thrives, proving a happy marriage for those who crave the opportunity to meet celebrities.

And the Premier Suite, upstairs at Bar Sport in the little Staffordshire town of Cannock, offers more of an intimate experience than most to meet the stars.

This is no huge hall, where feature attractions sometimes appear with those not in receipt of VIP access, often shunted into balconies or areas a good way away from the stage.

The Premier Suite holds just 300 people and the owner Scott Murray won't cram anyone else in to make a quick profit. So, at the most, you'll be watching a show with 299 others.

It's a decade-long love affair for Scott, who boxed at a decent level himself as an amateur. It's clear boxing fans know how to please boxing fans. We've shared a few years working together as 'reporter' and 'promoter', with me the scribe and him a former fighter who became a businessman.

Words and the sweet science became united for me from May 2008, when I started covering the sport for a newspaper in the West Midlands.

The *Express & Star* presented that opportunity and I became their 'boxing man'. Hundreds of shows and thousands of bouts followed and the passion remains.

It was by no means my first dance as a reporter. I'd been publishing works since 2003, but boxing became my niche subject.

I'd had a passing interest in boxing from childhood. My first memory, aged ten, was watching the Nigel Benn–Chris Eubank rematch on television.

A nice memory was completing my first scorecard, which had Benn winning. We'll cover that, from both sides, in the book.

Equally fulfilling was telling my mother, stepfather and anyone who would listen, as a mouthy teenager, that Lennox Lewis would beat Mike Tyson.

Years later, when I started covering boxing as a professional writer, it became clear that this was something to become properly immersed in.

Football had been my sport and where my journalism career started, covering games for newspapers, but all that changed and for the greater good.

Small hall shows were where I cut my teeth, until I met Scott and started to attend his events. The things you heard on stage always stuck with you.

As a reporter, the big question was how best to use the fantastic stories, anecdotes and controversial views that emanated from the fighters' public speaking.

Features of considerable length appeared in the sports pages, but such is the pace of a hard news operation that no matter how good the material is, it soon becomes tomorrow's chip paper.

How do you immortalise these things? The most pressing concern was to make sure that none of the entertaining tales from the ring told within those four walls ever went to waste.

That's where the premise of this book came from. Different stories, which can be picked up or put down at leisure, are where all of these great memoirs lie.

In this case, 12 chapters, each devoted to a different boxer, capture just how much fun this has been. All are undoubted stars or former world champions, and some Hall of Famers.

Bar Sport is, without doubt, more than holding its own in attracting the cream of the crop from the 'circuit'. Long may it continue for the locals.

It was where Floyd Mayweather paid his first visit to the West Midlands, an evening that Cannock, the local press and the media beyond went wild for.

By then, it was just the tip of the iceberg as a multitude of fellow world champions had already provided the Premier Suite with an insight into the 'wow' factor.

Mayweather appeared to have the time of his life, too, when it emerged he had whisked away a shop worker from Dudley he met on the night to his life of luxury.

His arrival was the stuff of legend as a fleet of luxury cars cruised through Cannock, including a black Rolls-Royce containing 'Pretty Boy'. Bewildered residents watched in awe.

Ray Mancini and Scott have become firm friends since 'Boom Boom' first came to town, and they remain close. His story about threatening Quentin Tarantino will take some beating.

I'd watched *Bleed for This* the day Vinny Paz came to town, which only made me want to meet him more.

Bar Sport have become heavily involved with the Ken Buchanan Foundation, too, so his visit proved to be just the start of something.

The whole Premier Suite turned Irish green the night Barry McGuigan was the special guest, and he was great value.

He loved it there and it wasn't the last time an Irishman appeared, with Carl Frampton, joined by Steve Collins, to follow.

Anthony Joshua has a soft spot for the place as his first after-dinner speaking engagement came there. He's been back again since.

You'd have to have been living under a rock somewhere, or simply too young, not to remember the Benn–Eubank rivalry from yesteryear, or the Carl Froch–George Groves feud of the modern day.

It was great to see Joe Calzaghe and Richie Woodhall – the latter permanently on hand as host and interviewer for the main event – reunited and still the best of friends.

Richie retired after losing to Joe in 2000, when the Welshman was putting together a record-breaking run as WBO super middleweight champion.

That was the first time Richie had posed questions to someone he'd traded blows with, which made it a trip down memory lane.

Enzo Calzaghe was there, too, and he is sadly no longer with us. It turned out to be the last time most of us ever saw him.

Richie is an integral part of the show and without his inside knowledge as a star and student of the sport, the offerings on the whole would certainly have been the lesser for it.

He takes his job seriously, just like with anything he's involved in. His research and general nous is outstanding. If you've seen him first hand, you'd argue he's the best pundit around.

A heartfelt personal thank you must go to Richie because, without him, this book wouldn't have been possible. He's a top bloke in every sense of the words.

My appreciation must also go to Scott, everyone at Bar Sport Cannock and James Ward who, with Gold Star Promotions, has been responsible for bringing most of the fighters over.

You'll see some great pictures in this book, too, and that is down to the work of Glenn Curley, a super snapper and a good friend of mine.

It takes two to tango with anything that goes on inside the ropes, and that premise has been adopted here. Richie's got the most out of all of them, including Mr Mayweather.

It seems fitting that the first chapter in this book is about Mayweather, while the last goes through the mental torment and recovery of Tyson Fury.

This takes nothing away from the other chapters, all of which have been a blast to research, transcribe and write.

It was towards the end of writing this book that Mayweather and Fury, before the latter boxed Deontay Wilder, were pictured together in America.

They had met at a Lakers basketball match in Los Angeles, a world away from Cannock. With 77 pro wins between them at the time, it was again the stuff of legend.

To get a proper understanding of where Mayweather, Fury and the other interview subjects have really come from and what they've been through, read on.

I could carry on waxing lyrical about the good times that have been had by all, but that's not what we're here for. That will soon become apparent.

CHAPTER ONE

WHEN PRETTY BOY MET PRETTY WOMAN – FLOYD MAYWEATHER

FAST cars, a hefty entourage and a life-changing story for one girl who attended – Floyd Mayweather Jr's visit had the hallmarks of a night of bling with the king of the ring.

'Money Mayweather' stayed true to type for the few short hours that his evening's duty called to attend a part of the world you can bet your bottom dollar he'd never heard of before.

Undoubtedly the biggest coup to that date for Bar Sport in Cannock was to attract the man who, at the time, was still the highest-paid athlete on the planet.

Only golf icon Arnold Palmer, Vince McMahon (owner of WWE pro wrestling, arguably not a sport), Formula One driver Michael Schumacher and golfer Tiger Woods had earned more.

The fighter who proclaims himself to be 'The Best Ever' had first hung up his gloves after his previous bout, exactly five months earlier, having banked a whopping $650 million for his exploits.

An easy points win over Andre Berto equalled Rocky Marciano's record-breaking undefeated record of 49-0 and, without question, earned him a place among the finest of all time.

You can never say never again in boxing, though, and Mayweather would indeed get back in the ring to take on Conor McGregor, but only when the money was right.

He netted a whopping $100 million to punch for pay one last time, with Irishman McGregor also earning his biggest purse of $30 million.

Mayweather's tenth-round stoppage win earned him his first KO since beating Victor Ortiz in 2011, the latter by count-out in the fourth after what many fans saw as a cheap pot-shot.

Some will argue that halting McGregor was Mayweather's first legitimate stoppage in nearly ten years, when Ricky Hatton was decked for the finish in the same round.

It was the right way to go for Mayweather, who probably knew deep down that he was always going to lace on the gloves again.

He had filed a number of '50-0' trademarks long before he agreed to fight again, and it was hard to envisage him walking away for good until he'd beaten Marciano's tally.

Timing can be everything, in life as well as boxing, and the only thing Mayweather is better at than boxing is drawing cash into his coffers. All of this came in his twilight years.

The writing had been on the wall since May 2015, when he settled the years-long debate over who would prevail out of him and Manny Pacquiao with another clear points win.

He was as Vegas as his flashy persona, having boxed his last 11 bouts at the MGM Grand Garden Arena in Paradise, Nevada, before taking on McGregor at the T-Mobile Arena.

He'd already been acknowledged as the best draw Las Vegas ever had when he toured the UK, as an after-dinner speaker, for the first time.

So what was he doing in Cannock again? Most people, initially, refused to believe that it would happen and that hurt ticket sales.

Others thought that it was some sort of con, believing the all-too-familar adage that if something is too good to be true then it probably is. A sponsor pulled out on such grounds.

It left promoter Scott Murray with a dilemma ahead of staging the event, which he'd originally planned for the larger Vox Centre in Birmingham with his business partners.

The Vox, which was newly opened at the time, would have cost a bomb to hire and the sums, even with the venue packed to the rafters, didn't make for great reading.

The obvious solution was to move the show to the Premier Suite which, while cutting the capacity to 300, offered level footing on grounds the organisers knew.

Bar takings and the like went back into the pot and if Scott could trust anyone to pull off Mayweather's appearance without major problems, it was his own team.

They'd endured the carnage that can come with big names before and have since. When football legend Pele came the next year, Scott didn't even try to take him anywhere else.

Just like that, Mayweather was Cannock-bound. The biggest problem was to make sure he actually turned up.

This is not like booking any celebrity. His lordship has the resources to please himself in any situation. What were you going to do, sue him? He'd already left Scott panic-stricken once.

After arriving in England, Mayweather suddenly boarded his private jet and vanished to Turkey. Turned out he was just popping to a friend's restaurant for a meal before flying back.

That's the lifestyle you can afford if you happen to be 'the Floyd', and there are few people you have to answer to if you're him.

Scott had him under contract, true, but whatever he'd have asked him for back would have been chicken feed to the defendant. And there's no compensation for the loss of reputation.

It was literally in Mayweather's always-formidable hands. All anybody could do was just wait and see how it panned out.

The start of the night went like any other function there, but without the meet-and-greet with the feature attraction that usually occurs in a private room.

There was the usual meal, raffle, auction and so on in front of a top table that Mayweather was never going to sit on anyway. He would appear, speak, pose for photos and be gone.

Everyone was on tenterhooks until just after 9pm, when a fleet of luxury black vehicles – along with a lime green Lamborghini supercar – cruised through the neighbouring streets.

They were all on loan from a company that took the late-notice job through Scott's friend and ex-boxer Richard Carter, who made the arrangements. Most drivers worked for free.

Mayweather drove one of the Rolls-Royces, kerbing both of the front wheels as he wrestled with the twists and turns in the roads of a good old English town.

After damaging the alloys, he was heard shouting 'he's going to kill me' when he reached his destination, referring to the co-owner of the Midlands-based Celebrity Super Car Hire firm.

They seemed to care about as much as anyone in Bar Sport did, after getting the star rub and a £1,200 tip to boot. With that, Mayweather proved true to his word – he was here.

Out, also, jumped his trademark entourage of 26 people, some of them the biggest of burly men, who were unlikely to have any problems keeping him safe.

He was ushered into the same room where the meet-and-greet normally takes place to 'chill' with his 'Money Team', providing a wish list of requirements that needed to be there.

With Mayweather fed, watered and feeling relaxed, the strains of 'Versace' by hip hop group Migos started to play around the stage and ended up on loop for a good 15 minutes.

In he came, just after 10.15pm, clad in a black jacket, red t-shirt and baseball cap, with a diamond-encrusted watch and star medallion ticking the 'bling' box.

Flanked by his security, he sat down to chat with fellow former world champion Richie Woodhall and appeared at ease, occasionally stopping to sip a cup of coffee.

We were in Richie's hands now. They seemed to hit it off and Mayweather spoke openly and candidly about most things he was asked. Like with this book, there was no point telling Floyd how great he was in the hour, or just under, that ensued. It was about getting to know him on a personal level.

He wasn't always rich; in fact at times he was thought to be dirt poor. The writing had always been on the wall, though, as he'd been born into a boxing brood.

He was originally Floyd Sinclair, of Grand Rapids in Michigan, before changing his name to match his father's and become Mayweather Jr, aged 11.

His upbringing seemed to be as much characterised by drugs as boxing. His mother, Deborah, was an addict. He also had an aunt who died of AIDS.

Floyd Mayweather Sr had once been shot by his brother-in-law after a feud while holding Floyd Jr as a baby.

The subsequent wound to the leg ruined dad Floyd's own boxing career and he would later turn to drug dealing to make ends meet.

Floyd Sr had been a former national amateur champion who turned pro while one of his two younger brothers, Roger, won two world titles. Both would later work as Floyd Jr's coach.

Their mum, Bernice, had another son, Jeff, who was also a world champion, albeit holding the lesser IBO belt to Roger's WBA and WBC honours. She encouraged them all to box.

Grandmother played as big a part as anyone in making Floyd Jr the success he is today, despite Floyd Sr and Roger's influence in the corner. The man himself tells you as much.

He said that night: 'My grandmother was one of life's fighters and she made me believe I was going to be a champion. We came from a fighting family, but she raised me.

'My mother was doing drugs and her brother shot my father. My dad used me as a human shield, once, because he knew he wasn't going to shoot me.

'But things happen and you learn as life throws obstacles at you, but I found something to dedicate myself to and work hard.

'The first flashy people I knew were the kids in the neighbourhood; we used to call them the "go-getters". When I was 16, I was the same.

'I encourage every young male and female to stay in school, because it's very important. I took a chance, but I always knew school would still be there.

'From the first day I went to the boxing gym, I knew I was going to be a mega superstar. I rolled the dice and it paid off.

'I kept focused, I had tunnel vision and continued to believe. I knew I could make money from the sport, but I wasn't sure to what level.

'I've put my family in a great position; my four children will have the best education money can buy and go to the best schools. By the time I was 20, I was a millionaire.

'It wasn't all about the money, it's just a great comfort for me. The first thing I did was to buy my mother life insurance and make sure she was secure.

'Eyes are the keys to your soul and I would rather be hated for being honest than loved for telling a pretty lie. As long as God knows what I'm doing, that's all that matters.

'All I want to do is work hard for the people who are inspired by me, because we all dream. If there's something you believe in that you know you can do, go for it.'

The younger Floyd had the boxing beliefs of his fellow Mayweathers drilled into him from the crib, but it soon became apparent he would become better than they could ever wish to be.

There's wasn't much common ground between the three, as they became a warring faction. Roger and Floyd Sr don't get on, and neither have little Floyd and big Floyd most of the time.

Roger claims to have made Floyd Jr the force he is, while Floyd Sr contests that it's down to him. The piggy in the middle had abilities neither could teach, though.

Speed and movement, cat-like reflexes, ring savvy and a slippery defensive style, even when cornered, that could make opponents move on to his punches made for boxing clinics.

Tales of him in the gym, aged just ten, standing on an apple box to reach the speed bag and then pelting the instrument, two handed without looking, became the stuff of legend.

He mastered the old 'shoulder roll' better than anyone before him and, as he rose to the top, comparisons with the Sugar Rays – Robinson and Leonard – and Muhammad Ali grew.

A high school dropout, it was boxing or nothing when Mayweather was an amateur. That saw three Golden Gloves national titles and a place at a home Olympic Games in 1996.

The year of his first Golden Gloves title, 1993, came with a bitter pill to swallow as his father was jailed for five and a half years for cocaine trafficking.

He was robbed blind at the Olympics after narrowly outpointing Lorenzo Aragon by a point to became the first US boxer to beat a Cuban in 20 years of the Games.

He would not get the gold medal bout that he deserved, later losing to Bulgaria's Serafim Todorov in a decision so controversial his country filed a protest.

It was a miscarriage of justice worse than fellow American Roy Jones Jr's defeat to Park Si-Hun at the 1988 Olympics in Seoul. Even the referee raised Mayweather's hand by mistake.

He turned pro and took on Roger as coach, which changed to Floyd Sr in 1998 when he was released from prison. They split in 2000 and reunited in 2013, with Roger back in between. It was Floyd Sr who led him to his first world title, in his 18th paid outing, later that year. It came against his son's boxing hero, Genaro Hernandez.

He picked up the WBC and lineal super featherweight crowns, after the champion's corner pulled him out in the eighth round. Mayweather paid for his funeral after he died in 2011.

He told the audience: 'From when I started to use the speed bag, people used to come to the gym and go "watch this kid".

'If you ask me who had the biggest influence of my career, I'd have to tell you it was my father. He taught me what the sweet science of boxing really is, to hit and not get hit.

'It's exciting to see two guys go toe to toe but, if you want any sort of longevity, you have to be a smart defensive fighter. Uncle Roger was more about offence. I was a mix of the two.

'The way I was performing, I would have won that gold medal. We all know I got ripped off, but it made me strive and work hard to ensure it didn't happen again.

'I turned pro and things started moving on along very quickly. The first time [debut against Roberto Apodaca, won by TKO in round two of four], I didn't know who I was fighting.

'He was making his pro debut, too. One of my heroes, Sugar Ray Leonard, was there and that made me want to showcase my skills even more.

'Genaro Hernandez was a legend, in my eyes, and is someone who I had so much respect for. Sadly, he's no longer with us.

'I remember, when I was a child, every boxing magazine I had I would take the centrefold out, because that was in colour.

'I'd stick them on my wall and the one I had above my bed, the champion that I used to watch all of the time, was Genaro.

'He was very tall and rangy, a good boxer and body puncher, and I used to think "no one can beat this guy". I was 15 and, six years later, I was across the ring from him.

'He was crafty, too, and you could see the difference between someone who was green and this great veteran. For me to win a world title at 21, against him, was a special experience.

'He suffered a severe injury [blood clot and a torn cartilage muscle] while he was still at the top level, so he could no longer fight. He was then hit by the cancer [head and neck].

'When he died, I got in touch with his family and we communicated back and forth. This guy gave me my chance to become a world champion, it was the least I could do in return.'

There was no stopping Mayweather from there. You could compose a boxing bible analysing his accomplishments and still not do it justice, so here's a summary.

He would win another 25 world title fights, with 24 against reigning or former champions, including International Hall of Famers Arturo Gatti and Oscar De La Hoya.

He was a five-weight world champion, winning 15 world titles all the way up to super welterweight, where he finished his career.

Translated into money, he generated 19.5 million pay-per-view buys and $1.3 billion in revenue – and that was before coming out of retirement to take on McGregor.

The reason he kept such a chunk of that revenue was that he cut out the middle man, buying out his contract with promoter Bob Arum in 2007 to go self-managed.

He only ever fought one Brit, Ricky Hatton, who he sent crashing down for a second time in the tenth round of their fight to retain his WBC welterweight strap later in 2007.

There could have been two, had Prince Naseem Hamed answered the call to meet him after Mayweather's 2001 coming-of-age victory over Diego Corrales by tenth-round TKO.

A young Mayweather was nearly 24 while a weight-drained 'Naz', then 26, would lose for the only time to Marco Antonio Barrera three months later.

Mayweather went on to become the fight game's biggest-ever star, while Hamed retired in 2002 and vanished from the spotlight for several years.

Mayweather said: 'I was on my way to the top when Naseem was there. He's a legend, I commend and take my hat off to him.

'He was a real showman and, since I was a kid, I was the same. Everything I talked about, I was able to execute. I was very interested in fighting him and I wanted to make it happen.

'I feel, a lot of the time, when you are flashy and flamboyant, people call it cocky. It's not cocky if you are backing it up.

'It was the way I'd fought my whole life, with razzle dazzle and a lot of flair. Earlier on in my career, I was very flashy and flamboyant.

'Over the second half of my career, I wasn't 100 per cent, but I carried on. To call yourself TBE (The Best Ever), you've got to take on the best and not every fighter is the same.

'Once you face me, it's all about the skills. I don't care how much heart you've got. A fight doesn't last for two or three rounds, there's 12 to play with.

'I'm like a chameleon – I can adjust and adapt to many different fighting styles. Every move is calculated and I know I can dictate any fight and handle the situation.

'If somebody gets the best of me for two rounds and I take the other ten, I'll still feel like I didn't do that good. I'll never settle for less. You can watch me and think, "When I get in there with him, I'll do this, this and this." When you try and make it happen, it's totally different.

'I've beaten more world champions than anyone in the history of this sport. My life, the only thing I focused on was my craft. From morning to night, I dedicated myself to boxing.

'I never worried about getting beat. Every time I went into a fight, I knew I couldn't lose. I'm the best and I was born to be the best.'

With those themes touched upon, the speech came to a close and Mayweather headed backstage for photos with guests. That should have been the end of the story, but it wasn't.

It was there that he met teenager Raemarni Ball, who was literally half his age at that time, and whisked her off to sample a life of luxury.

Raemarni, 19, got more than a memento and left her mark on the 'Pretty Boy', who took her and older sister Relissa Ricketts, 21, away from England on his private jet.

The rest of the audience were blissfully unaware that Raemarni had slipped away with Mayweather in one of the six white Rolls-Royce cars that were waiting outside for him.

The media had spotted her, though, as Mayweather stepped out of the building and made their own investigations into exactly who the mystery woman was.

She reportedly worked at the New Look shop on the high street in Dudley, where she lived in a two-storey semi-detached house with her five siblings and mother Mandy.

An aspiring singer and dedicated follower of fashion, the former performing arts student at Dudley College strived for stardom and this was her chance to get a share of the limelight.

All with a passing interest kept an eye on her social media accounts and she was most active on Instagram, where she had over 81,000 followers.

The first image posted of her and Mayweather pretty much confirmed when and where they had met, as she was clad in the same evening gown she was wearing before the event.

Subsequent updates revealed she had boarded Mayweather's private jet, which went back to the United States for stops in New York and Las Vegas.

They took holiday snaps in Miami, too, and were spotted at a basketball match between the Los Angeles Clippers and Golden State Warriors.

Raemarni shared an image of her less than a foot away from married superstar musicians Jay-Z and Beyoncé at the game. Others saw her wearing 'TMT' (The Money Team) clothing.

The last time they were seen together was at the end of that May – some three months after they met in Cannock – when she was still living the dream.

Mayweather was 38 at the time and, although he had never married, he has four children by two different women. His eldest son, Koraun, is a teenager himself.

It was never determined if they became intimate. All the claims that Mayweather had a 'girlfriend' weren't substantiated. Raemarni's mother flat out denied they were.

They could have just been friends who had fun in each other's company and, at the end of the road, went their separate ways.

Raemarni has come home to the Black Country since then, while Mayweather remains at his Vegas mansion or hot-foots it around the globe.

She had a boyfriend, AA rescue van driver Andre Brown, who apparently had no objection to her spending time with Mayweather. It's unclear whether they remain together.

She appeared to have struck up a friendship with Mayweather's personal assistant Marikit 'Kitchie' Laurico, who she has wished a happy birthday to since on Instagram.

Subsequent posts showed her back with her family, who are pictured in some images. One selfie showed her wearing a top that had 'no hard feelings' emblazoned across it.

Cryptic captions such as 'it's up to me to take a risk even if I lose it all' suggest she's reflected on her bizarre experience. Either way, it looks as if her 'Mayweather Mania' is over.

But that wasn't the last time they ever met, as she was on hand again when Mayweather returned to the West Midlands for a second UK tour the following year.

They embraced as old buddies, but there was never any suggestion that she'd be caught up in the whirlwind again.

They parted ways once again, on good terms, but this is how Mayweather lives his life. He's like a rap star with all the perks, except with boxing gloves. His wealth affords him that.

There was never any suggestion he'd be back at Bar Sport, but it wouldn't turn out to be too long before the West Midlands would indeed become Mayweather's stomping ground again.

Mayweather's return to the region had the big-arena feel, over at the ICC in Birmingham, which wouldn't have come cheap to anybody.

One noteworthy moment occurred, before he and Mayweather later locked horns, when the organisers brought out a Conor McGregor impersonator, who raised the necessary laughs.

But it was no longer a once-in-a-lifetime opportunity to meet Mayweather; you couldn't sell that as a bill of goods like the first time.

Those bragging rights remain in Cannock. After the first run, such an event would always lose its lustre.

As rubbing shoulders with the greats go, that was as intimate an experience as a customer was likely to get.

The common denominator in all of this is Mayweather, who will never lose his drive to earn big bucks. A move into promoting and managing was his next project.

At the end of it all, he considers himself The Best Ever and he'll only be too happy to tell you why if you ever see him. Few would argue he's the best defensively of all time.

His flashy behaviour aside, there's clearly a humble human being inside of Mayweather, on the evidence of what's presented here. But, for him, talk will never come cheap.

CHAPTER TWO

MADE A SCAPEGOAT FOR WHAT WENT WRONG – RAY MANCINI

RAY 'Boom Boom' Mancini will always refute that he's the reason the distance of world title bouts was shortened after his fateful fight against Deuk Koo Kim in 1982.

You can always be sure that the age-old debate about whether boxing should be allowed will rumble on every time tragedy strikes in the ring.

It was no different when Mancini's world title challenger Kim died as a result of their gruelling contest, which ended in the 14th of a scheduled 15-rounder.

The grim result of that war on 13 November didn't come as a complete surprise to anyone following their fortunes, held in the outdoor arena of Caesars Palace in Las Vegas.

It was Kim himself who was quoted as saying 'either he dies or I die' before the fight, and he's believed to have written the message 'live or die' on a lamp shade in his Vegas hotel.

He'd also taken liberties to get himself down to the 135lb limit so he could compete for the WBA lightweight crown. Severe dehydration was the inevitable outcome.

Italian-American Mancini told how he was expecting a 'war', and that's exactly what he got from his South Korean rival as they tore into each other, toe to toe, from the first bell.

Mancini, who was just 21 at the time, took a beating himself, with his left ear sliced open and his left eye swollen shut. At one point, the pain was so immense that he considered quitting.

He'd hammered away at Kim so hard that his left hand had swollen to twice its normal size. By the 13th, though, his blows had really started to take effect.

Kim, whose knees had buckled under one shot in the 11th, was bashed around as he took a flurry of 39 punches. Too brave for his own good, he fought back and saw out the round.

Mancini came out and settled matters in the 14th, charging forward to send Kim reeling with a right hand. Another stiff right sent him flying down, his head hitting the canvas hard.

Even then, Kim still tried to carry on, pulling himself up the ropes to rise unsteadily on to his feet. Referee Richard Green waved the fight off, just 19 seconds into the round.

Kim was a warrior in every sense of the word, but he was also an engaged-to-be-married man with a son on the way. A few minutes later, he collapsed and slipped into a coma.

He was rushed to Desert Springs Hospital, where emergency brain surgery was performed in an effort to save him.

It failed and four days later Kim was dead aged just 27. The neurosurgeon claimed the fatal injury was caused by one punch. Everyone connected with the situation was distraught.

It sparked a chain of events that would also claim lives, starting with his mother Yang Sun Nyo. She flew to Vegas to be with her son before his life support machine was turned off.

Three months later, she committed suicide by drinking a bottle of pesticide. The following July, referee Green also killed himself.

Whether what happened that night affected the man in the middle to such an extent that he took his own life is unclear, as he'd officiated again since the fateful fight.

It certainly took its toll on Mancini, who was consumed by guilt. He attended Kim's funeral and fell into his own depression. Random strangers would ask him if he 'killed Kim'.

Friends consoled him, pointing out it was an accident, as he struggled to decide whether he would ever lace on the gloves again.

Still a reigning world champion, he did box on but the old 'Boom Boom' was gone. Promoter Bob Arum admitted he was 'never the same'.

Mancini has had over 35 years to come to terms with what happened. Bearing the sorrow he feels has been like carrying around a bag of rocks at times, but it's a battle he's won.

He said: 'I made my peace long ago and I don't dwell on it. I fought on and, if I hadn't gotten over it, I wouldn't have been able to do that. If you hesitate, you get hurt.

'When I retired, it's because I had no love for the game anymore. It's not that I couldn't do it, I didn't want to. A big part of my success was my passion for boxing. It had become a job.

'I was financially able to do it, too. I've lived a good life. I'm smart and let my money work for me. My style of fighting was fan friendly, but it was never built for longevity.

'I came in at the right time, got what I needed and got out. I'm still healthy, when a lot of other guys are not.

'It was a war, we were banging heads, elbows, punches, all of it. That's the deal with a rough and tough fight like that.

'I was catching him so many times that I hoped the referee would jump in but, unfortunately, it didn't happen. He was a great warrior and a hero in Korea. They should be very proud.

'Because it was on prime-time television on a Saturday afternoon, there was an outrage because it reached such a savage conclusion.

'Only a fighter who has gone through that can understand how difficult it is, but they all know that these things can happen.

'I questioned everything and did a lot of praying at church but, ultimately, I came to the decision that I'd been blessed to be able to become a world champion.

'I wanted more financial security for me and my family, too. I came back, but that was the day that I lost the love for the game. I could still fight, but the passion was gone.

'I only boxed as a pro for five and a half years in total and, like in any marriage, when you've lost the passion, you've got to walk away.'

It didn't happen through his own hands, but Mancini had previously experienced a grief that was even closer to home.

It was Valentine's Day 1981 when his older brother, Lenny Jr, was killed by a gunshot wound to the head.

His girlfriend, who was just 17, pulled the trigger and claimed the weapon had discharged accidentally when he was showing her how to use the gun.

She pleaded guilty to negligent homicide after being remanded into the custody of the Ohio Youth Commission. The younger Mancini sibling boxed again less than a month later.

He said: 'It was my 17th fight, which was my first in New York City, and was at the Felt Forum, which is the small arena downstairs from Madison Square Garden.

'I was 16-0 and my opponent was "Stormin" Norman Goins, who had previously been a contender and was a good puncher.

'It was my first time in the ring since my Lenny had passed and everyone was worried about how I was going to react.

'Mentally I wasn't right but I didn't want to waste my career. I caught him with a couple of good shots and knocked him down in the first round, then stopped him in the second.

'I'd only had a month to regroup from my brother's death, but I was able to move on from that. He was a handsome kid and had also boxed, but he didn't have the discipline for it.

'He was only 25 when he died. We were very close and he was in my corner. He was always the first one to come in the ring and hug me when I won.'

A safety-first policy in championship boxing was implemented after Kim's death, with a number of measures brought in. Shortening the distance was just the start of it.

The standing eight count was introduced and medical tests for fighters became much more stringent. The days of just checking for a heartbeat and blood pressure were over.

In the fullness of time, all world title fights would be reduced to 12 rounds. The WBC, which did not even sanction the Mancini versus Kim bout, made the first move.

The governing body had conducted a study that claimed boxers tended to get hurt more severely in rounds 13, 14 and 15. WBC president Jose Sulaiman announced that its title bouts would be dropped to 12 rounds.

Its annual convention that year had been held in Korea, where Kim's story was later made into a movie called *Champion*.

But it wasn't until 1987 that the WBA, which governed the bout, and later the IBF, followed suit. The WBO went with 12-rounders upon their formation in 1988.

The last 15-rounder took place on 29 August 1988, when IBF minimumweight boss Samuth Sithnaruepol outpointed In-Kyu Hwang in Bangkok, Thailand.

Mancini asserts that only one change should ever have been made. The same-day weigh-in rule, abolished in 1983, should have been retained, he believes.

He said: 'I've always thought the true world championship distance is 15 rounds. With shortening the distance, the course of history in boxing has been changed.

'Think about it. If it had always been 12 rounds, Joe Louis wouldn't have beaten Billy Conn and Rocky Marciano would have lost to Joe Walcott the first time around.

'They were both behind in the 13th and had to turn it around. Sugar Ray Leonard wouldn't have beaten Thomas Hearns, either, as he was behind in the 14th round.

'I speak to some fighters now and they train for eight to ten weeks for 12 rounds. I tell them, "What are you getting ready for? A marathon?" When I was training, I'd be ready in six weeks. Every fighter has that time-frame where they peak, when they are in prime condition. It's a science and you can over-train.

'It's like sharpening a knife. You reach a point where it's at its sharpest but if you carry on sharpening it, it will dull the blade.

'When people claim I'm the reason world title fights got cut down, I laugh. The last 15-rounder was in 1988, so that's a long time to change!

'What happened affected me and my family, and it got people thinking and talking. The WBC were the first to act, but I thought that was a knee-jerk reaction.

'I actually think it was a TV decision. Everybody knows they control the game. If they wanted it back at 15 rounds, it would be done.'

Mancini's despair weighed him down from the moment he left the ring that night, but a long, drawn-out process would ensue before it got to unmanageable levels.

In the meantime, he still boxed. The next time he stepped through the ropes was less than three months later, a concerted effort to keep him busy but out of the firing line.

He would go to Italy, where he would face the newly crowned British champion George Feeney in a ten-rounder, without his title on the line.

Feeney, three days shy of his 26th birthday on fight night, brought with him the scalp of Ken Buchanan, having outpointed the former WBC boss in the Scot's last fight 13 months earlier.

The game Englishman was durable and it later took a detached retina in a European title shot to end his own career. He had been stopped before, on a thankless trip to Nigeria.

He stood firm as Mancini landed left jabs to the body, going upstairs with sharp combinations to the head. Feeney sucked them all up and responded in kind.

Mancini was cut above the left eye in the seventh and was rocked in the eighth as Feeney, behind on the cards, put his all into the finish. It nearly backfired in the tenth and last round.

The cards were called into play, with the three judges scoring 98-96, 98-96 and 98-95, all in favour of Mancini, who got the test he wanted.

The two were reunited at Bar Sport, over 30 years after they touched gloves, taking their places on the top table.

Mancini said, 'It was such a pleasure to see George again. He still looks the same! God bless him, he was a fighter English people should be proud of.

'He threw his punches in bunches and looked like he had a difficult style for a lot of guys. Styles make fights and he'd give anyone a headache.

'The famous English writer, Reg Gutteridge, actually called me and asked what I thought about George. I thought he was very strong and aggressive.

'Reg told me George was a hard man. I'd never heard of that term before. I knew then I was in for a difficult time.

'I was offered the chance to come to Italy and I always thought a world champion should box all over the world. I wanted to go somewhere comfortable, where I hadn't been before.

'I needed a decent test to see where I was at and there are certain guys you are not going to knock out. George was one of them. He was going nowhere. I wasn't even close.'

From there, Mancini tried to go about his career as he had before and wasn't afraid of losing. That had already happened before his crowning glory.

His world title success had actually come at the second attempt, Mancini having challenged Alexis Arguello for the WBC strap in October 1981. He was just 20 at the time.

On that occasion, he learned his own lesson about fighting an uphill battle against formidable Nicaraguan Arguello, by then a three-weight world champion.

Family ties had built up the bout for Mancini, who was a second-generation world title hopeful after his father, the original 'Boom Boom', Lenny Mancini.

Mancini Sr was the number one contender for the only world lightweight title (hence the 'lineal' term) in the 1940s before he was called up to fight for his country in the Second World War.

It cost him his shot at reigning champion Sammy Angott, who he'd already pushed close before losing on a split decision in a non-title affair.

Mancini Sr was awarded the purple heart for his heroics in the conflict but, crucially, had also been injured during his service. Much like Ray after Kim, he was never the same boxer again.

By the time Ray got the chance his father never did in 1981, Lenny was 62 and in a wheelchair at ringside, recovering from double bypass heart surgery. He lived until 2003.

He said, 'My father had signed to challenge for the world title in February 1944, but he got drafted. He was torn between wanting to defend his country and the fight.

'He offered to give all the money he got from boxing to the Army Relief Fund, but they told him, "We don't want your money, we want you."

'He got shot up in France at the Battle of Metz which, next to the Battle of the Bulge, was the most destructive war in the European Theatre of Operations. Consequently, he never got his opportunity and he was in hospital recuperating for almost a year in England, at a town called Harrogate.

'The doctors said he'd never fight again because he'd lost so much blood and had shrapnel all over his body. They weren't even sure he'd walk, as there was damage to his spinal cord.

'He came back, but he was a shell of what he had been. I've always believed he would have won that title had it not been for the war.

'His coach, Ray Arcel, is in the Hall of Fame and trained over 20 world champions. Of Joe Louis's 25 title defences, Ray was the trainer for 18 and he had confidence in my father.

'Ray later came to a press conference for one of my fights and everyone was asking him, "What do you think of the kid?"

'He told them he thought I was a wonderful fighter and I reminded him of my father, because of my style, but he also said that I would never have beaten my father.

'I appreciated those comments because I knew I was never going to be as good as my father was. I was proud of that.

'Ask my father how many chances you get to become a world champion, because he only got that one. I wanted justice for him.

'I was raised in a blue-collar town [Youngstown, Ohio] and growing up there was a wonderful life. They are the best people I know.

'I was from a middle-class background, but my father wasn't. Most fighters come from an economic need and, in the 1940s, it was necessity for most Italians in the United States.

'I just wanted to be something different. People always asked me, "What do you want to be when you grow up?" I told them I was going to be a world champion, for my father.

'I wanted to be like him so much. I used to read about his boxing career, as he used to keep all of his newspaper cuttings. He taught me a lot about the sport.

'But, believe it or not, he was the one who actually tried to talk me out of it in the worst way. He told me he had to fight, but I had other choices. I had an academic scholarship.

'My mind was set on boxing, though. I put my heart and soul into it and I was fortunate enough to achieve my dream.

'My father still supported me. He went to all of my amateur fights and, before I turned pro, he sat me down for a talk.

'He explained to me, "Raymond, it's a lonely and painful life being a boxer, you have to give up your family, friends and everything," but there was nothing else I wanted to do.'

Mancini turned pro and disposed of Phil Bowen in the first round on his debut. He boxed another 19 times before tackling Arguello two years later.

Only two men had gone the distance with him as he won and retained NABF honours.

But this was virgin territory and, as if to reinforce his views, he'd never been past 12 rounds.

Mancini, although never in command, took the fight to Arguello and claimed some of the earlier rounds, but when the champion established a foothold, he was done for.

Ironically, the 12th was when proceedings went properly awry, as Mancini took a knee after a right cross landed flush. He staggered back to his corner and was saved by the bell.

Blood oozed from the left eye, mouth and nose of Mancini, but he asked to carry on. He came under fire again in the 13th, as his corner pondered action.

Manager Dave Wolf climbed the steps with an orange towel but never got to throw it in, as he was pulled back by trainer Murphy Griffith.

Mancini survived another round to start the 14th but he would not see the final bell, as a left hook sent him crashing to the mat for a second time.

The referee Tony Perez stepped in with Mancini's sobbing mother Ellen trying to enter the ring. The contest had 76 seconds left to run but, above all, he had lived to fight another day.

He said, 'I turned over in 1979, but I had a pro style as an amateur. Fighters are born, they are not made. An ability to punch is a gift from God.

'My debut was special – I stopped him in the first and dropped him twice. If I hurt someone, I just tried to jump on them. As I went on, I was beating guys I shouldn't have so early.

'Anyone will tell you, if you have a lot of knockouts earlier in your career, it will extend how long you can get in the ring for late on. It keeps you from a lot of wear and tear.

'I'd be happy to get the job done early. You get paid the same no matter how long it lasts, but there are certain guys you are not going to knock out. I worked my way into a position for Arguello as, in the two fights previous, I'd beaten Jorge Morales [retired after eight rounds] and Jose Luis Ramirez [unanimous points].

'That was for my NABF title, but Morales was ranked number six and Ramirez number three with the WBC, so I was pretty much next in line.

'Ramirez had already boxed Arguello and knocked him down twice, but Alexis got the decision [split on points] as the hometown guy.

'The wrong man won, no doubt in my mind, and then I beat Ramirez convincingly. Where else was I supposed to go?

'When I took the Arguello fight, some people thought I was crazy, as I was only 20. I was never going to say no. If you want to be the best, you have to beat the best.

'It felt like we were catching him at the right time. I thought my youth and my strength would be too much for him.

'If it had been a 12-round fight, I'd have won the world title. I was on top after 12, but that's not the true championship distance, which I maintain is 15.

'His experience took over and, in the 14th, he stopped me but I knew I would be a world champion after that. I proved that I belong at that level.

'People were concerned about my safety, but fighters are smart enough not to get involved in the melee. I was just sad that my family had to see that.

'I lost to a great champion and it taught me more than in 20 wins. His experience made all of the difference. I lost, it hurt and I grieved for a while, but I knew I had to move on quickly.'

Believing he'd lost the fight but the war was still on, Mancini chased a return with Arguello, who went up another two weights to take on Aaron Pryor.

The WBA title changed hands later that year, with ninth-ranked Arturo Frias taking Claude Noel's belt. Frias was in the habit of finding ways to win, and often early.

He signed to face Mancini after he had settled the score with Ernesto Espana, who had taken his '0' before he came champion. He exacted his revenge by ninth-round technical decision.

Mancini trained for the distance, even though the likelihood was that it would come down to gunslinging in the centre of the ring. It would end more quickly than either had imagined.

He had also, perhaps literally, dodged a bullet in the lead-up to fight night, when armed men came looking for Mancini in his hotel room. He was then placed under police watch.

Mancini and Frias clashed on 5 May 1982, locking horns for all of two minutes and 54 seconds. At the time, it was regarded as the best round of boxing ever.

Just 15 seconds had passed when Frias caught Mancini flush on the chin, before a further flurry drew blood from his eyebrow. This was not the start Mancini had hoped for.

Fending off his opponent until he managed to recover, Mancini met Frias in the centre of the ring and dropped him with a combination of his own.

Frias shot back to his feet but hadn't regained his senses as Mancini had done. He got trapped on the ropes and was shipping punches.

The referee, ironically Richard Green, saw nothing coming back from Frias, who had six seconds to last until the end of the round, and intervened accordingly. Mancini had done it.

The joyous family scenes in the ring that both father and son had dreamed of could now finally happen.

His first defence would also come against Espana, whose second chance ended by sixth-round TKO in July 1982. Kim came less than four months later.

Mancini said, 'I wanted the rematch with Arguello, but he was going up in weight. Frias was another world champion, so we went for him.

'What went on outside of the ring was a true story. We were in Tucson, Arizona, and I was shadow boxing when a gentleman came into the gym.

'Turns out he was a US marshal and he'd had a call from the hotel because two men had been looking for me there. One of them was carrying a gun over his shoulder.

'They were asking if the receptionist knew which room Ray Mancini was in and, of course, she said no because she was nervous.

'They left and she followed them out to their car, where there were more men holding rifles. She thought they were going to kill me. They wanted me to stay in a room elsewhere under their guard but I was that focused on the title, I just carried on with my training.

'I still went out for a run and told the officers, "If you want to follow me, you can do." They got me out of there and I went to Vegas. It was less than three weeks before the fight.

'I just wondered who would have done it and why, but Tucson was close to the border and there had been kidnappings, where people were taken into Mexico for high ransoms.

'I was a high-profile athlete at the time, so that was one theory, although I never did find out the truth. I put it to the back of my mind.

'Another story was, when I got to Vegas, we only had one sparring partner and my coach was good friends with Eddie Futch [another Hall of Fame trainer].

'Murphy asked Eddie if he had any guys I could work with. He had one kid, but Eddie said he'd give me all the work I'd need. It was Freddie Roach [later to become a top trainer].

'That was how I became good friends with Freddie, because he slapped me around for two weeks! He wasn't a puncher, but was fast and had more heart and desire than anybody.

'Every fight was a war for him, because he wanted to stand toe to toe when he couldn't really hurt you. After a while, I caught up with his speed and then I knew I was ready.

'Going out to the ring against Frias, I thought of my father. I promised him from when I was a little boy that I would win a world title for him.

'Frias caught me early on and, when you're hurt, your instincts take over and you either cover up or you fire back. I chose to throw as many punches as I could. I took his best shot and when you knock a guy down, it's like a shark smelling blood. It was the greatest feeling in my life when the referee jumped in.

'I was able to accomplish my lifelong dream at a young age and that made it a good time in my life. I'd gone close once before, but everyone around me knew I'd come back.

'I was heartbroken that night against Arguello, but this made up for it. That celebration, with my family, was special and there are very few moments in my life that I can compare to that.'

Mancini's tenure would last for over two years and, despite lacking the ferocity of some of his earlier displays, he still had the power to blow his adversaries out of the water.

His give-one-to-take-one style remained and, after Kim, he successfully defended his title against Orlando Romero and Bobby Chacon.

Romero had his moments before he was flattened by a left hand to the jaw in a bombs-away ninth, while a bloodied Chacon had a number done on him in three rounds.

The man who ended Mancini's reign was Livingstone Bramble, who wasn't supposed to upset the apple cart. Talks about a super fight, with Mancini going up a weight to meet Pryor, were already under way.

Two of the three judges had Mancini ahead going into the 14th, but referee Marty Denkin took the fight out of their hands, Bramble landing head punches at will to force the stoppage.

Mancini never left his feet or stopped throwing back, but was hurt and flopped into his corner afterwards. The subsequent hospital visit led to 71 stitches around one eye.

He asked for a rematch with Bramble and got his wish. In what was a do-or-die affair, Mancini lost again, this time by a point on all three judges' scorecards, after 15 rounds.

Facing a long road back to the title, he called time in August 1985 at the age of just 24. His retirement would last four years.

Hector Camacho, who would have been another option, along with Pryor, had Mancini beaten Bramble the first time, lured him back in March 1989 with the chance to become a two-weight world champion.

An ugly spectacle ensued as Mancini tried to shake off the ring rust against Camacho, who hit and held effectively to take the first WBO super lightweight title on a majority decision.

Another three years passed before Mancini would see action again, against former two-time world titlist Greg Haugen for the NABF strap, again at super lightweight, on 3 April 1992.

That was a bridge too far. It was all too obvious that the snap in Mancini's shots and his punch resistance had both gone. Haugen halted him in the seventh with a right hand. Mancini admitted, 'This is it.'

His drawing power had also waned, evidenced by the $1.6 million he received for Camacho compared to the $450,000 on the table against Haugen. At the age of 31, leaving boxing for good seemed to be the right move.

Despite the relative inactivity later in his career, Mancini still made it into the International Boxing Hall of Fame in 2015.

He bore the Hall of Fame ring on both occasions he was at Bar Sport, in October of that year and in September 2017.

Mancini's first visit was a labour of love for promoter Scott Murray, a self-confessed fan of the boxer, who went to Paddington train station himself to meet him.

The second time around, it was a family affair as he brought his in-laws, his mother and father and his wife Tina. Mancini had actually wanted to come back a year earlier.

He also met one of his predecessors as WBA world champion, the aforementioned Buchanan, and admitted he was one of his idols and someone he'd always looked up to.

Career-wise, they just missed each other, so the prospect of them ever sharing a ring was unlikely. It was something that had crossed Mancini's mind, though. That was only because an American boxing magazine had run a story fantasising about dream fights under an 'any era, same division' banner.

The article pitted Mancini against Buchanan when both were in their primes, and it was the 'Tartan Legend' who came out on top.

Feeney, who joined Mancini both times at Bar Sport, can offer an honest opinion on the two, as he was the only man who had the distinction of touching paid gloves with both of them.

It was victory over an ageing Buchanan that got Feeney to the level where he was considered a decent opponent for the likes of Mancini.

Feeney brought his Lonsdale Belt the first time around and didn't realise, until his return, that he was the only man to box both Buchanan and Mancini in the pro ranks.

It can be difficult to put on the same public speaker to a similar audience, but Mancini had a few more stories up his sleeve.

It emerged he'd auditioned for the role of Mr Pink in iconic gangster flick *Reservoir Dogs* and got into a fiery argument with the director when Steve Buscemi landed the part instead.

That man was Quentin Tarantino, a household name to many movie-goers, who was concerned people would never accept a man as famous as Mancini in a fictional role.

Mancini said, 'I read for the part three times and, as an actor, you know when you stink the joint out and when you kick ass.

'In the entertainment business, if you get a second call back it means you did well enough to warrant it. If you come back for a third, they're interested.

'By then, they want to see what you can do for the role. Very seldom do you go past three auditions. I knew it was now or never.

'I knocked it out of the park again, but Quentin couldn't be convinced people would watch the film and see anything other than Ray Mancini if they saw me on screen.

'I asked him why he had me come back and he told me, "I was waiting for you to fail." I felt like he was trying to make a fool out of me.

'It was at that point I got up and pushed the table he was sitting at, threatened to punch out his liver and make him pee blood for a month! I leaned over the table and couldn't stop myself. I was like, "How about I beat you up here? That would be a story everyone would like!"

'On and on it went. "Let me tell you something, don't ever disrespect an actor like that! If I come across you again, you'd better give it to me or I'm coming after you."

'I realised there was a room full of people staring at me and he was scared himself. Word gets around Hollywood quickly and, if it got out, they'd all think I was a loose cannon.

'I started walking away and then I turned around and said "Hey, how was that for acting?" I wasn't joking, though. I was angry but I knew I had to do something to flip it.

'Steve Buscemi is a friend of mine and a wonderful actor, one of the best we have, but I knew I'd have been as good. Different from him, but as good.'

Mancini may have had a temper and a gung-ho streak in combat, but he was smart with it. He'd looked after his money and kept 75 per cent of the $12 million he'd earned.

His father had always told him 'one day the headlines, next day the breadlines' and his working-class roots had kept him grounded.

Mancini was a celebrity in his own right and Sylvester Stallone was the first one who wanted to take his life story to the screen. Yes, Rocky Balboa wanted to make a movie about him.

Mancini has starred in a film documentary, entitled *The Good Son*, which was released in 2013 and contained the emotional moment he met Kim's adult son, Jiwan.

It also touched on other father-and-son bonds and the trials and tribulations Mancini went through trying to live up to his own family name.

Mancini has acted and produced films regularly and will probably always be involved in showbusiness. In his heyday, he counted Frank Sinatra as a personal friend.

Perhaps most poignantly, he's still here with his faculties intact living a good life, when some of his former rivals are dead. He respects that every day.

CHAPTER THREE

WHEN THE TABLES WERE WELL AND TRULY TURNED – VINNY PAZ

VINNY Paz had to gamble with something far more valuable than his money to make the greatest comeback in boxing history.

The sport's miracle man can confidently call himself that after defying doctor's orders to fight again following a road accident.

To think that Vincenzo Pazienza's career was not cut short before he was 30 after what he went through is, quite frankly, astonishing.

Instead, a comeback of superhuman proportions happened and inspired most who know the story, which has now been immortalised on the silver screen.

The 2016 movie *Bleed for This* starred Miles Teller as Paz, who became famous like never before after his biography made it on to the big screen.

But this wasn't just about boxing. It was more a tale of triumph in the face of adversity.

The likelihood of a happy ending for Paz seemed unfathomable after a fateful day that nearly ended his life, as well as his career.

He was on top of the world as the new WBA super welterweight champion and flavour of the month before everything, literally, came crashing down.

There were doubts over whether Paz would walk again, let alone fight, after the near-tragedy 42 days after his crowning glory.

The celebrations for the wild man of the ring, inside and out, continued until he climbed inside friend Kurt Reader's vehicle on 12 November 1991.

They struck another car at speed and rescue workers had to prise open the passenger door to reach Paz in the wreckage.

He would later be awarded damages after suing Reader, who was cited by police for failing to control his vehicle.

Paz was left with a dislocated vertebra and two fractured vertebrae, spending ten painful days in hospital.

Once discharged, he had to spend three months wearing a halo, a circular metal brace screwed into his skill in four places and propped up by four metal rods.

But he starting training again, despite the immense discomfort, and made medical professionals look foolish in the process.

It was by no means easy. Many who suffer with ill health can relate to the mind being willing but the body failing, and Paz will know exactly what they are talking about.

He lived his life with reckless abandon, but this time he was playing with his health rather than on the casino tables where you'd often find him.

No one gave him the remotest chance of ever returning to the ring, not even his family, who had always backed him to the hilt.

Coach Kevin Rooney needed some persuading to have anything to do with his comeback, while other fighters in the gym initially refused to spar with Paz for fear of hurting him.

When the halo was taken off in a painful fashion that makes even the viewer wince in the film, people slowly started to be more hopeful, even more so when he was medically cleared.

Paz was back in action just 13 months after the accident on an emotional night one day shy of his 30th birthday.

He'd been stripped of his title, even though it still hadn't been contested by the time of his return. Julio Cesar Vasquez claimed the vacant crown six days later.

Luis Santana was picked as the opponent for Paz, who was not found wanting as regards fitness and put his man down twice in the ninth of their scheduled ten-rounder.

He settled for an almost flawless points victory at the final bell, which was greeted by huge sighs of relief as well as cheers. And, with that, 'the Pazmanian Devil' was back.

He recalled, 'When we crashed, all I could think of was, "I'm never going to defend my world title," even though I should have been dead.

'It was horrifying what was going through my mind. There's been plenty of times in my life when I've been lucky to be alive, but that was the biggest.

'The kid who was driving was a good friend, we'd just got done lifting weights. We got in his car, which had bald tyres, and he was going too fast. I should have told him.

'I remember holding on to the door handle and side panel for dear life, then a car cut us off and we started sliding into the next lane.

'He slammed on the brakes and I just saw all of this traffic coming. Boom, we got hit by a big town car. Afterwards, my friend was shouting "Oh my god, Vinny Paz is in there."

'When they pulled me out, the pain shot down my body and it felt like my neck was on fire. I was asking them to stop, it was that bad.

'Everyone has got problems, so I just got through it the best way that I could. It was ugly, I couldn't feel my arms or my legs.

'My surgeon was Doctor Cotter. He used to call me "son" all of the time, probably because he was around 80 years old himself.

'He felt for me and he was the one who had to tell me, at first, "Son, I'm sorry, but you're not going to box again." I told him he was wrong, that he didn't understand the man that I am.

'The halo wasn't pretty, either, but that's what I chose because I wanted to fight again. If I'd followed the doctor's orders, my career was over.

'As soon as I could, I walked down to the basement of my parents' house and sat on the bench, looking at the weights for about half an hour.

'I got up and lifted two 25lb dumbells and the pain just shot through my body again, like a hot flash. I just sat back on the bench and stared at the weights again, with tears in my eyes.

'After a while, I picked up two 20lb weights, it still killed me but I managed to do some reps this time. From that moment on, I was all in and I was working out until I got the halo off.

'The screws in the halo could get loose, but they would get really loose because I was starting to work out, lifting heavier and heavier weights.

'My mother started to figure it out, because my clothes were wet from sweat. I just told her everything was cool.

'I started going to the gym, but I didn't tell any of my family. When I walked through, people were like "Vinny, what are you doing?"

'I used to get checked out every week and Doctor Cotter must have known something. My body remained in shape and he'd just tell me, "Keep doing what you're doing."

'At the end of three months, I'd been working out for two of them and I finally told him. He just shook his head and said, "Obviously, you know better than I do."

'The most excruciating pain was when they took the screws out of my skull. When I had the halo removed, it felt like he was taking them out the wrong way. He was using a ratchet.

'I heard a click and it hurt like hell. I bent the chair I was sitting in trying to take the pain. Remember, bone had rebuilt around the screw. I don't do drugs, so I didn't have painkillers.

'I had determination and persistence to box and I made it back again. I'd had to relinquish my title, but at least I could carry on.

'It was a wild week leading up to getting back in the ring, but I had tunnel vision. I was either going to do this or die trying, but I felt about 100 per cent.

'When I got back in there, it was the best moment of my life. I was back, on national television no less, and I won. It couldn't have got any better. I tried to knock him down for a third time, but he had a chin like steel. I was sore afterwards, but the pain went away by the time the cheque had cleared!

'It was never a one-fight comeback. All I could think of was what I wanted to do from there. I was only just turning 30.

'As it went on, I knew the story was going to be big one day, but I thought Tom Cruise would be the one playing me!

'The title *Bleed for This* came from my father. I used to gamble, a little too much, and I'd win some and lose some.

'He used to tell me "Kid, you bleed for this money, you can't give it to those casinos. They'll take you for all you've got." I wanted to call the movie *Paz*.

'I'm a positive guy, I don't like to have negativity around me, but there was more than one time after I came back that I thought, "It can't get any better than this."

'I've got some serious fans and I take it to heart. I've got people who have named their kids after me and men who have put tattoos of me on to their bodies. It's quite amazing.'

Had the accident, or one more fight, been the end, Paz would have finished as a two-time world champion and a challenger on three other occasions.

A warrior in the ring and hellraiser outside of it, the Italian-American built up his reputation on the East Coast after being born and bred in Cranston, Rhode Island.

He was inspired to box by Muhammad Ali and idolised 'The Greatest'. He played other sports as a child, but concentrated on boxing after a fateful trip to the cinema.

Dad Angelo and mum Louise deemed studies more important and were hesitant at first, but became his biggest supporters.

There was no stopping him after he first got in the ring as he racked up 112 amateur bouts, with 100 wins, in an unpaid career that took him up to the age of 20.

He won a national championship and boxed for his country on a USA squad that contained the likes of future heavyweight greats Evander Holyfield and Mike Tyson.

Television exposure from that gave him the name recognition of a hot prospect when he decided to turn pro, which came with his paid bow on 26 May 1983.

He stopped Alfredo Rivera in the fourth and last round of his debut and went on a run of 11 straight TKOs, all but two in Atlantic City, New Jersey.

He also halted Emilio Diaz in Warwick, in his home state of Rhode Island, and David Bell in Beaumont, Texas.

The Bell fight was scheduled for eight rounds, the distance Paz completed when Mike Golden and Rich McCain then both saw the final bell in successive fights.

Both bouts were at the Sands Hotel in Atlantic City, a venue close to Paz's heart as he'd made his debut there.

He would box overseas in his next contest, in his father's homeland of Italy, with his power securing an early finish, this time against Bruno Simili in three rounds.

He would return less than a month later to take on Frenchman Abdelkader Marbi in Milan. Paz was cut badly in the third round and there was no way he could continue. Although he tried to box on to save his undefeated pro streak, his 15th outing ended controversially in round five.

The year 1984 drew to a close with Paz making a new year's resolution to bounce back. It proved a bump in the road as he started to build his legacy.

Paz said, 'I was five when I first watched Ali. He was like a saviour to me and, when I went to his funeral, I cried like a baby.

'I was born to fight and I watched Ali beat people and talk all kinds of trash. He was just unbelievable. After I saw him, that was it. Boxing was all I wanted to do.

'I mimicked him, Ali never got knocked out and Vinny Paz never got knocked out. I got up all of the time. When we met, I told him I was here because of him.

'I lived my life after that guy. He was the biggest influence on me ever and I had great parents and a good dad, who loved boxing like I did.

'I'm so lucky to have a good family, because you never know what can happen to people. My parents made me do the school thing, but I just wanted to box.

'The kids in the neighbourhood used to come down the cellar at my house and we'd all fight each other until someone got hurt!

'I went to see the first Rocky film when I was 14 and, the next day, I woke up my parents before school and told them I wanted to be a fighter.

'My father had always called me "champ" because of how much I loved boxing, and he took me to the gym a few hours later. That was it.

'I was an amateur for a long time and used to train at the Olympic centre with Holyfield and Tyson when they were coming through.

'My last year as an amateur, 1982, I fought in Cuba in front of Fidel Castro. He was sat on a throne in the Havana Dome smoking a cigar, two guys either side of him with machine guns.

'I was in there with Angel Herrera Vera, who won two Olympic gold medals. He was a man with muscles and I was an 18-year-old kid.

'I went at it with him and I landed a left hook that shook him up. I was like "Oh my god, I'm going to knock him out!"

'I went in to open up on him and he grabbed me in a lock, so he would have time to recover, and I was like a little kid. I couldn't move a millimetre.

'It went to a decision and I lost on a split. Inexperience of how to handle that cost me but not many even dared to fight Vera.

'A lot of promoters wanted to sign me because I was on the USA boxing team and had a few fights on TV.

'The Sands Hotel is now dust. I almost cried when I went back there after it had been demolished; it felt like I grew up there. It used to be a place of fun, like a mini Las Vegas.

'I just did my thing and I wanted to knock out everybody. When I turned pro, I stopped the first 11 guys in a row.

'That made me think I could knock out anybody but then a couple took me the distance and McCain was the toughest.

'In the last round, he literally had a golf ball on the side of his face because I'd broken his jaw, but I couldn't stop him. I was so mad at myself.

'I'd been the main sparring partner for Rocky Lockridge, who fought Eusebio Pedroza in Italy for the WBA featherweight title [rematch, Pedroza won again on points].

'Rocky told me all about it, so I went over and stopped Simili, who was the Italian champion. I didn't care about going there again but, this next guy, I didn't know anything about him.

'I asked what he fights like but I was told not to worry about him. All they said was "watch his head". What do you do about that?

'I go in there and, boom, he headbutts me. Next thing I know, I've got a cut from eyebrow to eyebrow. It was really bad.

'I was unbeaten, so I didn't want to lose, never mind get stopped, but it was ugly as hell. I don't know how the referee let me go on for another couple of rounds.

'I wanted to win and stop the guy. I hurt him a couple of times even after that [the cut] but I couldn't get him out of there.

'They ended up giving him the win, when it should have been a no contest. I got over it as fast as I could.'

Rebound Paz did in 1985 with a sixth-round stoppage of Antoine Lark, who was down four times. He also outpointed Jeff Bumpus in a ten-rounder and beat Melvin Paul in two that year.

Scalps were what he needed in 1986 and where better to start than Joe Frazier, not the iconic heavyweight but his son Joe Jr.

It was sold out at the Providence Civic Centre in Rhode Island when they clashed, with Paz delivering a performance that showed he was for real.

All Frazier Jr could do was show how tough he was as he got pelted with flurries of blows, with Paz throwing around 100 punches a round.

He was finally battered into submission in the seventh, his hands dropping again under fire not long after he'd taken a standing eight count.

A non-title bout between two unrated boxers had created major waves and the plaudits were all for Paz, not least from Joe Frazier Sr.

He said, 'We were up against a buzzsaw. If Vinny can keep making that kind of effort and sacrifice, he's going to be a world champion real soon.'

A better class of opponent had brought out the best of Paz and he wanted more of the same.

Harry Arroyo, a former IBF world champion trying to find a path back to the top, was chosen as Paz's opponent for a ten-rounder live on NBC television.

Paz nullified the tough, heavy-handed Arroyo with speed and power to run out a wide points winner, with open scoring that was not announced to a raucous crowd.

He would box for a third time in Providence that year in a world title eliminator against Nelson Bolanos, who was removed in six. The winner was supposed to get a shot at the WBA crown, which had passed to Edwin Rosario after he stunned Livingstone Bramble with a second-round knockout.

But instead Paz was lined up to fight new IBF champion Greg Haugen, who would become a recurring rival in the years to come.

Haugen, making his first defence, agreed to fight Paz at the Providence Civic Centre in 1987, and lived to regret it. Trash talking between the two had turned it into a grudge match and 15-round fights were still in effect, which cost Haugen late on.

Paz bossed rounds 12 to 15 and rolled over Haugen to become a world champion for the first time. The decision was unanimous, with all three judges posting the same score, 144-141.

He said, 'Frazier stood up to punches no lightweight in the world should have. It was unreal. Beating Arroyo put me on the path to a world title shot and Bolanos made sure of it.

'When my chance came along, it was one of the last 15-round fights in history. I compare it to running a marathon and getting socked every half a mile.

'When you think about it, 15 rounds is brutal. Perhaps the wildest thing I ever did was doing that distance.

'Training for it is also crazy. I had to do 15 rounds of hard sparring a couple of times in the gym to get myself ready.

'I knew I'd won that fight. If it had been a 12-rounder, he would have won, but I beat him in the championship rounds. From the 12th, I stepped it up so I could secure the decision.

'I had the best fans anywhere when I went to Providence and my first world title was for all of the "Pazmaniacs" back home.'

What his home supporters didn't know about were the trials and tribulations Paz endured making the 135lb limit. His title reign only lasted eight months.

A stocky lightweight at the best of times, it really showed when Haugen was granted a rematch in Atlantic City in February 1988.

It was another 15-round contest and this time an out-of-sorts Paz struggled, ending up well beaten on points. The most generous of the three judges had Haugen five rounds up.

As a former world champion, more opportunities would come Paz's way but even going up a weight left him drained.

In 1988, Paz went to Las Vegas to take on Roger Mayweather, the WBC super lightweight champion and uncle of future great Floyd, who was a fine adversary in his own right.

The movie shows how the fight was in danger of not going ahead, such were Paz's struggles with the scales. He nearly took a liberty too far.

Paz again faded quickly once the bout got under way and was down for the first time as a pro in the 11th, although he got up and heard the final bell.

Another one-sided points defeat saw him beaten by seven rounds on two cards, with the other judge giving it to Mayweather by ten rounds. Even worse was to follow.

He said, 'In the first fight with Haugen, I remember I was sick as a dog that day. I lost so much weight. I really wasn't a lightweight.

'After the weigh-in, I was gorging everything and got crazy sick, with vomiting and diarrhoea, then I fought him in the afternoon.

'The second time, I got it more wrong. I lost 13lbs the day before the fight, which was like suicide when you're the champion.

'I wasn't a drinker and I never did drugs, but I would go out until late. When I went to the gym, I kicked into overdrive. I trained like an animal but I didn't do much running.

'I didn't see the point in it. I wasn't preparing for a sprint, it was to fight. My hard work was all with boxing in mind.

'Mayweather had the greatest jab of anybody I'd ever been in the ring with, it was remarkable. It was like a cobra; it gave you whiplash.

'I couldn't make weight for that, either; three times I tried before I got there, and I passed out after the fight. I woke up in hospital.

'I went down, for the first time in my career, because I was so tired. I literally saw myself go through white clouds, like I was going to heaven, and it felt so good.

'The nurse said to my father "Mr Pazienza, we are losing your son," and he started to shout and shake me violently. Somehow, I heard him.

'Those are the times you get hurt. Think about it, the only time Roberto Duran ever got knocked out cold, face first and out like a light [against Thomas Hearns], was when he was dehydrated like hell.

'When I see things like that, I know I should be dead. To think I got up and carried on was crazy. Roger was a great fighter.'

The first of a few warning signs had come Paz's way but he stayed in the super lightweight division, thinking his power might not travel up any further.

Paz got warm-up TKOs under his belt in 1989 before getting back into the title picture, against WBO champion Hector Camacho.

They met in 1990 on a bill titled 'Put Up Or Shut Up' and it was Paz who was silenced again. As against Mayweather, he was left bloodied and frustrated after being outworked.

Again, the judges were unanimous in deciding against Paz, who was three rounds down on the closest card.

In his next fight, Paz moved up to 140lbs for a rubber match with Haugen, whom he beat on a unanimous ten-round decision, setting up a tilt at new WBA super lightweight boss Loreto Garza before the year was out.

Garza got ahead early, building a substantial points lead over Paz, who was again cut below the right eye.

Frustration boiled over when Paz picked up Garza in the 11th round and threw him across the ring. Referee Larry Rozadilla, who had already docked two points, disqualified him.

It looked to many like Paz had reached the end of the line as a contender. But that was before Kevin Rooney got hold of him.

His new trainer made him to go up not one but two weights, into the super welter division, and convinced him he'd still have the might to trouble the heavier men.

He dropped down to domestic level to capture the USBA strap on points against Ron Amundsen in 1991 and plotted his way towards another world title shot.

Opponents were running scared of new WBA super welter champion Gilbert Dele and the Frenchman was not afraid of facing Paz.

Hard-hitting southpaw Dele was so convinced he'd smash through the smaller man he agreed to defend his title at the Providence Civic Centre.

He hadn't counted on Paz's chin, as well as his power, making the transition and found out the hard way later in 1991.

What some called a 'freak fight' saw Dele's best shots count for nothing as Paz kept on coming, beating him to the punch before stopping him in the 12th and last round.

Paz had upset the odds to stun Dele but there appeared next to no chance of him winning his battle against the car crash that followed. Paz, as always, had other ideas.

He said, 'I literally almost died after the Mayweather fight and, if it wasn't for Kevin Rooney, I'd have probably carried on doing the same thing until I retired.

'I've had some good coaches come in and out of my life, but he was the best. I loved Kevin, he was the bomb. I got lucky to have him and my parents supporting me.

'Hector Camacho is no longer with us and he had his last great fight against me. He knew it would be a war with me.

'I remember we were doing a commercial and I was telling him I was going to hurt him bad. He said he would be ready for me.

'He was as fast as lightning in the ring, so hard to hit and real slippery, with real great boxing skills. He was a southpaw, too, which would help me later against Dele.

'I thought about retiring after Garza; if I had won, I would have. I just wanted a title again so, when it didn't happen, it might have been the end. Then Kevin came along.

'I beat the tar out of one of his best middleweights, a guy called Kelvin Prather, in the gym when Kevin and everyone else was watching.

'He told me to get on the scales and I was like an elephant, because I wasn't going to be fighting anytime soon. I thought he was kidding when he said I was going up to 154lbs.

'Beating Dele was the greatest night of my life; it couldn't have got much better for me at all. Everything about it was awesome.

'He was undefeated in 30 pro fights and he was knocking everybody out and putting them in the hospital. He was a bad dude but that was my time and what he'd done didn't bother me.

'I bought a house the same month that I fought him, so I could put pressure on myself. If I didn't win, the "for sale" sign was going up again.

'I beat him and stopped him in the last round, won the title and was on top of the world. Then I broke my neck in a car accident. It turned out to be a good thing. I made the rest of my career happen for the people who were worrying about me. That's the crowd I was fighting for.'

Coming back from the brink and getting back into the ring is one thing; trying to restore former glories in your thirties after suffering a serious injury is quite another.

But Paz was determined to give it his best shot and he went up a weight again in 1993, to ease the tension of training on his body.

He dared to dream of becoming the first Italian-American to win a world middleweight title since Jake LaMotta.

Brett Lally retired after six rounds against Paz before he was paired with Englishman Lloyd Honeyghan, a former undisputed world champion at welter with 26 stoppages on his record.

It was considered a measure of how Paz could bridge the gaps between weight divisions when the two met in a non-title match that June, which was scheduled for 12 rounds.

Paz did a demolition job on Honeyghan, dropping him to the canvas with vicious assaults in the third, ninth and tenth rounds.

With added belief in his own power, instead of pursuing his 160lb ambitions he travelled up yet another weight, campaigning at super middle for what proved to be the rest of his career.

Another acid test was lined up against a naturally bigger and more powerful rival in Robbie Sims, Marvin Hagler's half-brother, over ten rounds.

Paz worked his jab to perfection and peppered Sims with left hooks to win convincingly on points, establishing him as a force at either middleweight or super middle.

He said, 'Lloyd is a great guy. He was awesome at one time but I fought him towards the end of his career. I won and it was no big deal to me because he was past his prime.

'Robbie Sims was a bad ass, all the way from the amateurs. He was also Hagler's main sparring partner. He was probably the best fighter to never win a world title.

'One day, I just happened to go to Marvin's gym when he was sparring with Robbie. I watched them go at it for five rounds and I can tell you people would have paid to see it.

'I wanted to beat him [Sims] so bad; he'd hurt a couple of my friends in the ring and I was determined to do it for them.

'I beat him easy but it didn't happen like I wanted. I used to get jacked up for fights but I'd had stomach problems that were bothering me.

'I invited him back to my gym afterwards and I got ready for that sparring session like it was a world title fight. I battered him for three rounds and then his trainer, Goody Petronelli, took him out of there. We were supposed to box for five.

'My father was taking my gloves off and Goody goes, "Wow Paz, you've improved." I said, "Goody, are you out of your mind? I'm 33, I'm not going to improve now!"

'I just felt ill the day of the fight, I told him, otherwise that would have happened in front of the whole world.'

In what had already been a breakthrough year in the unlikeliest of circumstances, there was more glory to come for Paz in 1993 as another world opportunity came along.

It wasn't on the biggest of stages, a hotel in the Rocky Mountains setting of Aspen against the Canadian Dan Sherry for the vacant, and lesser regarded, IBO belt.

Paz neither knew nor cared about the details as he took full advantage with an 11th-round TKO that effectively made him a world champion for a third time.

It also made him only the second man in history to move up from lightweight to super middle and win world titles in both categories.

The first was the legendary Robert Duran and at the time 'Hands of Stone' was still looking to add to his impressive haul of world titles at a fifth weight.

Putting Paz and Duran together made for a perfect story, even though there were 11 years between them. The little-known IBC world title was at stake.

Paz was 31 at the time while Duran was in his 26th year as a pro when they first touched gloves in 1994.

It was still a rarity for Paz to be on the floor but he fell into the trap of thinking the older man couldn't hang with him.

Round five proved the old adage that the last thing to go is a fighter's power when Duran's trusty club put Paz down. Fortunately for Paz, he woke up and went on to become a clear points winner.

He said, 'I loved Duran because he could be an animal like me in the ring. Then I ended up in the ring with him. It was crazy to fight one of your idols.

'I joke around and tell people I fought him when he was 78 but, no matter how old he was, nobody ever hit me harder and I've been in there with guys who could knock down walls.

'When we met, we were at each other's throats. The first thing he tells me, after we barely shake hands, was that my girlfriend would be looking after me when he puts me in hospital.

'I had good legs, so I was moving around and pot-shotting him. He was 43, actually, and he could still fight, but not the way he used to. It's just impossible.

'You can get worse and not know it, because you're still young in your mind, but the last thing to ever go is a punch.

'I threw a bomb in the fifth, he got there first and, the next thing I know, the canvas is right next to my eyeball.

'I'm like "Oh my god, what am I doing down here? This is not where I'm supposed to be!" I jumped up and went to walk back to the corner.

'The referee was following me around counting and I still had time for a breather, so I went and put my head on the ropes.

'There were 15,000 people in the arena and there were celebrities and athletes there, so when I looked out to the audience I just happened to see Montel Williams [the talk show host] in the first row.

'I'd done his talk show with my mother a couple of months earlier and, afterwards, we went out to eat with him. He's a great guy.

'He caught my eye and he was shouting, "Vinny, come on, you can do it," and I'm thinking in my head, "Why don't you get in here with this maniac from Panama?"

'I never saw him again to tell him that [but] we'd have a good laugh about it. This was over 20 years ago. I thought I'd beat Duran a little easier; I was a little off but I got the win.'

Duran raged about the result, particularly the fact that none of the judges even gave him the fifth round despite the knockdown.

He argued that he didn't lose the fight at all, and added he wouldn't be retiring, throwing open the possibility of a rematch.

Paz took him up on his offer and in January 1995 they clashed for the IBC bauble for the second time in six months.

Duran could have no complaints this time, with Paz dominating the second half of the fight and making him look foolish by the end.

With no knockdown to call on, Duran was well beaten and Paz had done the double over him, although not without some more scary moments.

He said, 'When the second fight came around, he was much nicer to me. I think I'd earned his respect by then.

'How many people can say they earned a president of the United States millions of dollars? We did in the rematch, because it was at Trump Plaza in Atlantic City.

'I was moving well again and hit him with a big left hook in the first round, but he took it like it was no big deal. Then he gets me with a right hand, dead straight on the jaw.

'He was so different than the first fight; his defence was still unbelievable and it brought me back to the days when I was an amateur. That inspired me for the rest of my career.

'It was like hitting an oak tree and when he got you back, he was solid as a rock. After another right hand in the sixth, I couldn't have told you where I was for about a minute.

'I outworked him in the end, which was the way I could win as the younger man. Duran wasn't in shape that time.'

It was Paz's turn to be the old tiger against the young lion in June 1995, when he challenged Roy Jones Jr, the reigning IBF champion.

Billed as 'The Devil and Mr Jones', the fight saw Paz's track record of staying upright vanish as the champion did a number on him, dropping him three times in the sixth for the finish. Beaten but as determined as ever, Paz refused to give up on further success and lined up a bout for WBU world honours in 1996.

Paz and Dana Rosenblatt soon took a dislike to each other, which added spice to the affair. Untested but unbeaten, Rosenblatt was ten years the younger man.

That seemed to tell early on as both threw wild bombs, with little regard for skills. It was certainly a slugfest.

Down went Paz in the very first round but all that did was make him mad, as he immediately shot up and decked an off-guard Rosenblatt, even though it was ruled a slip.

Rosenblatt completely outboxed Paz until the fourth round, when a great equaliser, a huge right hand from Paz, bowled him over.

A dazed Rosenblatt wobbled as he answered the count and shipped a ton of punches before referee Tony Orlando stepped in, nearly catching a stray blow from Paz in the process.

Paz's only fight across the pond came in 1997, when he was matched with Herol 'Bomber' Graham for the WBC international title in London.

His trip to England was fun until the end of the 12 rounds, when Paz feels he was unjustly treated by the judges at Wembley Arena. Graham won by some distance on the scorecards.

Paz went back to the States and put together a five-fight winning run, which set up a return with Rosenblatt for the IBO world belt in 1999.

Rosenblatt exacted his revenge on a split decision after Paz had run him close for 12 rounds.

Fellow veteran Aaron Davis came next in a ten-rounder.

Davis handed out a beating like the one Jones gave Paz, who was pulled out of a bloodbath in the eighth by the referee and ringside doctor.

Paz had now turned 39 but gave it one last push, with a tilt at WBC champion Eric Lucas in 2002 undoubtedly his last stand.

Standing on 49 pro victories from 59 contests, Paz wanted to make it 50 wins before he hung up his gloves. Not for the first time, it went away from him on points.

He would get that 50th victory, outpointing Tucker Pudwill two years later at the age of 41 in his swansong. Now a five-time world champion, Paz had boxed 25 times since the crash.

He said, 'I knew I'd have to be lucky to win the Jones fight. It would take for me to be at 100 per cent and him to be at 80 per cent.

'They got me good; they promoted the show so they picked everything from the size of the ring to the gloves we used.

'I was told we'd be on about 9.30pm to 10pm, so I'd been in my dressing room ready from 8pm. There was no fight until ten minutes after midnight.

'When we were told to go out there, my father had to wake me up because I was asleep on the massage table. I felt about dead walking to the ring.

'It was one of those "My God fights" as in, "My God, please let the other guy have a bad night." I probably had about five of them.

'The first rematch with Haugen, Roger Mayweather, Loreto Garza and Aaron Davis were the others. It's not a good feeling.

'Rosenblatt, I hate that guy. He was some kid who used to look through the dictionary for big words so he could look smart. I used to call him "Rosen-splatt".

'With Graham, I beat him clearly and there's still no doubt in my mind about that. You know if you've won or not.

'I was in England and I knew I'd have to knock him out. If I hadn't have come over with a porn star I would have, but that's a whole different story!

'I didn't get the decision that I should have, but I thought I would stop him. I'd been close to coming to England to fight Nigel Benn before that, but it never came off.

'I would have loved that. Can you imagine me versus Benn? It would have been "the Dark Destroyer" and "the Pazmanian Devil". Sounds like something from an after-school club!

'Lucas was under-rated but I just wasn't the same anymore. All through it, I kept thinking, "If I was ten years younger, I'd kick his ass," but I wasn't. I was nearly 40.

'My last fight was the weirdest of my career, because my mother and father were both gone. I'd always call my mum before I got to the ring and my dad used to walk me out.

'Pudwill was going for his 40th win and was beating me after five rounds, but I turned it on and stepped things up.

'I was confident I'd knock anybody out. I won 50, all told, and got 30 TKOs. It's a good ratio. I joke a lot that I had 60 pro fights, five world titles and three brain cells left.

'There are four reasons why I won five world titles and that was I had persistence and determination, I worked hard and I never quit. Boxing is a crazy game but I still love the art of the sport, where two fighters duke it out until one wins. It just gets ugly sometimes. There's an old adage that if you work at the donut factory, you get sick of the donuts, but there's nothing better than a good fight and that's going to last until the end of time.

'I got to 50 wins and I was content and happy with what I'd done, so I knew it was it. I didn't want to fight any more.'

It was a long and winding tale that Paz laid bare at Bar Sport, in front of an audience that knew of him for different reasons.

Some hadn't heard of him until seeing *Bleed for This,* while others hadn't watched the film but remember his fighting days.

All searched which of those they weren't up to speed on after their visit to the Premier Suite, where Paz enjoyed light-hearted fighting talk with his interviewer.

Richie Woodhall was WBC champion at his weight from 1998 to 1999 and Paz had looked into becoming a challenger for him.

He joked, 'I kept watching Richie because I thought he was going to hit me with a sucker punch! He was a bad ass [but] he was kind of good looking as well.

'I just thought, "I want to mess this dude up" and years down the line, we are sitting next to each other. It's crazy.

'You can almost see how boxers live their life by how they fight. I was a wild man, in and out of the ring. I'd do anything to win; I wasn't worried about getting hurt or cut.

'Looking back now, I wonder how the hell I did all that. I won 100 as an amateur and 50 as a pro. It's a crazy amount and I'm lucky enough to still be in reasonably good health.

'They called me the "Pazmanian Devil" for a reason; I was aggressive and that was the only way I knew how to fight. I wanted it that way, to entertain people.

'Everything I've ever done, I did it big in life as well as in boxing. I'm different than the average person; I'm not better than anybody, but no one has had more fun than me.'

There ends the lesson from Vinny Paz, with the second half after the crash lasting longer than the first. Now you know what kind of man he is.

CHAPTER FOUR

THIS COULD HAVE BEEN DIFFERENT – BARRY McGUIGAN

IT was hotter than any *Hell's Kitchen* when Barry McGuigan lost his world title in the searing heat of Las Vegas.

The WBA world featherweight champion had no idea what he was letting himself in for when he landed in the United States to defend his title.

But the Irishman was soon under no illusions about what was ahead when the humidity hit him in the face as soon as he got to Vegas. The Strip was in the middle of a heatwave and there was no running for cover where he was going. The contest was to take place outside, in the open-air arena next to Caesars Palace.

Many big fights have been staged in the same place, before and since, including three *Ring* magazine Fights of the Year and the fatal bout between Ray Mancini and Deuk Koo Kim.

None of those could match the sweltering heat that McGuigan and his challenger Stevie Cruz would endure on 23 June 1986.

Cruz, a plumber's mate from Fort Worth in Texas, was more used to the conditions and better equipped to perform than the pale-skinned McGuigan.

That said, Cruz shouldn't really have been in with McGuigan at all. He was stepping in for Argentinian Fernando Sosa, who withdrew from the fight after detaching both of his retinas.

'The Super Kid', who was ranked number nine by the WBA, had been drafted in by promoter Bob Arum to ensure McGuigan, tied into an iron-clad contract, would appear on his show.

Not much had been done to offset the burning sun, with a canvas canopy rigged with 74 television lights around the ring only making things worse.

There was no turning back as the fighters made their way to the squared circle, with the temperature 43C (110F) before they even climbed through the ropes.

Referee Richard Steele mopped sweat from his brow before the first bell, when McGuigan bombed out of his corner, just like any other night. But the pace was unsustainable.

His usual aggression kept him on the front foot from rounds two to five before they took it in turns to fade, McGuigan in the sixth and seventh and Cruz in the eighth and ninth.

McGuigan had already poured everything he had into the bout and, come the tenth, was down in a neutral corner after being bowled over by a short left hook.

The champion, who had seldom been on the floor, was stunned but not beaten, and showed his grit to take the fight back to Cruz from rounds 11 to 15.

But the last round, with McGuigan ahead on two cards despite having a point deducted for low blows in the 11th, took the fight away from the Irishman. He literally had nothing left as he walked on to a two-punch combination from Cruz, and tried to hold on in desperation before stumbling away.

Cruz stalked him and connected with a left hook to the head, following up with a big right hand that decked him for a second time.

McGuigan used the mandatory eight count to try to get some breath back and then ran for cover, but Cruz caught him again.

Two right hands had very little power behind them, but they were enough to send McGuigan tumbling on to the ropes as he dropped to the canvas again.

He shot back up and saw the round out, ensuring that the cards would be needed, but the result now had a far different complexion.

All three judges went for Cruz by margins of 143-142, 143-139 and 142-141, but that was with three knockdowns and a docked point taken into account.

The elements had conspired to rob McGuigan of his crown. He was a spent force, with the fatigue too great for him to stand.

Tearful and beaten, he was taken to the Valley Hospital suffering from dehydration and concussion. Father Brian D'Arcy, who prayed with him before every fight, was by his side.

The decision to try and crack America had backfired, with McGuigan's belt gone and a rebuilding process now ahead of him.

He'd already proved a huge draw back home, dethroning the division's kingpin Eusebio Pedroza to become champion a year before in front of 18 million BBC television viewers.

In his first two defences, McGuigan retained his title on both sides of the Irish border, halting Bernard Taylor in Belfast and Danilo Cabrera in Dublin. His fight with Cabrera attracted 18.3m BBC viewers.

McGuigan said: 'There were millions of people watching me [versus Pedroza] on television, which was incredible. No fight in England had seen a bigger audience watching than that.

'I didn't have much time before I made my first title defence against Taylor, then I had a short break before getting ready to take on Cabrera.

'More [on the BBC] watched my second title defence against Cabrera. That gives you an idea of how popular boxing was in those days. It was amazing.

'Then I went out to Vegas and that was a mistake. It was unfortunate that I had to fight in those conditions and, if I had to do it again, I wouldn't have.

'It was so ridiculously hot. It was outside and the conditions were phenomenal. It was 110 degrees anyway, and the heat of the television lights made it 125.

'I didn't fear for my life but others who were with me, and my family and fans, were concerned about it, particularly as it went the full 15 rounds.

'It had dropped from 110F to 100F by the tenth round, but by that stage I was done anyway. I decided to have the fight, though. I was roped into a contract and couldn't get out of it.

'It was something I had to get on with, but when I look back at my career one regret is that I went through with it rather than going home.'

Cruz hadn't just caused an upset, he'd scuppered McGuigan's hopes of winning more titles and, ultimately, going up a division in a bid to become a two-weight world champion.

It had been thought that WBC featherweight champion Azumah Nelson might be interested in a unification bout but instead he ended up giving Cabrera another opportunity.

There was also talk a contract had been agreed with WBA super featherweight boss Wilfredo Gomez before the Puerto Rican lost his crown to Alfredo Layne in Puerto Rico that May.

After the Cruz defeat, McGuigan was out of the ring for nearly two years. In 1987, his world was turned completely upside down when his beloved father, Pat, died of cancer.

It wouldn't be the last time that tragedy would befall the McGuigan family. In 1994, Barry's elder brother Dermot committed suicide.

It happened on the 11th birthday of Barry's son, Blain. His daughter Danika was then diagnosed with leukaemia but got the all-clear in 1999.

Family means everything to McGuigan, who is the third of eight children and has two other sons, Jake and Shane, the latter now a pro boxing coach. He married wife Sandra in 1983.

Losing his dad hit McGuigan hard and it became difficult for him to contemplate boxing again. While he hadn't hung up his gloves, he didn't look like he was planning a comeback.

Pat had set the tone for every pro bout McGuigan had been involved in, singing his rendition of 'Danny Boy' as his son made his way to the ring. He was also famous in his own right, a popular singer who came fourth representing his country at the 1968 Eurovision Song Contest.

Things would never be the same for McGuigan, although he eventually returned to the ring after moving to England to work under a new trainer.

Under the management of Frank Warren, he would fight out of London, where he beat world title challengers Nicky Perez, Francisco Tomas da Cruz and Julio Cesar Miranda.

But the rebuilding process came unstuck in Manchester in May 1989, when he was cut badly and stopped in the fourth round against Jim McDonnell.

It was a world title eliminator and McDonnell went on to get a shot against Nelson, who had since become WBC titlist at super feather. Long punches were McDonnell's main weapon and a swinging left hand inflicted a cut by McGuigan's right eye at the start of the second round.

Realising the wound was getting worse, McGuigan piled on the pressure but it was to no avail. Just over halfway through the fourth, referee Mickey Vann stepped between the boxers and, after inspecting McGuigan's injury, waved the fight off.

Once again, the underdog had won and McGuigan was facing an uncertain future. But this time he knew what to do next.

He had stated beforehand he would call time on his career if he lost again. Just 30 minutes after the final bell, McGuigan announced his retirement and stuck to it. He was only 28.

He said: 'If Cruz hadn't happened, I would have held on to the belt for a lot longer and I would have gone up a division and won the super featherweight title.

'I have absolutely no doubt that would have happened, but circumstances took two years out of my life. I never retired during that time, though.

'My father was extremely close to me and, when he died, it was like someone had cut off my right arm. It was a very bad time for me.

'He was such a great man and died at just 52, which is no life at all. It was a very sad time. My brother later took his own life and my daughter got ill and almost died.

'I moved to England in November 1987 and rekindled my career, training with Jimmy Tibbs, but my father had gone and my mother, Kate, was unwell, although she recovered.

'I had four more fights, winning three by knockout and losing one on a cut, but it just wasn't the same. I worked very hard, but there just seemed to be something missing.

'When I did retire, I knew it was the right thing to do. I have no regrets about that. When I went into the ring, all it reminded me of was my father and I didn't have the same passion.'

McGuigan had achieved a good number of his other ambitions as a man and a fighter, in both his pro career and the unpaid days that had come before them. He was dubbed 'the Clones Cyclone', after the town where life began for him. His strong background would never allow him to stray far from his values.

Ireland was gripped by the Troubles, a war in his homeland that began in the late 1960s when he was a child and raged on until the Good Friday Agreement of peace was signed in 1998.

His entire boxing career came and went during the conflict and he first saw the disturbing cost of the bloodshed when he was barely a teenager.

It caused him to leave Wattlebridge Boxing Club, in the Northern Irish county of Fermanagh, and join Smithborough of the Republic. His mother insisted and for good reason.

In adulthood, he courted controversy by becoming a British citizen so he could win the British title and tying the knot with a Protestant, despite him being a Roman Catholic.

Fears McGuigan could be made a martyr for the Troubles also heightened, particularly around the time he beat Pedroza.

He returned to Ireland to a hero's welcome, hailed by a public reception in the streets of Belfast that attracted over 100,000 people.

He was named BBC Sports Personality of the Year in 1985, becoming the first person not born in the UK to win the award.

He said, 'I first went to my local boxing club, which was in a school. There were two ways of getting there, the longest being a cycle ride for nine miles.

'You could take the short route and that was half the distance, which me and my friends would inevitably do.

'One night, we were coming home and we saw a guy who had been tarred and feathered and was dead at the side of the road. The police and army were there.

'It was a dreadful ordeal for us and, by the time we arrived back home 30 minutes later, it was all over the news. My mother made me find another club.

'It was euphemistically termed as "the Troubles", but the reality was that people were dying every day. I was just sick of being told I had to be on one side or the other.

'I really didn't want to get involved in that. Too many people were suffering and they were being threatened by it, in many ways.

'You'd have a Protestant friend on the other side of town, but you couldn't bring him back to your house for their own safety. It was the same for Roman Catholics in some areas.

'I knew that existed but I was determined not to take sides. It was important to take a stance. I wore the flag of peace and our anthem was "Danny Boy".

'It meant a lot to the people and the more successful I became, the more pressure there seemed to be but I didn't mind that. It was still a really special time for me.

'It was an attitude that no one was thinking about at the time. Segregation and separatism are nasty things and some of the things I saw scared the life out of me.

'I wanted to bring people together through boxing and, although I never got threatened at any time, there was a red flag on me. I just wanted to bring people together through boxing but, for a while, there were guys in plain clothes 50 metres behind me everywhere I went.

'I was given a gun and it was a serious threat, both in the north and the south of Ireland. Thankfully, nothing happened.'

Another bone of contention for some people was that McGuigan had boxed for Northern Ireland, both at the 1978 Commonwealth Games and 1980 Olympics.

He would make history with Commonwealth gold and wanted to put himself firmly on the map by repeating the feat at the Olympics, going up to feather from bantamweight.

He had injured himself before and did so again taking out Issack Mabushi in the third round of his opening bout. He had no chance of recovering for Winfred Kabunda, who outpointed him in the next round.

Instead of waiting another four years for a second chance at the Olympics, McGuigan turned pro. He removed Selwyn Bell in two rounds of his debut on 10 May 1981.

He said, 'Although Clones is in the south, there are three counties in Ulster that are not part of Northern Ireland. There is Monaghan, where I'm from, Cavan and Donegal.

'Even though I was not from the north, I boxed in the Ulster championships, which was in Belfast, and it was always a dangerous thing to do in those days.

'I was 17 when I became the youngest Commonwealth Games gold medallist of all time. I had five fights in Canada.

'The guy I fought in the final, Tumat Sogolik, was the size of a tank. They kept us away from each other until the final and realised why when I first saw him.

'At international tournaments like that, you'd have bouts one after the other in different divisions like, for instance, a bantamweight contest and then a lightweight contest.

'We'd warm up in the same room and I looked across at this guy and thought he was one of the lightweights! It was only when I got in the ring that I realised he was my opponent.

'He was knocking everybody out, he was such an incredible puncher. He caught me with a right hand at the end of the second round and it felt like a house had fallen on top of me.

'I had never been hit like that before, we didn't have headguards on, and I held on for dear life. I rallied between rounds and beat him on points.

'That Commonwealth Games produced three Hall of Fame fighters in me, Azumah Nelson and Mike McCallum. Mike fought one of my team-mates, Ken Beattie, in the final.

'Ken was a really good welterweight but never turned professional and he told me Mike was the hardest fight he'd ever had.

'I won two more multi-national titles and, in 1979, moved up to feather because I couldn't do bantam anymore. I'd broken my hand, too, in the Irish seniors before the Olympics.

'The Americans boycotted the tournament that year and when people ask me what it was like out in Moscow, I tell them it was metallic and surreal but still an amazing experience.

'I stopped the Tanzanian kid in my first fight but I broke my hand again and I went in again a couple of days later after having a local anaesthetic.

'That was no excuse; I thought I won but I didn't get the decision. The Zambian fought what turned out to be the gold medallist next and, for me, beat him clearly but lost on points.

'I knew, by that stage, that I had the ability to be world class as a pro and three rounds were never enough for me. I thought I would be a lot better over that longer distance.

'I knew my fan base was going to be in Belfast. That's where I won most of my provincial titles, so it made sense, but I made my debut in Dublin. It was raining as it was outdoors.

'When I was walking to the ring, I had plastic bags on my feet so they wouldn't get wet and then the floor manager comes running towards me.

'He went, "You can't go out now, we've got to get the main event on!" It was on the undercard of Charlie Nash against Giuseppe Gibilisco for the European title.

'I had to turn around, go back to the dressing room and listen on the intercom until Charlie got stopped in the sixth. That was disappointing as I was such a fan of his.

'Then I had to go out and take on a guy who I stopped in two rounds. That felt good to see my fans and my family jump up and down.

'I remember reading *Boxing News* the next week and Harry Mullan, the old editor, had covered my fight for the magazine.

'He had written, "You'd think McGuigan had just won a world title, not become the 43rd guy to beat Selvin Bell." He later told me he regretted that after I did win a world title!'

McGuigan looked a hot prospect but his '0' would not last long. He scored just one more victory, a fourth-round TKO of Gary Lucas, before he ran into Peter Eubanks.

The crafty Eubanks – older brother of future world champion Chris – hustled his way to the cards and took the decision by a half of a point.

A smarting McGuigan exacted his revenge with 20 seconds left of another eight-rounder four months later before going into 1982, when he was active regularly.

A life-changing night on 14 May of that year put everything into perspective, though, after he touched gloves with Young Ali in his 12th professional contest.

McGuigan hit him on the bridge of his nose and saw his eyes go. The punch was among a number of damaging blows traded before Ali was knocked out in the sixth.

He never recovered, falling into a five-month coma before passing away on the day of McGuigan's first wedding anniversary.

That was the first time McGuigan contemplated giving up boxing, but he continued and ended up dedicating his world title victory to Ali.

McGuigan said: 'When that young man died, I felt as if that was it for me. I never got into boxing to take people's lives. Nobody wants to do that.

'We all want to make boxing as safe as it can be. It's the greatest sport in the world but when you go into the ring, you take those risks.

'If I was a racing car driver, someone could tell me you can't race because you run the risk of dying. I wouldn't care. You can't walk across the road with a guarantee you'll get there.

'My wife was pregnant [at the time of the Ali fight] and I hadn't got a bean. I had given my whole life to the sport, so I decided to carry on.

'I did also make a pact that if I ever became a world champion, I would dedicate the fight to Young Ali. I was in tears on the night, thinking of him, when I won the title.

'If I did win something very special, I was determined that I would remember that kid the night it happened. It was very important to me.'

Ali would certainly have been proud of the performance against Pedroza, who had spent years looking unbeatable.

The pride of Panama had held his belt for seven years and made 19 successful defences, a record in the featherweight division.

McGuigan was facing the biggest step up possible after claiming British and European titles, with 23 stoppages from his 26 wins, against the sole defeat by Eubanks.

A sell-out crowd of 26,000 packed into Queens Park Rangers' football ground at Loftus Road to watch the action up close.

People from England, who had been dragged into the Troubles, Northern Ireland and the Republic gathered under one roof and agreed, 'Tonight we leave the fighting to McGuigan.'

It was McGuigan's finest hour, with victory looking more likely from the seventh, when Pedroza hit the floor from a right hand.

The champion attempted to battle back but knew he had to stay away from the challenger, who was proving he carried the greater power.

A fantastic display of guile got Pedroza through to the final bell but he was widely outpointed on the cards, with at least seven rounds the difference with all three judges.

Pedroza showed his sportsmanship by throwing his arms around his nemesis and telling him, 'You will be a great champion.'

It never got any better than that for McGuigan but, even then, events were transpiring outside the ring that could have spelt disaster.

He said, 'I was going to stay in England until the middle of the following week, but the night I won the title my mother's house burned down because of an electrical fault.

'My mother and aunty Brid smelled the smoke and got out. In the grand scheme of things, it wasn't that important, as no one got hurt.

'I had tried to get a world title fight earlier. Pedroza agreed and went off and defended against Jose Caba in Italy and then again when he drew with Bernard Taylor.

'Ever since I turned pro, I knew Pedroza would still be the man to beat if I ever got to world level. He just had such wonderful technique.

'He was in the country with his manager when I defended the European title against a pretty hapless French guy [Farid Gallouze]. I either had to give him a shot or I'd be stripped.

'I remember looking around for him, it was the first time I'd done that, and he wasn't there. The same day,

England were playing football against the Republic of Ireland at Wembley.

'Quite a few of my fans were going to the game and had to run to make it to Wembley Arena in time for my fight. Worse for them still, it was over in two rounds!

'Negotiations had broken down for Pedroza and he made it clear there was absolutely no way he was going to Belfast, but he would go to London. Eventually, they signed a deal.

'Two weeks before my last spar, I threw a long left hook with my hand open in training and pulled all of the tendons in my elbow. Up to the fight from there, I had physio twice a day.

'The "Danny Boy" song means an awful lot to me but that time I didn't listen to it because I was that focused, but people in the crowd were crying.

'Irvine Welsh, who would write *Trainspotting* [a book that was turned into a film], was there that night and he was a young man at the time. He told me later how special it was to him.

'Most of the time, when I got to the top level, the other guy was better than me technically, but I had a better engine than all of them.

'I knew nobody could fight at my pace. I was a terrific body puncher and I worked forever to try and perfect that. I walked them down and kept my head moving as much as I could.

'When I went up against Pedroza, I wasn't going to match him for talent. The only way to beat him was to stay on him. I knew he'd blow a gasket after half a dozen rounds.

'He'd thrown everything he had at me before then and, in the fifth, he hit me that many times I thought there was two of him.

'It suited me to close that distance and put pressure on him. Being in the pocket, short to mid range, was where I wanted to be.

'Pedroza hardly never missed you; he was fantastically skilful but a lazy counter puncher. In the sixth, I nailed him with the left hook to the body.

'He was jumping around on his feet, trying to get some relief, and it was the first significant shot I had landed. That gave me heart.

'I remember practising a shot we used to call the "Smithborough Special", where I'd drag a hook to the body towards the head. I caught him flush on the chin with it in the seventh.

'I thought I had him then and he was in bad trouble in the ninth but, the amazing fighter he was, he went the distance. When the fight ended, I already knew I'd won.'

On the basis of all the evidence, and how the fight unfolded, it was always unlikely that winning feeling was ever going to be matched. At Queens Park Rangers, McGuigan was the king that night.

The year 1985 will always be the year McGuigan holds most dear, but life went on for him as it did for everyone else.

He had endeared himself to most of the general public and not just in the boxing community, but fighting was not where his talents ended.

He came from a family who were devoted to showbusiness, which is where he would have most likely plied his trade had he not taken up boxing.

Reality television came calling in 2007, which put him in the public eye for the first time since his glory days.

Cooking rather than fighting was the name of the game in ITV's *Celebrity Hell's Kitchen*, but McGuigan showed his versatility and ended up winning the competition.

He has repeatedly turned down offers to appear on *I'm a Celebrity, Get Me Out of Here!* but, much like boxing, you can never say never.

McGuigan said, 'I've actually got a very good voice, so I could have been a decent singer. I didn't play any musical instruments, though.

'My sister played piano and my mum sang in a choir, so we come from a musical family. My eldest son was in a pop band and my youngest is a decent guitarist. My daughter is an actress.

'You are in sport or some form of entertainment, that's the way it seems to be in our family. I didn't realise this until 20 years ago, but my grandfather was also a great sean nōs singer.

'That's the old Irish ballads where there seemed to be about 20 verses to a song. We always had musicians in the house, all of the time.

'We were right on the border, so bands would often stop with us as they were travelling to the north. We grew up with them.

'*Hell's Kitchen* was more of a popularity contest, it wasn't really because of my cooking skills. I wasn't good before I went in and whatever I've learned I've forgotten.

'It reintroduced me to the British public, if you like, and they put you in all sorts of awkward positions to see how you react under pressure.

'Most people end up falling apart and we had Jim Davidson [comedian and television presenter], who was arguing with everybody. I was the referee of that, more than anything.

'The viewers seemed to take to me and it was lovely to win the competition, but it doesn't mean an awful lot.

'I've had my time on television, I'm not going to do that again. They asked me three times to go into the jungle and I turned it down. It's just the thought of making a clown of yourself.'

There wasn't much McGuigan didn't talk about at Bar Sport, with the Premier Suite decked out in Shamrock green for the evening.

Every effort was made to ensure he would feel at home and everything had an Irish feel to it, including a good number of the crowd, who originally hailed from the same motherland.

In a fitting but unintentional tribute, Irish guests of both a Catholic and Protestant persuasion broke bread in the same room and enjoyed themselves.

There was a Clones connection, with singer Wayne Scott's mother hailing from the same hometown. Scott's version of 'Danny Boy' was personally saluted by McGuigan on the mic.

The laughs came from funnyman Mike Cash, also from Clones and once touted by the late Bernard Manning as 'one of the best comedians I have come across'.

A good night was had by all, and you left with the impression that the star of the show will have fans wherever he goes.

That's Barry McGuigan. Fighter, promoter, manager, aspiring singer, reality television performer, family man. And there's no chance of him ever resting on his laurels.

CHAPTER FIVE

IT'S UNDISPUTED
HE'S A TARTAN LEGEND
– KEN BUCHANAN

KEN Buchanan still bears the scars from the fateful night Roberto Duran put paid to his reign as world champion almost half a century ago.

Buchanan came into battle as the star that evening in 1972, climbing through the ropes as the WBA world lightweight champion who had given up his 'undisputed' status.

The fight venue, Madison Square Garden in New York, had become a home from home for the Scot, who had already appeared there twice, including retaining his title in the second of two defences in the US.

Buchanan's crowning glory had seen him dethrone Ismael Laguna in 1970 then outpoint him again in a rematch the following year. He hadn't seen the last of Latin-American opposition. Next came another Panamanian in Duran, who had just turned 21 but was already an undefeated puncher with 28 wins, 24 of those by stoppage.

Buchanan had already given up the WBC belt – the only other world title available at the time – in order to take the return fight against Laguna.

It took a then-record purse for a lightweight of $125,000 to get him into the ring with Duran on 26 June 1972.

A crowd of 18,821 generated a gate of $223,091, of which Duran received just 15 per cent. Having taken a financial hit, the challenger wanted to make Buchanan, a 2-1 favourite, pay.

As early as the first round, there was a sign of things to come when Buchanan wilted under a right and touched down, breaking his fall by putting both gloves on the canvas.

A vicious Duran continued to charge forward, determined to hit the champion with everything he had in his arsenal.

For Buchanan, that was the problem. The challenger scored with plenty of punches but there were just as many headbutts and low blows flying in. Without a doubt, he fought dirty.

Referee Johnny LoBianco issued only one warning, for the low blows. As the rounds wore on, Duran built up a good lead on the scorecards despite his rough-house tactics.

Buchanan, as tough as they come, used all of his guile to hang in there but even he could do nothing about what happened at the end of the 13th. The two fighters carried on trading blows after the bell had gone, which led to Duran unleashing a right that landed way below the belt.

Down went Buchanan writhing in agony on the canvas as all eyes turned to LoBianco, who subsequently ruled it a clean punch. Only television replays after the fight could convince him otherwise.

With no time to argue, Buchanan frantically tried to pull himself together but the man in the middle was having none of it, despite him being back on his feet.

In the corner before the 14th was due to start, LoBianco ignored Buchanan's pleas to continue and declared Duran the winner. Buchanan had been robbed of his title.

LoBianco, who was officiating in his first world title fight and went on to take charge of four more, had it eight rounds to three for Duran, with one drawn session.

There were two judges, with Bill Recht scoring the contest 9-2-1 and Jack Gordon calling it 8-3-1, both in favour of Duran. In reality, only a knockout could have saved Buchanan.

The referee only had to look down to see how badly Buchanan was hurt from the low blow, which was so hard it dented his groin protector. The physical problems it caused him remain to this day.

The WBA didn't order a rematch, despite the controversy, and Duran's camp turned Buchanan down flat for a return.

Duran went on to rule the 135lb division for seven years before moving up the weights, becoming a legendary four-division champion over five decades.

Buchanan would never win a world title again and, for him, the glory days were over. It bothered him so much down the years he tried to track Duran down, at the age of 50, in 1995.

His wealth gone, Buchanan was back working in his first trade of a joiner. Goodness only knows what would have happened had he found Duran on that two-week trip looking for him.

He said, 'Every time I think of Roberto, my balls hurt. I was in hospital for ten days afterwards, because I couldn't stop urinating blood. He was a big puncher, as we all know.

'It was discovered I had burst a testicle, which will never fully heal. I still get a shooting pain from it, once or twice a month, up my body. Whenever that happens, I think about that fight.

'I tried to find him, long after I'd finished boxing. I'd heard he was training in New York and, one day, I just went off site. I got on the plane there and somehow ended up in Harlem.

'I found myself in a bar with all these black guys wanting to know if I'd heard of this Scottish fighter called Ken Buchanan. I said I knew him pretty well.

'Some years later, Roberto was in the UK and we finally came face to face again. He's apologised to me and we've become friends.

'He knew he'd made a mistake, he's told me as much through his interpreter. He's never spoken English, he doesn't speak Scottish either!

'As soon as I heard that, I felt like a great weight had been lifted off my shoulders. It wasn't justice and it wasn't a rematch, but at least he did the honourable thing.

'It was his manager who wouldn't give us a rematch. I had nowhere to go with it, but I couldn't ever forget what happened.

'In boxing, you are always guided by the bell and, when it went, I dropped my hands and turned to move away.

'Roberto had committed himself and the punch was so low, it was only about six inches off the floor. He hit me illegally, right between the legs. He should have been disqualified.

'I believe he was ahead on points. I thought I was getting beat but he hadn't hurt me at that point. It was unfair to lose like that.

'I had no protection from the referee, apart from him saying "you're not coming out" after I told him I could keep boxing. Even when we clinched, he let Roberto keep me there.

'Roberto went on to become one of the all-time greats and I still considered that nice to see, as he was the man who beat me for the title.

'He would have fought me again, but I think he knew I would have boxed his head off. I underestimated him and I wouldn't have taken him so lightly twice. We'll never know now.'

Buchanan remains famous through his accomplishments, which are still remembered in his native Scotland, where he's regarded as their most successful boxer of all time.

He proudly sits alongside Alan Minter, Lloyd Honeyghan and Lennox Lewis as Brits who have reigned as undisputed champions, and is still the only Scot to do so.

His rags to riches story – and then rags again, depending on who you speak to – began on 28 June 1945 in the Edinburgh suburb of Northfield.

Parents Tommy and Cathie were staunch supporters of his sporting aspirations and a trip to the cinema with his father saw a young Ken watch *The Joe Louis Story*, a boxing biopic.

His aunts, Joan and Agnes, were shopping for Christmas presents in 1952 and bought him his first pair of boxing gloves, so he could have playful spars with his cousin Robert.

An aptitude for boxing led Ken to the local Sparta gym in the winter of 1953. He was eight years old.

Buchanan's amateur career would last until 1965, when he won the ABA senior title as a featherweight. He'd grown from a 3st 2lb boy into a young man who had just passed his teenage years.

He'd boxed internationally, too, in two European Championships but a controversial defeat to reigning Russian Olympic gold medallist Stanislav Stephashkin proved the last straw.

Buchanan was keen to become a pro but didn't want to leave Edinburgh, so turned over with Eddie Thomas, who paid him £500 for his signature.

Thomas lived in Wales but let Buchanan stay where he was, getting him his first ring time at the National Sporting Club in London on 20 September 1965.

Two-bout novice Brian 'Rocky' Tonks was dispatched in two rounds, with Buchanan going on to build a 16-0 record, six wins coming by TKO, before getting his first title opportunity.

The vacant Scottish area lightweight belt was on the line between Buchanan and John McMillan, who made a better fist of it than expected.

On 23 January 1967, Buchanan had his first outing in his homeland, at Glasgow's Central Hotel. He won on points, by a round and a quarter, in the opinion of referee George Smith.

Buchanan had compiled a winning streak of 22-0 when he narrowly outpointed Jim 'Spike' McCormack in a British title eliminator, earning him a shot at champion Maurice Cullen.

They clashed at the Anglo-American Sporting Club in London on 19 February 1968, with Cullen making his fourth defence.

Cullen was a stylish boxer but was overwhelmed by Buchanan, who put him down twice in the sixth and ninth rounds.

The game Cullen attempted to battle his way back but in the 11th was decked again by a perfect left hook. Buchanan claimed the crown by count-out.

The next step up was for European honours, which meant a trip to Spain to take on the reigning titlist Miguel Velazquez in Madrid on 29 January 1970.

The decks were always stacked against Buchanan, even more so when he went down in the ninth round from a sweeping right hand.

Their clash went the distance, with home spectators invading the ring to hoist their countryman on to their shoulders at the final bell.

A riot might well have ensued had Velazquez not retained his crown, which he did on a card that referee Signor Piero Brambilla initially refused to declare.

The sport can move in mysterious ways and the loss of Buchanan's '0' actually got him a world title fight, with Laguna and his camp confident he was beatable.

It was all on their terms, which meant that Buchanan this time had to travel all of the way to San Juan, in Puerto Rico, for the opportunity.

They touched gloves on 26 September 1970 in a sweltering Hiram Bithorn Stadium, which should have beaten the pale-skinned Scot before he started.

Instead, Buchanan's fleet-footed movement and trusty left hook worked arguably at its best against Laguna, who had been the undisputed world champion himself until a few days prior.

Buchanan had endured his own problems outside of the ring, too, and ignored an order from the British Boxing

Board of Control, who were at odds with the WBA, not to fight Laguna.

The champion had been stripped of the WBC belt for not fighting Mando Ramos instead of Buchanan, whose camp tried to negotiate with both Ramos and the governing body.

Buchanan went ahead anyway and was the underdog against Laguna, who set the pace bobbing and weaving in an effort to land chopping right hands and short blows on the inside.

Buchanan started to come on strong from the fifth round, moving in behind a snapping left jab, and dominated to great effect in the 12th.

He shook Laguna with a series of solid shots to the head that forced him to hold and continued his assault, which his opponent was struggling to block, until the bell.

The three judges were again called into play as the fight went the full 15 rounds. Away from home, it was by no means guaranteed they would go with Buchanan after a close fight.

All had just one point in it. Waldemar Schmidt scored it 144-143 for Laguna, while the other two, Pito Lopez and Jose Soto, had it 145-144 and 144-143 respectively, both for Buchanan.

The new champion immediately set his sights on the vacant WBC crown, which was to be contested by Buchanan and Ramos.

Ramos withdrew after being injured in a car accident and with the fight date fast approaching, in came Ruben Navarro as a late replacement on 12 February 1971.

He had just 72 hours' notice and had previously not been due to box until 13 days after, when he was scheduled to take on Jimmy Robertson at the Olympic Auditorium in the city.

Navarro had to train for five hours the day before to make the weight and put all his efforts into getting Buchanan out of the fight as early as possible.

It looked to have paid off in the very first round when Buchanan hit the floor, but referee Arthur Mercante said it wasn't a knockdown.

Navarro, after winning the fans over in the first three rounds, faded after the midway point, with the dancing and jabbing Buchanan pouring it on to win clearly on points.

A unanimous decision went his way, with two judges and the referee having Buchanan up by at least five rounds. He was the undisputed world champion at long last.

The WBC ordered Buchanan to defend against Pedro Carrasco, who had been campaigning as European boss at super lightweight, by 25 June of that year.

Buchanan instead wanted a rematch with Laguna, who was hardly flavour of the month with the WBC. By the end of it, the organisation took action and stripped him of their belt.

Buchanan said, 'Boxing has been in my blood since I first started at eight years old, in 1953. I've found it very difficult to give it up.

'I tried to get a trade doing joinery when I was an amateur and it was the longest apprenticeship you've ever heard of. It lasted eight years! That's how I ended up becoming the Fighting Carpenter and, little did I know it, I would go back to the tools when I couldn't box any more.

'I turned pro in 1965 and I was always boxing, which is4 why it took me so long to learn joinery. I'd won an ABA title that year and also a bronze medal in the European Championships.

'Stephashkin hit me very hard, he was very strong and the fight was 50-50. I could have beaten him, I could have lost. It was hard to call. I was ready to turn pro after that.

'I was nervous before every fight and, on my debut, I was up against a guy who had just come off three wins in a row. He was experienced but I was too fast for him.

'My manager was Eddie Thomas, who was Welsh, and he was taking care of Howard Winstone, who he'd already got world title fights for.

'Everything I did in boxing was leading up to becoming a world champion. It's the dream of everyone who puts on a pair of boxing gloves.

'My chance to do that had only come along to begin with because Laguna had won the world title, he wanted to defend it and they were looking for a patsy [slang for fool].

'They picked me, because I'd just lost to the European champion Miguel Velasquez in Spain. What they didn't know was I'd been robbed there. I wanted to go for Laguna and I did.

'We flew over 4,000 miles and, as soon as we came out of the airport in Puerto Rico, the humidity was that bad it nearly knocked me on my back. It was like walking into a wall.

'I always remember my dad [Tommy Buchanan] saying, "How are you going to fight in this heat, son?" If he didn't know, neither did I!

'I trained hard, though, and I spent the last two weeks getting ready over there. I got used to the conditions as much as I could.

'We went to San Juan, where the show was taking place in an outdoor stadium, and it was 125 degrees at 2pm. The heat was unbelievable.

'Laguna thought I'd go down dead easy, with the heat and everything, and he certainly didn't think I'd go the full 15 rounds.

'He spoke to me years later, through an interpreter. He admitted as much. He expected me to collapse after eight or nine.

'He was crafty. He'd gone out to the ring first and stole the corner that was shaded. I was burning up in the other corner.

'My dad had actually got hold of a parasol from a woman and, between the rounds, was holding it over my head.

'My manager was rubbing Vaseline on to my head and my dad was rubbing suntan lotion into my back. People don't believe me, but that's what happened.

'I pressured Laguna, stayed on top of him and, at the times he wanted a breather, that's when I went after him.

'He was a great champion, he knew the ropes and had fast hands. I still don't know how, but I just kept on going. It was a hard fight and, at the end of it, I was absolutely knackered.

'Laguna was complimentary towards me, he thanked me and we hugged. I was really happy with myself. Next to Duran, he was the best man I ever fought in my life.

'It was something that I'll never forget. I did what I wanted to do to become a world champion, but I had one big regret.

'I had promised my mother [Cathie] that I would do it for her and, 11 months after her death [from cancer], it happened. It was great, but I wish she had been there. That's life.

'My dad said she was looking down on me and, when I was getting tired in there, he was telling me to go out there and throw a few for my mum. I might not have done it otherwise.

'It was a great feeling to get the win and I expected a hero's welcome when I got home to Edinburgh, but there were only five people at the airport waiting for me.

'My wife was there, along with her mother and father, my brother Alan and my baby son, Mark, who had been born while I was away!

'I joked there was one more person in the house when I got home to when I had left. My dad, of course, was with me when I flew back.

'I wasn't undisputed, because they hadn't taken the WBC belt off Laguna. It was only a few days earlier when we found out.

'The WBC was vacant, so I was still the only world champion at that time. They wanted me to fight in Los Angeles, which I wasn't bothered about because I was getting a fair deal.

'It wasn't even supposed to be against Navarro, who they'd pulled in and fair play to him for having a go, but I beat him well on points.

'With that, I retained my title and won both belts, so I was finally the undisputed champion. Even if it was only for a short time, I've still got my place in history.

'I never actually got a say in it. The WBC just stopped recognising me as their champion. There was a letter I'd had, the boxing magazines also got hold of it and it just happened.

'Pedro Carrasco had to get his fight by a certain date [25 June 1971] or else. I thought that was a wee bit unusual, as he'd been boxing heavier for titles just before that.

'They never got their belt back, because the WBC make a new one for each champion. I kept it, as I did for every one I'd ever won.'

After becoming boxing royalty as a global ruler, Buchanan lived the high life and revelled in his new-found fame.

Madison Square Garden was his playground but he was still the Ken people knew and loved, particularly with fans across the pond.

Muhammad Ali knew all about that when the two were acquainted in New York on the night of 7 December 1970, with both due to be in the home corner.

It was only Ali's second fight since getting his pro boxing licence back, after his refusal to join the United States' Armed Forces for the Vietnam War led to a four-year ban.

Ali was still in possession of the *Ring* magazine and lineal heavyweight titles, which he'd retained in Las Vegas on his comeback against Jerry Quarry less than two months earlier.

His next defence was against Oscar Bonavena on the same card as Buchanan, then the new WBA lightweight boss, who was topping the bill in a ten-rounder with Donato Paduano.

Ali's legend had not preceded him that evening, though, and he arrived at MSG to discover he hadn't been allocated a dressing room.

The fighter formerly known as Cassius Clay ended up sharing with Buchanan before he went to work, eventually stopping Bonavena in the 15th and last round.

Buchanan followed with a unanimous points win over Paduano, despite giving away weight to Canada's welterweight champion, and was already in good spirits.

He said, 'I always looked at it that if you're fighting someone a stone heavier, then it's a stone slower. I was much faster than Paduano. I had Ali's number, too.

'It was my first time fighting at the Garden, but I had a dressing room and he didn't. When Ali got there, his coach Angelo Dundee came in and asked if he could share mine.

'I thought he was joking, so I played up to it. He had handlers with him and I was pretty clear that lot weren't coming in as well.

'There was an ashtray with a piece of chalk in it, which I took, bent down and drew a line with on the wooden floor.

'By the time I got to the end, Ali was standing there and went, "Hey man, what are you doing?" I told him, "Muhammad, this is my dressing room and I'm letting you share it, right?"

'He goes, "Yeah, but what's the line for?" I go, "Well, that's my side of the room and this is yours. If you dare cross that line!" I showed him my fist.

'The room went dead quiet for a few seconds. He did that tight-faced thing and burst out laughing. I thought, "Thank God he saw the funny side and he's not going to batter me!"

'Ali won, but it was a terrible fight. The fans weren't happy but they were brilliant to me. They loved seeing me in my tartan dressing gown and shorts. The Americans like all that.'

It may have been Buchanan's first time at the Garden, but it certainly wouldn't be his last and he experienced both triumph and heartache under those lights on four other occasions.

He also boxed at the Felt Forum, an arena underneath the Garden, making it six times he fought on the grounds.

He was Britain's highest earner in 1972 ahead of racing car driver Jackie Stewart, pop star Mick Jagger and golfer Tony Jacklin. He had become Ken Buchanan MBE the year before.

That breakthrough 1971 saw him voted British Sportsman of the Year, in the same year Princess Anne won the BBC Sports Personality award. They duly met at a function.

He said, 'I got the keys to the city in Edinburgh in 2017, too, so I've got the freedom of the city now. I still have to pay for my food and drinks, though!

'I went to Buckingham Palace, which was nice, and I knew I was getting rewarded for all of the hardships I had gone through as a boxer. It felt like I'd done something for the sport.

'I got that from the Queen Mother and I danced with Princess Anne at an event I was at, where she came in to receive an award.

'I've got two left feet when it comes to dancing, and I was so nervous, but I was still determined to strut my stuff.

'I had told her that I had come from a long line of dancers and it was in my blood. It wasn't long before she noticed otherwise.

'She said to me, "I thought dancing was in your blood? If that's the case, you've got poor circulation, because it hasn't reached your feet yet!" We had a good laugh about that.'

Despite their successes together, Buchanan's relationship with Thomas was becoming increasingly fractured. Right from the off, they hadn't always seen eye to eye.

Thomas once instructed Buchanan to urinate into his hands and run it into his face after one training session, supposedly to make his skin harder.

Jack Dempsey had previously used salt water for the same purpose, but Buchanan's dad, Tommy, suggested he use petroleum jelly around his eyes to keep his skin supple.

The fact Thomas was spending more time with another charge, the aforementioned Winstone, also irked Buchanan, who was often trained by other coaches on Thomas' team. They split after the rematch with Laguna, with his father taking care of his affairs from there. Buchanan versus Laguna part two had been a bruising battle.

Taking place on a Monday night, 13 September 1971, at MSG, Buchanan this time prevailed unanimously on points, ending Laguna's career.

He almost got him out of there early after a two-fisted barrage that lasted nearly a minute, driving Laguna through the ropes until he caught the top strand to pull himself back in.

Buchanan was bleeding and battered around both eyes himself, though, and could have been rendered unable to continue due to cuts. He went to great lengths to carry on.

It was a second and last defence of the WBA belt after the Navarro fight, in which his title had also been on the line. Then came Duran.

Buchanan said, 'The boys going into fights these days are not getting really hurt, because there's not a lot of blood flying about. It was different in my day.

'Against Laguna, my trainer took out a razor blade after eight rounds and slit my eye open, because the swelling was that bad.

'Sylvester Stallone stole that off me, because the same happened in the *Rocky* film. Rocky was into the corner yelling, "Cut me, cut me", although he never told me what he was doing!

'He just told me to hold on to the ropes and the television commentator was going, "That's amazing, there was no blood from Ken's nose or mouth and now it's running down his face."

'Scottish blood is the best going, I joked, and I just carried on.'

After Duran, Buchanan was back in action twice by the time 1972 was out, but it was clear that a path back to world titles was blocked.

He had to rebuild, but stoppages against Carlos Ortiz and Chang-Kil Lee at MSG before the year was out almost did him a favour.

Still in his twenties, Buchanan dropped down to domestic level for a much-anticipated battle of Scotland against Jim Watt.

They are friends now, but that wasn't the case when they battled for the British title, a crown Buchanan had refused to relinquish even when he became a world champion.

That angered the up-and-coming Watt and his manager Jimmy Murray, who stoked the fire by calling Buchanan 'over-rated' and 'easy to put on the floor'.

Watt instead had to box and win an eliminator against Willie Reilly, while the British Boxing Board of Control tried to get their belt back.

But Watt then cut his eye against Reilly in a rematch for the strap, forcing a tenth-round technical stoppage. The title was again declared vacant.

It finally went to Watt after he halted Tony Riley in the 12th of another challenge. When he eventually locked horns with Buchanan on 29 January 1973, he was the defending titlist.

It took place at the Albany Hotel in Glasgow, amid much fanfare in their home country. It wasn't Edinburgh, where Buchanan always wanted to box as a pro and never did, but it was close. With a dethroned world champion back on the domestic scene pitted against a hot prospect who had aspirations of stepping up, there was more than just the belt on the line.

There was a gulf of pro experience between the two, with Buchanan in action for a 48th time while it was Watt's 18th outing.

There was only four years in age between the two, though, with Buchanan the senior of the two men at 28, while Watt was 24.

The St Andrew's Sporting Club had only just been formed when it staged the fight and there were only 500 tickets sold, so it was a relatively private affair.

Watt exceeded expectations to make the score far closer than predicted after 15 rounds, but was two points behind Buchanan with referee George Smith.

Buchanan said, 'It was an east versus west encounter and I brought a busload from Edinburgh with me, so I had good support.

'I wanted to beat him to win the Lonsdale Belt outright. I didn't think the fight would go the distance, I thought I'd knock him out.

'I'd never lost to a southpaw in my life, because of how good my left hand was, and I caught him with some nice shots early on.

'He was hanging on to my waist while I threw my arms in the air and it was good to see him do that, because he was using his head there.

'George was the referee and Jim had been like "Aye, another boyo from Edinburgh," but he was the top referee in Scotland at the time.

'When I got the decision, I told Jim not to be so daft. He was a better man than I thought and he made me work hard, but I was in no doubt that I'd won.

'I gave up the title after that, so Jim could fight for it. People used to think, "Ken hates Jimmy and Jimmy hates Ken," but that had nothing to do with it.

'Imagine that fight now. I was a former world champion and Jimmy was going to become the world champion down the line with a victory over me. I couldn't allow that to happen.'

Buchanan got momentum after the Watt victory and went on a ten-fight winning run, including righting the wrongs of attempting to win the European title.

He was eight contests into that hot streak when he travelled to Cagliari in Italy to take on Antonio Puddu, with both in pro action for the 56th time.

They went hell for leather and shook each other at the start, but it was Buchanan who emerged from a gun-slinging contest with the belt after stopping Puddu in the sixth.

He put down Winston Noel six times in two rounds for another TKO and then made Leonard Tavarez's corner throw the towel in during round 14, all three fights coming in 1974.

The latter was a European title defence, but an opportunity at the WBC world title was to come Buchanan's way as 1975 rolled around.

He would have to travel even further afield to the Metropolitan Gym in Tokyo, Japan, for Guts Ishimatsu's third defence.

Ishimatsu had been beaten by Laguna and Duran before winning world honours at the third attempt, halting Rodolfo Gonzalez to finally claim glory.

Buchanan knew he was in the last chance saloon with the odds stacked against him, but his range deserted him on fight night.

The fast left jab was in full effect but too often the follow-up right hand missed its target. Knowing he was behind on points, Buchanan went for the knockout in the last two rounds.

It was Ishimatsu's left hand, though, that curried more favour, as he'd worked body and head and combined his shots with the right cross.

The three judges all had it for the champion by scores of one round, two rounds and eight rounds respectively.

Dick Young had it 144-142, British official Harry Gibbs scored it 145-144, while Seji Ebine was the widest of the trio with 149-141. It made for a unanimous decision.

The latter scorecard seemed far-fetched, as even Ishimatsu wasn't sure who was ahead come the 15th and final round.

Buchanan's vision had been impaired from the sixth round, a Japanese sparring partner having apparently injured his left eye beforehand.

But that was the end of his career at the very top level, although he still had the European strap to fall back on.

That took him back to Cagliari in Italy, this time to tackle Giancarlo Usai. He halted him in the 12th and retained, but it wasn't to be for long as he soon retired and vacated.

Buchanan will be the first to tell you that leaving boxing behind left a big hole in his life, and his personal affairs fell apart from there. Divorcing his first wife, Carol, as a father-of-two, accounted for much of his fortune and he had to sell the Edinburgh hotel he owned to meet the settlement.

His return to the ring in 1979 was as much about necessity as it was desire, although after a couple of warm-up affairs he picked up where he left off with the European crown.

He clashed with Northern Irishman Charlie Nash in Brondby, Denmark, and again it went away from Buchanan on points.

Most had it close, referee Robert Desgain scoring 116-115 while judges Knud Jensen and Fernando Paredes both had it 118-116.

That was it for Buchanan on the big stage, the remaining six pro bouts of his career coming in small halls with little fanfare.

The last was an out-of-sorts points defeat in 1982 to George Feeney, who later got a non-title fight with one of Buchanan's successors as WBA champion, Ray Mancini.

The three were reunited at Bar Sport, with Buchanan in his seventies and free of the personal issues that had plagued his life.

He'd drifted off into unlicensed boxing after his pro career had drawn to a close, partly due to the eye problems that stopped him from retaining his licence.

He went back to work as a joiner and withdrew from public life, but burning the candle at both ends had become a habit.

Buchanan had long felt unappreciated in boxing, particularly in Edinburgh, where he'd dreamed of headlining and never did. It was an ambition that went unfulfilled.

It was only in later life that he got the plaudits his efforts deserved, starting with induction into the International Boxing Hall of Fame in 2000.

The Ken Buchanan Foundation has been established to raise funds for a statue of him in Edinburgh, so his achievements will never be forgotten.

Bar Sport became big backers of the project, with owner Scott Murray's late father, Alan, a Scotsman who regarded Buchanan as one of his heroes.

Buchanan has been to hell and back, but is still here to tell the tale. It's only when others have tried and failed to emulate him that his feats have got their full respect.

He said, 'I've heard all sorts of stories about me being in the gutter, but that's a load of rubbish. Let me tell you, I've never even been bankrupt.

'I've used drink as therapy, in the past, when I got fed up and it's played a big part in my life. It caused the break-up of my second marriage, but not the first.

'I went back to work as a joiner, which pulled me out of it a wee bit. As the years have gone on, I've been able to look back at boxing and be proud of what I achieved.

'When you retire, you get time to sit down and reflect about what you've done in the ring. I just wanted to be a world champion; the money didn't really matter to me.

'I'd always enjoyed working on the tools but because I was working on a building site, people thought I was bringing myself down a wee bit. I was quite happy, though.

'The Hall of Fame changed my life completely, it was like being reborn. It's great now to go here and there and talk about my career.

'I love boxing and, if I could, I'd do it all again from tomorrow but, if I knew what I was doing, I'd make a few changes.'

And, through it all, Buchanan is finally at peace. Scotland will certainly have to produce a fine fighter if he is ever to have a true equal.

CHAPTER SIX

BUILDING AN EMPIRE, BUILDING A LEGACY – ANTHONY JOSHUA AND CARL FRAMPTON

IT'S not just the MBE status of Anthony Joshua and Carl Frampton that stand out – both are history makers in boxing.

Heavyweight idol Joshua has won all sorts of accolades, picking up his gong before he had even turned professional for winning a gold medal at the London 2012 Olympic Games.

You'll gather just how far Joshua has come from the upgrade to an OBE at the start of 2019, such have been his services to boxing already.

A stack of titles and a personal fortune running into millions quickly followed his entry into the pro ranks, which saw him become a world champion in his 16th contest. Of the 120 rounds he had been scheduled to box up to that point, Joshua needed a combined total of 32 to beat every opponent put in front of him.

Next to feel Joshua's power was American Charles Martin, who was beaten in less than two rounds in April 2016 for the IBF world crown. It was a victory that suddenly put Joshua, then still only a prospect, on a much higher pedestal.

He had won a world heavyweight title faster than anyone in British boxing history and was the fifth quickest worldwide, taking two years and seven months to achieve the feat.

Leon Spinks is the fastest in just 13 months followed by Mike Tyson (one year and eight months), Ray Mercer (one year, 11 months) and John Tate (two years, five months).

Many believe Joshua is already among the best fighters Britain has ever produced and his thrilling victory over Wladimir Klitschko, the modern-day gatekeeper of the division, reinforced that view.

The clash with Klitschko in 2017 was notable for three reasons – Joshua dropped for the first time as a pro, how he came back to prevail and the huge commercial success of the fight.

Klitschko caught Joshua with a straight right hand in the sixth and sent him to the canvas, having been down himself a round earlier.

Joshua will freely admit he barely knew where he was for a few minutes afterwards, but Klitschko was too hesitant to capitalise.

Wladimir's brother Vitali should apparently shoulder the blame, after telling his younger sibling to bide his time before going for the stoppage.

Rumour had it Vitali was so upset about how the game plan backfired that he considered coming out of retirement to avenge the defeat. An uppercut from Joshua nearly took Wladimir's head off in the 11th and Klitschko was floored twice more in the round before the finish, ending one of the most entertaining heavyweight affairs for years.

It came in front of 90,000 spectators at Wembley Stadium in London, setting a new post-war record attendance for a boxing show.

Carl Froch versus George Groves had drawn 80,000 to the same venue two years earlier to set a precedent. Froch wasn't half gutted it had been surpassed.

If his career ended tomorrow, Joshua would be financially set for the rest of his life and could easily make the transition into television or movies. Indeed, the camera loves him.

Everything he's ever done has been box office and, with the help of promoter Eddie Hearn, he's taken the sport to new levels in Britain.

Bar Sport holds the distinction of being Joshua's first-ever public speaking engagement, the first time in 2015, before he'd climbed to the top of his profession. It was one for the ladies, too, with most of those who met Joshua at the private meet and greet declaring he was the man of their dreams.

He returned in 2016, all of 18 days after dethroning Martin for his first world title, on the same day his first defence against Dominic Breazeale sold out in 30 minutes.

Whatever happens from here, Joshua will be able to look back at the good times and he'll never forget his first world title victory.

He said: 'People always talk about game plans, but it's all the same to me. Boxing is not complicated. I train the best I can and, if I can, I'll get the win.

'Almost every fighter comes into the ring in their peak physical condition, but mindset is the most important thing to me.

'I want to make the biggest impact I can. There's no turning back now. People believe I will beat the opponents I'm going in with and I appreciate the level I've been put on.

'Back then, I was knuckling down to training and we were talking about fighting an American, someone like Bryant Jennings. Then Charles Martin started calling me out.

'A world champion was asking me to take him on. I believed I could beat him, but it was how I would be going about my business after that. We would be going into a serious league.

'If it had been anyone else's decision, I wouldn't have ever fought him. I trust the people who train me and guide me and I listen to what they say.

'If anything goes wrong in the ring, it's me who has to pay the price but it was me who was pushing for it. That's just the sort of fighting person I am. We had three sparring partners over from America and, if it wasn't for them, I don't think the performance would have been as clinical as it was.

'Think about cycles, too. I knew I'd stand a good chance as I'd had a better pro grounding than people thought. If I was still an amateur, I'd be preparing for the Olympics again.

'Then there's the media attention you get. When you're an unknown, no one cares about what you're doing. When you're in the public eye, they are waiting for you to fail.

'It's a catch 22 situation and it comes with the territory but, on the night, there were no nerves. I had my music on and my cousins were in the changing rooms with me.

'It all felt a bit routine and I was a lot more edgy about the Olympic final. It was a home tournament and I'd only been boxing for just over four years.

'By the time of the Martin fight, I'd been around eight years and I was a lot calmer, because I knew I'd learned my profession.

'When the bell rang, Martin was standing side on and I thought, "I'm just going to pepper him for the first three rounds."

'It didn't surprise me when I was catching him with shots, because I know what I can do when I want to slug. I put him down twice and the second one was for good.

'I thought he was capable of getting up, because he wasn't out cold. If he wanted to, he would have, but he'd have got a serious beating.'

He may come across as a wholesome athlete now, but it hasn't always been like that. Like everyone, Joshua has a past and there are parts of it he's not proud of.

He was born Anthony Oluwafemi Olaseni Joshua to Nigerian mum Yeta and Nigerian-Irish father Robert on 15 October 1989.

There was trouble in his teens and brushes with the law up until he was 20, when he knuckled down and dedicated himself to boxing.

He was always a keen sportsman, a promising footballer and sprinter who could run 100 metres in just over ten seconds.

He started boxing in 2007, when he was 17, when his cousin Ben Ileyemi took him to Finchley Boxing Club in London.

But his antics outside the gym continued and came to a head in 2011, when he was arrested for possession with intent to supply drugs. Police spotted him speeding in his Mercedes-Benz and, after they pulled him over, found 8oz of herbal cannabis hidden in his sports bag.

He was suspended by GB Boxing, whose tracksuit he was wearing at the time, but not cast aside, giving him some hope.

Team GB had fast-tracked the double senior ABA champion through their programme to get him ready for the Olympics and weren't giving up on him.

Prison was a possibility but Joshua escaped with a sentence of 100 hours of unpaid work and a 12-month community order.

Having come so close to ruining his career, Joshua stayed on the straight and narrow and tried to avoid the wrong path.

The following year, he became famous at London 2012 when he squeezed past Italian Roberto Cammarelle to win gold in the super heavyweight final.

He'd also beaten the Italian in the 2011 World Championships en route to a silver medal, but it could have been second place in the rematch.

Cammarelle won the first and second rounds, leaving Joshua with it all to do for the third and final session. He won on countback, a decision which was criticised in some quarters.

He turned pro in October of that year, having previously turned down a £50,000 pro deal to become an Olympian.

Hearn won the race for his signature, promising to produce the biggest boxing star Britain had ever seen. That part turned out to be easy.

He racked up 15 wins, all stoppages, before challenging for the world title, with only one opponent going past three rounds with him.

That was old enemy Dillian Whyte, who had beaten him in the amateurs and promised to do it again in their grudge match for the British and Commonwealth titles.

Whyte had dined out on his bragging rights over Joshua, who he had knocked down en route to a points decision and was one of only four men to have beaten him in the amateurs. Joshua redressed the balance against Whyte in the rematch but only after the fight had descended into chaos at the end of the first round.

After the bell, Whyte continued to attack Joshua, who was being held by referee Howard Foster. It led to both sets of entourages, followed by security, invading the ring.

With order restored, the action hotted up again with Joshua hurt for the first time by a left hook in the second.

But Joshua regrouped and dropped Whyte in the seventh with a savage uppercut to leave his rival brutally beaten.

Whyte was vanquished but had given Joshua his first real test as a pro. Both have since risen to world class, but there will always be a competitive edge between the two.

Joshua said, 'There is no sport like boxing and I didn't take it up for money. I didn't turn pro before the Olympics as I wanted to win medals. Turning that £50,000 down was easy really.

'I like a game of chess and it's the same type of thing in the ring, taking your opponent's pieces and then counter-attacking. You need to be two moves ahead, all of the time.

'I have a bricklaying qualification, which is what I'd be doing if I wasn't boxing. I would probably be trying to start my own company, like those people who go around the estates.

'There is still more to do, I've got to keep making an impact. I know it's my era and I just want to make a legacy. Maybe I already have.

'There are two sides to opponents; you've got that competitiveness between two men and then you've got your rivalries.

'When I started boxing, I never classed myself as a boxer. I was just training. I remember having my first two fights and winning them both by knockout.

'I thought boxing was easy up to when I fought Dillian [as an amateur]. We got the call on the Thursday night and, in this sport, you can't ever show any fear.

'I wanted to take the opportunity, even at 24 hours' notice, I went up there and had a good scrap but lost. I took it a bit lightly and got dropped, but I was never getting stopped.

'It was one of those bumps in the road you contend with and I saw it as a positive, because I took a lot away from the experience. It wasn't really a level playing field anyway.

'We were supposed to fight again as amateurs, but he got banned and went down the pro route. There wasn't any rivalry at that point. I was just meant to get my own back.

'It did make me take my boxing more seriously after that and I achieved what I achieved, but Dillian was one of the first pros to start mentioning my name. Even his coach was doing it.

'When anybody calls me out, I take it seriously but they were doing it when I was still an amateur. When the British title came up and we'd both turned over, it was easy to make.

'The second time, you could have had that fight in a car park, it was such a brawl. Whenever it's me and Dillian, I just like to go to war. He brings that side out in me. I tried to box but it soon went out of the window. I'm not shy of a little scrap and Dillian brings that to the table.

'There was so much emotion and that made for a mental environment inside of the ring. It was hard to keep your mind straight.

'I put so much into it. Even at the end of the first round, I went back to my corner and my heart was beating fast.

'He hit me with that left hook in the second and I was like, "That wasn't in the script!" I held myself together and managed to carry the power through, which is important.

'I nearly took his head off in the end and I enjoyed the fight 100 per cent. We've always had a proper grudge match going.

'I'll always want to do it again. In my mind, let's just keep this rivalry going and carry on entertaining people. It's never over between me and Dillian.'

Joshua and Whyte continued to rise in stock, but the trilogy showdown has still yet to materalise, although at least one offer was made.

On the back of success over Klitschko, Joshua would make a successful first defence against Carlos Takam in Cardiff, removing him during round ten. A unification fight would follow, again at the Principality Stadium, where he added the WBO strap to his stash by outpointing Joseph Parker.

The one thing that Joshua did concede was his perfect knockout ratio, in pro bout 21, before returning to Wembley to take on Alexander Povetkin.

He got Povetkin out of there in seven, but didn't look unstoppable in the process. Perhaps the seeds had been sown for what would come next.

Joshua was supposed to crack the United States, headlining at Madison Square Garden against Jerrell Miller. It first went south when Miller got banned, after failing a drugs test.

In came Andy Ruiz Jr, a late replacement considered overweight who, on appearance alone, had next to no chance of winning. Whyte, at one point, had been tempted to fill the breach.

A few extra pounds count for little in heavyweight boxing and Ruiz, the most unfancied of outsiders, pulled off one of the biggest shocks of the modern era.

It looked to be going to plan when Joshua floored Ruiz with a left hook in the third, but he hadn't banked on the counter-punches that were coming back.

Joshua went to pieces, never really recovered and was dropped four times himself before the end came. The '0' of the 1-25 favourite went with it, as his recorded changed to 22-1.

Coping with defeat is something Frampton can relate to, but he'll always be a hero in his native land as the first Northern Irishman to become a two-weight world champion.

His route to the top was more conventional, but he's had the box office fights as well. The people of his country have every reason to be proud of him.

He arrived at Bar Sport in 2017 without a belt, though, after losing for the first time as a pro to Leo Santa Cruz in a rematch.

Despite the setback, Frampton was in good spirits and loved spending time with former world middleweight champion Steve Collins, who was brought on to the show down the line as an added attraction.

The two shared a common bond as Collins was the first and only other boxer from Ireland to win world titles in two weight classes.

Collins is as formidable a joker as he is a fighter and he had Frampton in stitches after a comment he made to a kickboxer he had met backstage.

'The Jackal' tweeted as much the following day, recalling Collins' quip, 'I tried kickboxing once, couldn't get the gloves on my feet!'

Frampton already had the respect of the audience in the Premier Suite and has proved a force to be reckoned with in multiple divisions.

He was brought up in a loyalist part of Belfast called Tiger's Bay, separated from the nearby nationalist New Lodge area by 30ft-high fences.

The Troubles were deemed to be over after the Good Friday Agreement of peace in 1998, by which time Frampton was 11 and had already started boxing.

He represented the Midlands Boxing Club and, on occasion, would spar at the Holy Trinity gym on the other side of the fence.

Frampton started out as a flyweight, with the Irish Amateur Boxing Association governing the sport in both the Republic of Ireland and Northern Ireland.

He was a part of the All-Ireland High Performance squad, starting up a domestic rivalry with Paddy Barnes that saw Frampton knocked out of the ring in one contest.

They later became the best of friends after Barnes went up a weight and Frampton served as best man at Barnes' wedding.

Frampton won his first national title, the Irish senior flyweight prize, in 2005 at the age of 18 and would go on to become an amateur centurion.

He had previously boxed internationally at the 2003 World Cadet Championships and did so again at the 2005 European Youth competition, but failed to medal in both.

It wasn't until the 2007 European Union Championships, held in Dublin, that Frampton got on to the podium, claiming silver as runner-up to France's Khedafi Djielkhir.

Frampton had gone up to featherweight by then, where he stayed until the end of his amateur career in 2009.

His final year on the unpaid circuit saw him claim another Irish senior title at feather, finishing his amateur career with 114 wins from 125 fights, with 11 defeats.

He said, 'I've had fans supporting me from all over the world. They come from Belfast, Dublin, Manchester, Leeds, Glasgow, Lisbon and even Cannock!

'I was brought up in Tiger's Bay, a working-class area, and I used to mess around on the street, like any normal kid from those surroundings. I had a few fights on the school yard or street corner to settle disputes, when I got frustrated, but I was never your brash type. Being small, I'd have been easily picked on.

'I stayed out of trouble because of boxing, which I got into from the age of seven, but I had mates who went down that route. It just taught me how to defend myself in a tough area.

'I grew up at the back end of the Troubles and Belfast is one of the best cities in the world now. I had a good childhood.

'The quickest way to Belfast city centre was through New Lodge, but I wouldn't go that way when I was a kid – you'd take the long way around.

'I tried to stay out of all that stuff as much as I could. Holy Trinity was only a five-minute walk, but we'd always go by car. There's still a bit of tension here, but mostly it's fine now.

'I get asked all of the time, "Would you have liked to have represented Great Britain?" The answer is no. I was looked after by Irish boxing from 11 years old and I was very proud. I had a decent amateur career but I don't really feel like I dedicated myself. If I'd put the effort in, I'd have done a lot more.

'I was a teenager and more interested in chasing girls than going down the boxing gym five nights a week.

'I wanted to go to the Olympics but I wasn't good enough at the time and I loved the thought of becoming a professional champion.

'I admired Wayne McCullough as a kid; he'd won world titles and was from Belfast. He was my hero in boxing.

'From the age of ten, I knew that I wanted to be a pro and by 15 or 16, I had attributes that were better equipped to the pro game – a good chin, big heart and heavy punch.

'Even as a young kid, I punched harder than most my own age. Real concussive power is largely a God-given thing that comes from a combination of timing, speed and strength.'

Frampton slimmed down after turning pro in June 2009 and settled into the super bantamweight division, debuting with a second-round TKO win over Sandor Szinavel.

Coming under the management of Barry McGuigan, himself a former world champion and Irish hero, drew inevitable comparisons.

McGuigan's fight nights had seen peace prevail between warring spectators at a time when the Troubles were firmly in the public eye.

The conflict had long since died down when Frampton turned over, Yannis Lakrout becoming the first man to take him the distance in his second fight before 2009 was out. The following year, McGuigan took Frampton to the King's Hall and Ulster

Hall in Belfast, where he had memorably made his own name nearly 30 years earlier.

After a win over Yuriy Voronin at Ulster Hall, Frampton returned to the venue less than three months later to stop Scotland's Gavin Reid in two rounds for the vacant Celtic title.

The win over Reid might have been easy but Frampton would have to work far harder to outpoint Robbie Turley and successfully defend in his opponent's backyard of Wales.

Scott Quigg and Rendall Munroe were both namechecked as potential opponents before Frampton decided to go for the Commonwealth crown later in 2011.

That was when his rivalry with Kiko Martinez was initially due to begin, but the Spaniard's withdrawal for personal reasons meant another vacant title fight against Aussie Mark Quon.

Quon went down in four to Frampton, who would retain against Kris Hughes and Prosper Ankrah by TKO, the latter notable for Quigg's presence on punditry duties.

Frampton called out Quigg, who was managed by Ricky Hatton at the time, with McGuigan and promoter Eddie Hearn – who would later switch sides – following suit.

The fight didn't happen in 2016 but Frampton moved on to improve his standing with the IBF by winning their inter-continental title.

Unbeaten Mexican Raul Hirales was picked to face Frampton but was completely outboxed in what was almost a whitewash points victory.

Frampton closed out 2012 with a sixth-round stoppage of former IBF champion Steve Molitor and looked odds-on to land a full world title shot with the organisation.

He said, 'I had a lot of top-class sparring when I turned pro with guys like John Simpson, Stevie Bell and Choi Tseveenpurev, who hit me with an uppercut I felt for about a week.

'Sometimes I got beat up but I learned my trade and it benefited my career. I think some kids today get off too easily and they'll come up short when they get thrown in the deep end.

'My debut was at the Olympia in Liverpool. I was on about 6pm in front of about ten people on a televised undercard.

'You see guys now stepping past the domestic scene and going for international titles, which are nice belts to walk around with but you never really fight anybody for it.

'I fought for the Celtic title and, although it wasn't a major belt, it was a big deal for me. I knew Gavin was tough and to stop him in two made a big statement.

'I defended it against Robbie Turley and it was my first fight live on Sky Sports. He was the most awkward opponent I'd ever fought in my life. It was a hell of a fight for me and I learned so much from it. I won but Robbie made it as tough as he could.

'Quon was comfortable but I had to give the lad credit as he'd stepped up to the plate at late notice. It took something spectacular to get rid of Hughes [a right hook], but I delivered.

'The rivalry with Quigg started when I beat Voronin and then Gavin for my first title, in my sixth and seventh pro fights.

'Quigg had beaten them in his 15th and 18th fights4, but I got rid of them before he did. When he won the British title, people started putting our names together.

'My grandad, Jimmy, was a big boxing fan and he'd always wanted me to win a Lonsdale Belt, because he thought it was the most beautiful belt in the sport.

'I agreed with that and I wanted to do it, but Quigg was the champion and he wouldn't fight me at that point. I was looking for him all of the time.

'I certainly don't believe I was given anywhere near enough credit for my win over Hirales, or for getting Molitor out of there.

'I boxed the whole of the Hirales fight off the back foot, which I always preferred when I was international as an amateur.

'Molitor was a world-class opponent. I knew it was a big test and I passed it with flying colours. No one could have expected anything more.'

In the meantime, Martinez had got his hands on the European title for a second time and, without ever touching gloves, there was unfinished business between him and Frampton.

Frampton got home advantage, too, when they clashed in 2013 at Belfast's Odyssey Arena, but the champion wasn't worried.

Martinez had previously demolished Irishman Bernard Dunne in one round at the city's Point six years earlier and fancied his chances again.

Frampton, though, was to prove a whole different proposition and the 8,000 fans who turned out to watch him went home happy.

He led on all three scorecards, two by four rounds, going into the ninth. Martinez had never been put over but down he went from a devastating right hand.

He stumbled around the ring after climbing to his feet but referee Anssi Perajoki spared him further punishment and his title went to Frampton.

Frampton put up his newly won title and IBF bauble against Jeremy Parodi, ranked number four by the organisation, in what was billed as an eliminator later that year.

The manner of victory was even more emphatic, with the Frenchman counted out in the sixth after taking a body shot in front of a crowd of 9,000 fans at the Odyssey Arena.

In the meantime, Martinez had somehow beaten Frampton to the IBF world title by dethorning Jhonathan Romero, himself considered a fortunate world champion, in six rounds.

New manager Sergio Martinez, a pound-for-pound middleweight great with name recognition, got him that opportunity.

Frampton instead pursued WBC honours in his first outing of early 2014, with Santa Cruz holding that status at the time. They would do battle later and up a weight at feather.

A final eliminator saw Frampton take another former world champion in Hugo Fidel Cazares, who was floored in two by a left hook to the head.

Again, a world title shot didn't materialise, so a smarting Martinez was approached and he was as game as ever.

Martinez again brought his belt to Belfast, where a temporary outdoor arena was erected at the Titanic Quarter to house 16,000 people.

He promised he was an improved adversary and moved away from Frampton's jab early, but a cut on his left eye caused by a punch in the third saw him slip back into hot-head mode.

Frampton had him on the mat again with a booming right hook in the fifth but, on this occasion, there would be no surrender from Martinez as he heard the final bell.

Two scores of 119-108 and one of 118-111 with the three officials reflected the margin of Frampton's victory on a night that had been a long time coming.

Martinez, as always, was a good sport. He let Frampton keep hold of the belt to show off to the legions of fans while, as always, a fresh one was made for the new champion by the IBF.

Not everyone was on the edge of their seats, though. Frampton's baby daughter, Carla, fell asleep at ringside in the arms of his expectant wife Christine.

Frampton said, 'I've kept telling her about it ever since. It's a night I'll never forget and all I could hear was noise. I'm usually calm in there but it was emotional for me.

'I've never cared about getting hurt. I'm fearful of not boxing to my best, losing and being embarrassed by someone who shouldn't be beating me. I just don't want to let anyone down.

'You need to put that pressure on yourself and I knew how huge my first world title shot was for me. I'd already knocked Kiko out for the European title, so people expected me to win.

'Everyone thought all I had to do was turn up, so the pressure was massive on me. Kiko had gone on to become a champion and his confidence was high.

'It didn't surprise me he did that because he's a good fighter and it was a great performance that won him that world belt. He was at his best against me, yet I thoroughly outboxed him.

'I think it was one of the better performances of my career. I didn't stop him but it was easier than the first fight, where he just wouldn't slow down until I got him out of there.

'I dropped him and I was hoping he wouldn't get up. He did and the referee wouldn't let him continue. In the rematch, I felt completely in control. I'm not going to say it was the perfect performance and my face afterwards would tell you that it wasn't. I got hit a fair few times but that's going to happen against a guy like Kiko.

'I couldn't pick out many faults. I don't want to sound big-headed, but I stamped my authority on the fight and I could have gone for 15 rounds. The messages of congratulations I got after were unbelievable. I got tweets from Naomi Campbell and Sheamus [WWE wrestler]. Bono [U2 singer] also sent me a nice gift.

'It was the best year of my life. I won my first world title, had a lovely civic reception and my second daughter, Rossa, was born that November.'

Frampton was still making it clear that he wanted to take on Quigg, who didn't become a world champion until he clobbered Martinez in two for the WBA crown on 18 July 2015.

That February, Frampton's first challenger, Chris Avalos, took a one-sided beating until he went down swinging in round five.

Looking to make his mark across the pond, Frampton then travelled to El Paso in Texas for his second defence, against Alejandro Gonzalez Jr, at the Don Haskins Convention Centre.

His American debut against second-generation boxer but huge underdog Gonzalez was supposed to be routine, but certainly didn't look it after the first round.

Frampton hit the floor twice under the weight of Gonzalez's blows but shot up again quickly. Down but not hurt, he responded by dominating the rest of the fight.

Gonzalez had two extra points he scored for the knockdowns taken away for low blows, and at the final bell Frampton was named the victor with scores of 116-108 (twice) and 115-109.

Quigg revelled in the problems Frampton endured, quipping that he was 'up and down like a yo-yo'. Smelling blood, Frampton was offered £1.5m to fight him at the Manchester Arena.

Hearn paid his own fighter £500,000 plus a share of the pay-per-view revenue – which Frampton had no stake in – if the numbers reached 500,000 buys.

Frampton and Quigg finally touched gloves on 27 February 2016 in a world title unification contest, live on Sky Sports Box Office in front of a sell-out crowd.

Frampton bossed the early rounds and broke Quigg's jaw with an uppercut in the fourth, which wasn't known to those watching until after the fight.

Quigg rallied and took the fight to Frampton in the second half, but Frampton gave as good as he got before it went to the cards.

The announcement of a split decision heightened the nerves as it was read out that one judge had it 115-113 for Quigg, with the two others going with Frampton by scores of 116-112.

Hearn and Quigg had been made to regret their course of action. Frampton had silenced his rival and made big money doing it.

He said, 'The best thing that happened was me, in relation to Quigg, going to El Paso in Texas to fight Gonzalez. I was dropped twice in the first and then got up to win.

'Quigg had been watching and saw weaknesses that he thought he could exploit so, all of a sudden, it was on.

'I always believed I could beat him. Sky Sports were making people believe like it was a 50-50 fight, but I kept telling everyone in the build-up that it wasn't.

'I beat him in his backyard but it felt like I was in Belfast that night because I had so many of my fans in the crowd.

'I remember going back to my corner at the end of the sixth round and he was starting to blow a bit, but I was as good as I was at the start.

'I was winning the rounds by doing very little but that was down to Quigg not wanting to get too involved with me. He got his tactics wrong that night and I never got out of second gear.

'He came forward a bit late on but I already had the fight won by then. It was comfortable for me in the end. I couldn't believe it was a split decision, I had no idea what that judge was watching. He needed to have a long, hard look at himself.

'I knew I'd beat him and I knew it would be a boring fight, but I couldn't let on because we had to sell it. Quigg is an OK fighter, that's all. I always expect to see him in the crowd somewhere, he follows me everywhere I go. I've moved on from him.'

Frampton became a double super bantamweight champion, but would never contest the WBA title or his IBF belt again.

The WBA ordered him to defend against Guillermo Rigondeaux in July and wrote to him when reports suggested he had no intention of doing so.

Frampton didn't respond and none of his team contacted Rigondeaux's representatives. The WBA stripped him in April.

Negotiations were instead under way for Frampton to go back to feather and take on the WBA boss at that weight, which was now Santa Cruz.

Frampton had to vacate the IBF strap before he climbed through the ropes at the Barclays Centre in New York on 30 July 2016.

A fight of the year contender developed, with Frampton boxing smartly as Santa Cruz bombed forward, striking the cleaner punches despite throwing fewer.

It was Frampton's hand that was raised as he won a majority points decision. One judge had it a draw, 114-114, with the other two going with Frampton, 116-112 and 117-111 respectively.

Santa Cruz immediately chased a rematch, with Frampton wanting to fulfil his lifelong dream of headlining at Windsor Park back home.

Instead, the chance to box in Las Vegas presented itself and as it was an opportunity to crack America, Frampton gave it the nod.

The rematch took place at the MGM Grand on 28 January 2017 and, this time, Santa Cruz had a game plan that was outside of his norm.

He held back and invited Frampton to come after him, which he did, but his punch accuracy deserted him. An indifferent performance again led to a majority call.

One judge had them level, 114-114, but the other two picked Santa Cruz by 115-113. Frampton had lost for the first time as a pro after 23 outings.

Not used to defeat, it hit him hard and in the months that followed, a well-documented split with McGuigan unfolded.

Frampton went on to pick up an interim WBO world featherweight title under Frank Warren, who had a greater tussle in mind: Frampton vs Josh Warrington, the IBF champion.

Three days before Christmas 2018 the pair met in Manchester, with Frampton losing a thriller on points. Frampton, though, had already left his mark.

Reflecting on his rivalry with Santa Cruz, he said, 'People forget that Santa Cruz started at bantamweight, while I'd been as low as flyweight. He's not a huge puncher, but he gets on top of people and beats them up.

'He thought he was going to overwhelm me and be the stronger man when we first met, but I reckon I'm the strongest fighter he's ever fought. I hurt him, but he wasn't hurting me.

'I heard him wincing when we got in close and I was pushing him around. The way he fought that night suited me.

'The second time, I thought it was going to be more of the same [but] he outsmarted me and stayed on the back foot.

'I'd had some bad rounds early on, so I was trying to force the fight and that's not my game. He was switched on all of the time.

'When you're in close with Santa Cruz, you need to keep punching but he was throwing three or four shots and then moving away.

'I probably performed at about 75 to 80 per cent and, when you're a world champion, you need to be at the top of your game to get your hand raised. My tank was still relatively full.

'He definitely won, you looked at the two corners and they were celebrating, while I thought I lost the fight convincingly.

'When I watched it back, it was closer than it seemed when I was in there but he deserved it. I won the first one by doing one thing, I lost the second because I got that wrong.

'I was properly gutted to lose, so I went on the drink and forgot about it. We had a good night and enjoyed ourselves.

'We were in the Irish pub across from the MGM, then I went back to my suite with a few close friends. We had a few more drinks, then a few tears with a few jars in me.

'I didn't let it upset me too much. I got beat by a three-weight world champion on a bad performance for me and it was still relatively close.

'I was more disappointed for the fans. I don't know if there is another fighter in the UK now who would bring that support to Vegas.

'Would Anthony Joshua bring 5,000 to Vegas? Maybe he would, but for me to do it as a little featherweight makes me very proud.

'I do appreciate it and going out and having a drink with them in Vegas wasn't for show. That was a thank you from me.

'I put a tab on in New York but there were that many people in Vegas I would have lost my purse. Hopefully, everyone got a drink.'

There would be plenty more written about the careers of Joshua and Frampton, with the end game long removed from their visits to Bar Sport, but it was already a great body of work.

CHAPTER SEVEN

FROM THE DARK DESTROYER CAME LIGHT – NIGEL BENN

THE road to righteousness proved to be long and winding, and littered with pitfalls, before Nigel Benn finally found his calling in life. There's no doubting what the Dark Destroyer brought to the ring in his heyday and the legacy he left when he hung up his gloves.

But it's clear that the fight really began when the thrills and spills of in-ring combat were over, as he battled with personal demons.

There had been black marks against him, even during his boxing career, and some of the company he kept was questionable.

Sport kept him on the straight and narrow and, when it was gone, much murkier surroundings and situations often followed his actions. That was where the problems really started. Benn took up DJ'ing, partied hard and lived the high life with the same gusto he had shown in boxing.

He became an addict, not to drink or drugs but to sex. The consequences drove him to a suicide attempt before he was saved by religion. From there, the only thing that mattered was his faith and his family. But the thinking was he couldn't stay in England as too much had happened for that.

Benn couldn't have previously imagined leaving the country of his birth behind for good, even during all of those training camps in Spain.

It was to the Iberian peninsula that he headed first, but that didn't prove to be the fresh start he'd anticipated. He needed to go further afield.

Australia was certainly far enough and it's felt, to him, like the only other place on Earth where he could really settle. They had tried a few places before arriving Down Under.

There's plenty of God's work there for him, too, as he advises on the pitfalls he encountered while wandering down that perilous path.

Benn and his second wife, Carolyne, are still together and counsel couples facing marriage issues. Benn works with fellow addicts and young people at risk.

He hasn't completely left his past behind and still enjoys trips back to the UK. His son, Conor, followed him into pro boxing and lives in Brentwood, Essex.

Dad rarely misses watching him in action and, while he's in England, there are still plenty of fans, young and old, who want to meet Benn Sr. So it proved when he came to Bar Sport.

He still commanded respect as a world champion at two weights who, at one point, was one of the most marketable boxers in Britain.

He lifted the WBO middleweight title and went on to become one of the greatest WBC super middleweight champions.

He was only the third holder of the strap he defended nine times. His image was enshrined on to the organisation's sixth-generation 168lb belt.

It was St George's Day of 2015 when Benn starred in the Premier Suite and he hadn't changed all that much. He was still in great shape two decades after this retirement.

What was different and came over loud and clear was that, for the first time, he seemed to be truly happy. Mending his ways brought an enlightenment.

He couldn't be content had he not learned from the trials and tribulations along the way. Coming out on top is the biggest victory he's ever known.

He said, 'I've achieved way beyond my dreams of what I set out to do. To win two world titles was a dream come true, but that's a part of my life that has finished now.

'I got the call to become a born-again Christian and it changed my life forever. I am not unique, other boxers have as well. There's Evander Holyfield and Andre Ward, to name two.

'I've been to Spain many times and lived there for a while, but God moved me to Australia and it's a lovely country. I have been there for years now and it's been the best experience.

'To tell you the truth, my wife suggested it. I thought she must be mad, because everything is venomous over there. Then I worked through it.

'We lived in Miami, Los Angeles, Jamaica, Hawaii – you can put them all together and they don't add up to Australia. I absolutely love it there, I feel at home.

'I wouldn't come back to England, ever [to live]! I live in Sydney but I am about 45 minutes away from the city. It's the quiet life and no one really knows me, which I like.

'It's peaceful and different to how things have been, so I am enjoying it. I have my family time with my wife and kids, and work for the Lord. That's about it.

'I'm chasing nothing any more. My Porsche has gone, my Cadillac's gone, I've got rid of everything, but what I have is contentment.

'It's only through Jesus that I'm still married. If it wasn't for her [Carolyne], I'd be six feet under or in a mental hospital. I was one of the biggest sinners. Now a lie is something I can't live with.

'I was 41 when I had my first encounter with Him. I came home to my wife and admitted to all of the times that I'd been unfaithful.

'The life I had before wasn't healthy – I burned the candle at both ends. With fame and success, there was sex and temptation.

'It was just crazy, like being on a merry-go-round. It never stopped until I retired. I partied hard. All through my career was a dark place.

'When I was training, I had peace. When I wasn't, I'd be in what I thought were some of the best clubs going. It was all self inflicted, but now it's all changed. I'm in a different place.

'Me winning world titles was never going to get me into heaven, it doesn't mean anything. The life that I have now is a blessing. When you talk about Jesus, you are always on the up.'

While Benn may live on the other side of the world, he's never forgotten his roots. But his humble beginnings were, at times, a test of character.

He has experienced the good, the bad, the ugly and the tragic to get where he is today, and is testament to the proverb, 'What doesn't kill you makes you stronger.'

Benn was born – for the first time, he'd claim – on 22 January 1964 in the East London suburb of Ilford. He was part of a tough sporting family that also produced a famous footballing cousin in Paul Ince.

Father Dickson had arrived in Britain from Barbados eight years earlier, wife Mina joining him a year later. Nigel was the sixth of seven children, all boys.

He loved his upbringing but tragedy sent him off the rails. Older brother Andy died when Nigel was just eight. It was an event that deeply Nigel and put a tremendous strain on the family. Some of the wounds have never healed.

With his future looking bleak he became Private Benn, joining the army at 17. The move became one of his saving graces and he grew up quickly.

He called on the grit instilled in him through his upbringing when touring war-torn Ulster for 18 months of his near five-year term. It was where Benn laced on gloves for the first time, too. He'd previously had a keen interest in martial arts but never seriously considered boxing. As it turned out, he never lost a fight in the army.

Leaving the forces, Benn still needed the discipline that only boxing could provide. He didn't fancy a 'proper job' either, so it made even more sense.

He had already showed extraordinary power, winning titles from welterweight all the way up to heavyweight while still in the forces, representing the Royal Regiment of Fusiliers.

After serving his term, Benn joined West Ham Boxing Club in 1985, the year he suffered his only unpaid loss.

Benn only walked into the gym for a light-hearted spar with his mates. They boiled him down to welterweight for his first club contest.

He would feature in that year's ABA tournament and went up against former stablemate Roy Andre, who had switched clubs, in the area phases. He rolled over him accordingly.

One of the best-ever London ABA finals, screened on BBC *Grandstand*, saw a brave Benn battered from pillar to post by two-time winner Rod Douglas, who took a third title on points.

The beaten contender contemplated quitting boxing and then swore revenge, meeting Douglas again in the ABA area semi-finals the following year.

Once again, they went toe to toe in a compelling war but this time Benn had his hand raised on points. Big puncher Mark Edwards went the same way in the London final.

All of a sudden, he was in there with Johnny Melfah at Wembley Arena to decide the national title. He bashed him around with aplomb to become champion.

Benn's ferocious performance attracted offers to turn pro, but the 22-year-old dreamed of representing his country at the 1986 Commonwealth Games in Glasgow.

Amateur politics reared their head again as Douglas was picked ahead of Benn, whose 'do-or-die' style failed to find favour with the selectors. That told Benn all he needed to know.

Douglas was the only man who had ever beaten him as an amateur, but Benn believed other forces were at work. He nearly quit the sport altogether over it.

He turned in the vest, took on Burt McCarthy as his manager and went pro. With that, the Dark Destroyer was born.

Benn said, 'My childhood was great. We never had much, but we were happy. I was a handful, though, and I did some naughty things.

'I never lost any respect for my parents, but I changed when my brother died. I carried a lot of anger from then on. Even in my 20s, I was still cut up. We don't all talk about it, even now.

'I was always fighting from a young age, in school and everywhere else. I didn't have any fear of anything like that. I could really hurt people.

'I started to go to areas where I shouldn't have been, like in Dagenham, where there was a lot of support for the National Front. I didn't look for trouble, but I'd fight them.

'I would shoplift, brawl and end up in the police station time and again. I remember one time when I was arrested for a street fight.

'I had took on an Indian guy and the colour drained out of my face when my dad came. But he told me, "I can stand fighting, but if you nick anything off anyone you are in big trouble."

'I was out of control, no doubt. If it hadn't been for my family, I would have been holding up banks and everything. I never had a chip on my shoulder – I thank my dad for that.

'I had to join the army, I knew I would be inside [in prison] or dead otherwise. I needed something to channel my anger and it worked for me. It was a wake-up call and I never looked back.

'That was when I first took up boxing. If you are good at sport there, you haven't got to spend all of your time doing that soldier business.

'I did my fair share of that, too, with three years in Germany and 18 months in Northern Ireland. Proper army training taught me to be second to none. It became my rule.

'When I was out on patrol, and it was sleeting, the rain bouncing off my chest, I thought, "I'm a warrior. This is me." I was determined, nothing stopped me.

'It gave me that little bit extra as a boxer. It was never a case of, "It's a bit cold out there, it's raining, I'm not going running."

'The army taught me how to switch on and off. If I had been on civvy street, before boxing, I would have been switched off all the time.

'I was able to go out partying and then switch back on and get back into hard training. The army gave me that determination, that will to win.

'I came out of the army and got a job as a store detective in Woolworths, down in Hackney, along with doing cash in transit as a security guard.

'I did well as an amateur and I desperately wanted a place at the Commonwealth Games. I beat everyone, only ever lost one fight, and still didn't make it.

'I think it was down to favouritism. There were fighters who seemed to be ahead of me, no matter what I did.

'I came to the conclusion that I was better off as a pro because, first and foremost, they get paid for getting into the ring. That was the decider!'

McCarthy managed Benn for the entirety of his debut year, 1987, in which Benn boxed on average once a month to go 12-0, all wins by stoppage. Promoter Frank Warren then took up the mantle and got Benn his first title opportunity in April

1988. By then, Benn had squeezed in another four bouts, all TKO victories.

With all 16 of his fights ending by knockout, only three going past two rounds, Benn met Ghanaian Abdul Umaru Sanda for the vacant Commonwealth middleweight title. Sanda suffered the same fate, decked twice and halted in the second.

Benn's next five fights – including two title defences – all ended early. But one clash for the Commonwealth title, against Anthony Logan, didn't tell the whole story.

Logan was arguably the first opponent not to be scared of Benn, who was in trouble in the very first round when he was floored by a hammer of a right hand.

But if that was dire straits, it was nothing compared to the flurry that came his way in round two. A whopping 22 blows from Logan found their target and had Benn wobbling.

But for the first time in his career, Benn was about to show what he could do when he was hurt. A left hook, out of nowhere, flattened the Jamaican.

One-round wipe-outs of David Noel and Michael Chilambe, again with the Commonwealth belt on the line, appeared to have restored normal order.

Benn was building a reputation as a fearsome banger and looked unbeatable. But another London middleweight, Michael Watson, had other ideas.

It looked, to all intents and purposes, that Watson would be the last hurdle before Benn got a world title shot. Indeed, both had obtained world rankings with the WBC.

Watson had no '0' and was a humble individual, while Benn became increasingly cocky and brash after the fight was made.

Benn was a 3-1 favourite with the bookmakers, but Watson would stand for no nonsense. He threatened to leave the ring if his opponent's entrance lasted any longer than two minutes.

He was a man with a plan when they met for the Commonwealth crown in 1989 and, after the bell rang, it worked to perfection.

A fired-up Benn burned himself out throwing hooks, which were absorbed by Watson's tight guard. Watson, a tough, skilled operator, picked his shots when firing back.

Benn piled on the pressure without getting anywhere, and showed the frailties in his defence by dropping his guard. Watson used his right hand to pop away at him.

A stiff jab in the sixth froze Benn and sent him down. Misjudging his rise, he was counted out by referee John Coyle.

Benn's aura of invincibility was gone. He was still a dangerous customer but he'd now been beaten. He would soon head across the pond to rebuild his reputation.

Rather than going back to the drawing board on his own turf, Benn went to the United States, where he would respond in the same devastating fashion as he did after the Douglas defeat.

American promoter Bob Arum had already hailed him as 'the most exciting fighter in the world' and couldn't wait to get him on his shows. Arum held the cards he needed. He was a fan of Benn's style and later dubbed him 'the English Marvin Hagler'. Benn had long dreamed of taking on the 'Marvelous One', but had just missed him.

Benn's first fight Stateside saw him go the distance for the first time, a ten-rounder with the teak-tough Jorge Amparo. He was later retired by the state commission.

Jose Quinones then folded in a round before Benn was given a real test by the experienced Sanderline Williams, who used his guile as Benn again went the full ten.

Benn was now ready for what he had come for – to become an overseas star. Ironically, he and Watson would both compete for global honours in the same month.

In April 1990, Watson was completely outboxed and stopped by formidable WBA boss Mike McCallum at London's Royal Albert Hall. He'd undoubtedly ended up with the harder route of the two.

Two weeks later, Benn was up next. Arum had worked with WBO champion Doug DeWitt before and persuaded him to go up against Benn on US soil.

DeWitt was the favourite, but thought to be beatable and past his best. That considered, Benn still looked to have chinks in his own armour after the Watson setback.

Arum imagined fireworks when two contestants with little regard for caution clashed, and they duly delivered, with thrills and spills on the way.

Benn was dropped to his knees from a looping left hook to the jaw, with the bell to end the second round bailing him out.

Showing what would become a trademark trait in big fights, Benn recovered swiftly, clubbing DeWitt to the floor in the third with a right hook.

He then exploded on DeWitt in the eighth, dropping him three times with right hands before referee Randy Neumann waved it off. Benn had done it.

If winning the title didn't established him as a star, what Benn did to Iran Barkley in his maiden title defence certainly did.

'The Blade' was a former WBC world boss, albeit thanks to a lucky punch that took out a near-prime Tommy Hearns inside three rounds.

Barkley had also gone the distance with Roberto Duran for the IBF crown. On this night in Las Vegas, though, he was clearly running scared. He was on the floor within seconds from a right hand and although he fought back to hurt Benn, he went down twice more before the first round was over, the three-knockdown rule ending the bout.

Benn recalled, 'I turned pro and started knocking people out left, right and centre. All I thought was the old adage, "You don't get paid for overtime."

'That was more down to aggression, because I was a very angry boy back then. I didn't want the attention, it was all about making money.

'I wanted to earn a living through boxing, I didn't think about where it would take me. I thought I might be a Southern Area champion, perhaps even [get] a shot at the British [title].

'All I wanted to get [was] a terraced house, like my dad, but I wanted to go one better and get a BMW as well. I was getting thousands of pounds per fight.

'I was looking at it thinking, "Wow, that's a lot of money, man!" Remember, when I was 16 years old and signing on, I was getting £36.40 every two weeks.

'I came across Watson in my 23rd fight and, after 22 KOs, I thought I was the best thing since sliced bread.

'I never imagined I'd lose to him. I was that confident that, on the day of the fight, I went to get my hair plaited. I wasn't even thinking about the fight.

'I went out all guns blazing, expecting him to go, but it just didn't happen. I came back to my corner at the end of the fifth and I was exhausted.

'I remember trying to catch my breath and I saw Michael look over and wink at me, as if to say, "I've got you now, boy."

'His punches didn't hurt all that much, but Michael was a good fighter who knew what he had to do to beat me. It left me in a position where I had a lot to learn as a boxer.

'I went to America and it turned out to be good for me. It's the land of truth over there. Guys off the street can give you a tough spar. Reputations mean nothing.

'You get into a war, whether you like it or not. That's what really made me. I didn't believe that I could ever do ten rounds and the first time I did, that was it.

'I wanted to do something people back home would remember. I wasn't the first, but not far off. Lloyd Honeyghan beat Don Curry there in 1986, a Brit upsetting an American favourite.

'It's still my number one fight. I went over to Atlantic City on the Boardwalk and won my first world title. No one had given me a hope.

'DeWitt walked over to me in the ring and said, "You're going down." I replied, "I might be going down, but you're staying down!"

'We both threw hooks at the same time [in the second round] and, next thing I know, I'm on the floor. I got up and I was really mad then. I could have walked through anything after that.

'Iran beat himself, really. He was a lovely kid, but he never should have been in the ring with me that night. I wanted to trade punches with him, to see if I could dull "the Blade".

'I went to stare into his eyes when we touched gloves and he looked away. From then, I knew what was going to happen.

'I ran across the ring as soon as the bell went and floored him with a right hand. Twice again he went after that. Had it not been for the rule, it would have been worse for him.'

There was talk of Benn immediately jumping up a weight to challenge his WBO counterpart at super middle, which just happened to be a huge name in Hearns.

A unification bout with McCallum was discussed, too, but neither came off. Meanwhile, an offer came in to defend his newly won title back in England.

Benn wanted to come home and Barry Hearn already had a contender, a new kid on the block by the name of Chris Eubank.

Eubank had burst on to the scene with 24 straight wins, including 13 stoppages. He had meat in his gloves but it was a 'granite' chin that would prove his signature.

He'd been calling Benn out since his tenth bout and Benn told him to be careful what he wished for as mind games began between the two.

It captured the imagination of the British public, who hadn't seen Benn fight at home since the Watson defeat.

He had it all to lose, namely his world title, and another result like the Watson loss would certainly mean going back to square one again.

The fighters finally touched gloves at Birmingham's National Exhibition Centre in November 1990, in what was an all-British world title fight for the ages. Benn was like a bull at a gate from the moment he emerged and didn't change much after the bell went, throwing haymakers akin to the Watson fight.

Benn was just ahead on the cards and looking for the finish in the eighth, Eubank vigorously protesting a slip after going down in the corner from an overhand right to the top of the head.

Another dubious blow, this time a left hook to the backside, felled Eubank again in the ninth. He wasn't penalised, but Benn was smelling blood.

Once again, he walked on to a shot, a left hook staggering him and inviting Eubank to pounce as Benn grimly clung on.

A right hand over the top followed as the corners were preparing for the end of the round, sending Benn into the ropes, where an exhausted Eubank followed up with hooks.

Richard Steele stepped in to stop the fight, leaving a devastated Benn with his head on the referee's chest. He only had five seconds left to survive of the ninth.

If the British public demanding they meet the first time was clamour, the momentum that called for a rematch was something else. Still, it took three years to happen.

Benn put together a six-fight winning streak to get himself back into world title contention, this time up at super middleweight.

He halted Hagler's half-brother Robbie Sims in seven and Dan Sherry with one punch inside three rounds, and also scored a close points win over new rival Thulani Malinga.

That got him a shot at WBC ruler Mauro Galvano in October 1992 with one rather large catch – it was to take place in the champion's homeland of Italy.

A focused Benn went into the lion's den determined not to let the fight go the distance, remarking he would 'have to knock him out to get a draw'.

What could have given him that idea? Only two Brits had ever won a world title fight on points in Italy, and they were both flyweights.

It didn't get any less hostile after the bell rang, with the home corner and their fighter responsible for what appeared to be heinous acts.

Galvano pushed Benn out of the ring in round three, while the Italian's trainers also called for a doctor to inspect a cut to his right eye at the end of the fourth.

They wanted their man out of there on a technical draw, despite the wound being caused by a punch. It backfired spectacularly when Benn was awarded the win.

Hearn came over to inform his delighted challenger he was the victor after the Italians had tried to pull a fast one. Benn stuck his head straight out of the ring to speak to someone else.

Eubank was at ringside. They shook hands with Benn declaring, 'Now we can do business!' The war to settle the score was on.

Benn defended his title against Brits Nicky Piper and Lou Gent in the meantime, as well as seeing off Galvano for good in a rematch on British soil.

He and Eubank finally got it on again in October 1993 at Manchester United's Old Trafford ground, with 47,000 people in attendance and 18.5 million watching at home on ITV.

The bout failed to reach the giddy heights of their first encounter, with both fighters perhaps showing too much respect after the pain they had inflicted on each other before.

Both fighters boxed for the most part rather than brawled, and it seemed as if Benn had come out on top, the judges called into play after 12 rounds.

The final session was thrilling, with both told they needed to take it to secure the victory. The bout ended on a high but there would be more controversy.

One judge had it 114-113 for Benn, another 115-113 for Eubank. The third had it a draw, 114-114, which was the result. All had to take a point off the Dark Destroyer for low blows.

He said, 'It was just so volatile between me and him, it really was. He was a big, strapping lad, bigger than me, but I knew I could still have him on the cobbles.

'It could have kicked off at any moment, it was that close. I'm not saying he was scared of me but he kept it cool because he knew I was on the edge and about to jump on him.

'What annoyed me most was the way he looked down his nose at everybody. He thought he was an eloquent man, but really he needed elocution lessons. It was the way he conducted himself. It was like he was born with a silver spoon in his mouth, when he was just another kid from London.

'To him, the Queen should have been living in Hove and he should have been living in Buckingham Palace. We clashed on absolutely everything.

'I'm the sort of bloke that if my sausage falls on the floor, I'm picking it up and putting it back on my plate. Chris would want a whole new breakfast.

'That's just his image and, now he's retired, he has to continue to portray that image, but that's not really him. I know the real Chris Eubank, but he's not a bad man.

'I just never understood where he came from. He seemed to drop out of the sky one day. He was looking down on me and I couldn't hack it.

'I have to admit now that he won that first fight fair and square, though. When he fought me, he was a tough cookie. More power to him.

'He was harder than I expected. He caught me in the eye with a thumb and I couldn't see a thing out of it. What a tremendous fighter he was. I can't knock him for the way he worked.

'Let me tell you, he had a jaw like granite. He felt like any other fighter to the body, but you just couldn't hurt him to the head.

'I was in trouble, that's why I got stopped. Chris was simply the better man that day. The rematch was a different story.

'It took a lot of work to get there. I needed another world title to get him back in the ring. We took Galvano and knew the risks.

'I trained 13 weeks for him, we got in there and he didn't catch me with anything. I was in there, I saw their tactics, thinking they could stop it and rob us.

'I was over the moon that justice was done. I knew in that moment that I had my belt and Chris had his, so we were definitely going to get it on again.

'I knew it would be big when it did happen, but I couldn't really appreciate how massive it was until I went out there.

'I remember walking to the ring and the crowd were chanting my name. It sent tingles down my body. I thought, "This is it, you dare not lose."

'And I didn't. Even Chris has admitted since that I won that fight. The most disappointing thing for me was I thought I had him. The point off changed everything, that's a fact.

'I just walked straight out of the ring, shaking my head. People came up to talk to me and I told them to go away.

'Looking back now, we brought England together. It was what the British public, in fact the boxing world, wanted to see.

'I detested him before we got into the ring, true, but how could I hate him after? He made me a lot of money, huge figures for back then.

'The second time, I kept the belt around my waist, even if I didn't win. We never really did each other's career anything but good. I love Chris really and we're old men now, so we can laugh and have a joke about it but, truth be told, I needed him as much as he needed me.'

When the dust settled, Benn went back on his tear-up as the WBC champion, but he'd unwittingly made an enemy out of Don King.

Benn was now under Hearn's stewardship and had been used as a bargaining chip to get the Eubank sequel on. King had been hoodwinked when he looked all set to acquire him.

The wild-haired American had brokered a deal where he would pick up the contracts of both the winner and loser of the fight. He hadn't banked on a draw.

King looked to the countrymen in his camp and, eventually, sent a man dangerous enough to hurt the big hitters at super middle.

Gerald McClellan had people running scared in the middleweight ranks. He'd become WBC world champion and scored five stoppages defending his title, four of those in the first round.

He fancied his chances against Benn, even though the Briton was a weight above him. He noted that Benn had been taken the distance in his last three outings.

In the meantime, Benn and Hearn parted ways. Now a free agent who didn't appreciate being used as a bargaining chip, he rejoined Warren.

The two had an on-off relationship down the years, but he would remain under Warren for the rest of his career. He'd just turned 30 at the time.

There was no doubt he was the winner in the two points victories that followed the Eubank sequel, over Henry Wharton and Juan Carlos Gimenez, but it wasn't vintage Benn.

King had brought over Michael Nunn, the WBA title holder at his weight, to feature on the same bill, putting up his title against Steve Little.

Nunn versus Benn in a unification bout looked to be the plan, until Nunn blew his lines by surprisingly losing to Little, who wasn't chosen to fill the breach.

Benn snuck in another defence in the meantime. Ugly scenes of violence outside the ring marred his clash with Gimenez, who absorbed all of Benn's attacks and kept on coming.

Some criticism came Benn's way for not getting rid of Gimenez early, but he settled for a convincing points win instead. Another contender was waiting in the wings.

McClellan was definitely coming after him and Benn, despite a lot of advice to the contrary, accepted the challenge. He'd been offered the chance to fight Nunn instead.

They locked horns on 25 February 1995 in what proved a life-changing experience for McClellan, who had been dubbed a 'miniature Mike Tyson' by King. The result was not expected by anybody. Indeed, most of the so-called experts had given Benn little chance against the huge-punching American.

The predictions looked accurate when Benn was knocked through the ropes in the first round and again in the eighth before a stunning comeback saw him drop and stop McClellan in the tenth round.

McClellan was uncharacteristically blinking before he sunk to his knees from a fairly innocuous right hand. He even answered the count.

Two right hands returned him to the deck and he appeared to quit, not even trying to rise to his feet. McClellan was winning on the cards but no one knew how seriously hurt he was.

McClellan had suffered a serious brain injury and later collapsed in the ring before being taken to hospital. Nearly 25 years on, he still needs round-the-clock care. He's now almost completely blind and uses a wheelchair full time.

An emotional Benn said, 'It was 2007 before I saw him again. We raised $250,000 for Gerald and that was such a joy. The benefit night was a complete sell-out in London.

'It was so difficult because I had to shout in Gerald's ear so he could hear what I was saying, but he told me it was an accident, that it wasn't my fault.

'I was so happy to see him but my emotions were up and down. I didn't know whether to be happy, cry or be sick.

'I've never experienced so many emotions at one time in my life. I held Gerald's hand and his sister, Lisa, told me all of the stories about his after-care.

'I always felt the American people [boxing fraternity] should have looked after him better.

'If he'd been British, his house would have been paid for and he'd be getting the best of care.

'He was the first real threat to me after Eubank. Wharton and Gimenez gave me a good workout, but that was about it.

'Wharton was stronger than I thought, but Gimenez was so tough. I'm talking as strong as an ox. As soon as I hit him, I knew I wasn't stopping him. He was going nowhere.

'Then Don King threatened to bring Gerald over and I told him to bring it on. That was my attitude. I wasn't scared and I wasn't going to lie down for no one.

'The first time I ever looked at him, I was just like, "He ain't big." He was just a slim guy. I didn't understand where all his power came from.

'I'd done my homework. I came out fighting, because almost everyone tipped Gerald to win inside three rounds. That got my back up, because they were forgetting what I'd done.

'I remember him hitting me, I fell into the ropes and I felt all of the ligaments around my neck stretch. I would never give up. If I'd have gone, it would have been on my shield.

'Even when I was knocked down again, in round eight, I knew I had to get up and win. It was necessary to secure my family's future and the lifestyle I wanted. I was ecstatic to beat him.

'I remember being interviewed in the ring after, reminding Don King that he'd brought him over to bash me up. He said, "You've made a believer out of me."

'There was such animosity and resentment towards me afterwards. I went from a high to the lowest of lows. I said on the night that I was very sorry, but also rather him than me.

'I came out with damaged nerves and jaw, urinating blood for three days and a shadow on my brain. Gerald came out paralysed, blind, 80 per cent deaf and in a wheelchair.

'All of that punishment, plus I led a hectic lifestyle outside of the ring. My wife wanted me to quit boxing because she was nudging me through the night in case I'd fallen into a coma.

'Some of the things I heard afterwards were ridiculous. I collapsed after the fight, too, but that was purely down to exhaustion. It was the hardest of hard fights.'

Whether he liked it or not, Benn had found his punching power again, evidenced when he TKOd Vincenzo Nardiello and Daniel Perez in his next two title defences.

McClellan was still in hospital when he tackled Nardiello and it was under the same roof as that fateful fight. The London Arena watched him demolish the Italian in eight rounds.

Perez seemed ill-equipped to deal with the rigours of world boxing when he was stopped in seven, having already been down before the finish.

Unfinished business with 'Sugar Boy' Malinga came next, four years after their original ten-round battle in 1992. This time, the WBC title was on the line.

Malinga believed he had Benn's number, having long felt he was the rightful winner of their first meeting, which Benn won debateably by half a point.

It turned out he did. Benn was nearly ten years younger but it was Malinga who rolled back the years to leave the result in little doubt at the final bell, even though he'd been on the floor.

One judge, Chuck Giampa, scored it 114-112 for Benn, but he was overruled by Chuck Williams (118-109) and Omar Mintuum (111-115), who both went for Malinga.

Malinga thus became the first man to outpoint Benn, who had put in a lacklustre performance. It ended his four-year reign and an unbeaten run that stretched back to 1990.

With one eye swollen shut, Benn retired in the ring after the fight, but not before proposing to his then-girlfriend Carolyne. It looked as if he would then ride off into the sunset.

His retirement didn't even last the rest of 1996, but it would still be the year Benn hung up his gloves for good, although he'd fit in another two fights by the year's end.

Like Eubank, Benn had set his sights on halting the division's new driving force, Steve Collins, who in the end made them both regret it.

Both had two attempts at dethroning the heroic Irishman and Benn's failures were more emphatic than Eubank's, ending on his stool on each occasion.

The full-frontal brawls that were expected for Collins' WBO belt never quite happened. It certainly began to look like Father Time was catching up with Benn.

The original plan was for Benn and Collins to meet in a unification bout, with the Malinga bout considered a warm-up. But the plan backfired, meaning he conceded bargaining power.

Benn had to play ball with all parties to get a last chance at global glory with Collins, who still saw Benn as enough of a scalp to make it worth his while.

That meant Benn had to listen to the wishes of his promoter and manager as Warren handled both of them and could have left him out in the cold. The intention had always been for a summer showdown at what is now the Manchester Arena. Come July, it went ahead as planned.

Benn was labelled the old gunslinger, the veteran who'd lost some of the spring in his step but retained the puncher's ability to bang.

There was some truth in this, but skill hadn't really been his forte anyway. His boxing brain had improved but his trusty dig so often got him out of trouble.

Much was made of the fighters' ages in the build-up, but Benn was still only 32 and, in fact, only six months older than Collins. 'Shopworn' was one term used.

It was all conjecture until the two went at it but the first clash was a non-event. Benn injured himself, another sign his body was failing him.

Such was his momentum as he threw an overhand right, which missed the target, that he landed awkwardly and fell to the floor clutching his ankle.

They were allowed to box on but Benn was in so much pain that his mind wandered and he turned away from his opponent. The referee then stepped in to signal the finish.

It counted as a TKO but was an unsatisfactory ending to the proceedings for both parties. Benn had been stopped, Collins had beaten a one-legged man.

Some wondered if Benn would just leave it at that, but his own pride wouldn't allow him to. If he was going out, it was with no excuses.

They were back in the ring under the same lights four months later, with Benn fully healed. It would be hard to explain away another defeat. The mind was still willing as Benn came forward and he had success in flashes when he went hell for leather. Many before him had fallen, but Collins hung tough.

With his best shots getting him nowhere, Benn tired quickly. That gave Collins the incentive to fire back with his own punches.

Fatigued, Benn wasn't reacting quickly enough to get out of the way. Coach Kevin Sanders told him before the fifth that if he had one more round like that, he would pull him out.

Collins had a point taken off for use of the head in the fifth, when Benn asked for one more round at the end of the session. Little changed in the sixth, so he was retired on his stool.

No one was asking him to continue, either then or in the immediate future. His boxing career had ended, but his journey through life was only really getting started.

There's long been talk about a third comeback and he has even taken part in exhibitions, but Benn hasn't had a licensed boxing match in over 20 years.

He said, 'It wasn't more than a few hours after Malinga that I knew that wasn't the end. I retired after that, the first Collins fight and the rematch. It was only the last time I meant it.

'Malinga was just my bogeyman, he was very difficult for me. I won the first time, but I could easily have lost it. I think I got the decision because I was on home soil.

'I trained so hard for him when we did it again that I overdid it. I was knackered and jaded by the time we got in there.

'I can't really take anything away from him. Give me a guy who stands there and wants to fight and I'll be victorious, but I knew he was slippery.

'I could see his punches coming, but I couldn't do anything about it. Even when I knocked him down, I was shattered. He deserved to win. He's a lovely man, actually.

'When I first met Steve, he was trying to psyche me out, like he did with Eubank, but you can't do that with me. There was no bad blood between us, it was just his way.

'I'd watched him against Cornelius Carr and Neville Brown and thought to myself, "He's struggling with middleweights." I was a big, powerful super middle.

'I didn't go in there stiff and rigid [in the first fight], I was going in there to have a good time. We were throwing punches, I twisted my ankle and that was that. It was very disappointing.

'I knew, deep down, that wasn't me and it wasn't the way I wanted to be remembered. I've got to know when to say "the end".

'I didn't really get the chance to do anything to Steve in the first fight, but he took everything I had the second time. It just wasn't there for me any more. I knew that was it.

'I never really got closure because I wasn't living the life then. At one point, I was a world champion smoking 20 fags a day. I'm fitter now than I ever was back then.

'I gave people value for money. When they watched me at home or in the pub, they wouldn't go and get a cup of tea or a beer because it might be over when they got back.

'I was proud to be British and whatever it took to win, I was willing to do. I couldn't stand there and box, I was a fighter.

'It's funny, I had a trainer once who tried to get me to box. I won't mention his name. I tried it but I just felt the punches instead. Boxers don't like getting hit. I soon got rid of him.

'I was an aggressive, come-forward fighter – that's me. There's no going backwards, though, and everything changes. There's more knowledge now.

'I used to want to stay in the public eye – not nowadays. Being number one is being second to no one; I learned that from the army. I was hard but I had low self-esteem.

'I struggled but I've come out of the darkness and now I'm walking in light. I thank the man upstairs for a lot of it.

'I won two world titles, filled Old Trafford, owned a Bentley and a mansion, DJ'd at Ministry of Sound and served proudly in the British Army. I look at my life now and I feel blessed.'

So here's to the future of a man who gave so much to boxing and now attacks the good life with similar thrust.

Nigel Benn doesn't do anything by halves.

CHAPTER EIGHT

AN ENIGMA WRAPPED IN A RIDDLE – CHRIS EUBANK

THERE might not be another person on this planet, never mind in boxing, who is quite like Chris Eubank.

Eccentric, stubborn, strong-willed, unique, fascinating and supremely confident, with an air of madness thrown in, all apply when describing the well-known parts of Eubank's psyche.

A wannabe aristocrat, an attention seeker and a deluded man on the biggest ego trip of all are some of the less flattering terms you could use. Maybe only he knows the true answers.

The world has been known to shy away from people they don't understand and hate is always a strong word to use about someone you've never met.

Those in attendance at a sold-out Bar Sport can at least make their own minds up after an evening in Eubank's company. Some are still none the wiser, such is his flamboyant nature. There remains a furore all around him whenever he's out and about, and this night was no exception. He commands respect and feels it's no less than he deserves.

The man who was once quoted as saying 'boxing is a mug's game' was derided as the biggest mug of all by those who felt he was spitting in the face of the sport.

His arrogant mannerisms and outlandish comments only raised the ire further, but there has never been an equal in terms of personality. Maybe he's just misunderstood.

There's certainly only one Christopher Livingstone Eubanks, who took the 's' out of his surname that was shared by boxing twin brothers Simon and Peter.

The siblings spent most of their childhoods beating each other up, with Chris never far away from trouble. He was born on 8 August 1966 in south London, but didn't stay there long.

He lived in Jamaica from two months to six years old before returning to England, living in the country's capital. His mother, Rachel, left when he was eight to move to New York.

Chris endured a troubled education, particularly at secondary level, where he was suspended 18 times in one year and then expelled from Thomas Calton School in Peckham.

He spent some time sleeping rough and at Orchard Lodge Regional Resource Centre, London's last secure children's home. His father, English, whose name he later inherited, reached the end of his tether. The teenage tearaway was sent to stay with his mother, who had relocated to the south Bronx area of the Big Apple. It was as impoverished as Chris had ever experienced.

His life was to change forever when he walked into Jerome Boxing Club, where he would have to clean the gym for membership as he couldn't afford the fees.

By the summer of 1983, he was ready to start his amateur career and went on to box for Jerome 26 times, losing seven.

Flashes of the traits he would later show were starting to become apparent, but all Eubank wanted to do was prove that he was simply the best.

He said, 'I always apply good manners. When you are well-mannered and can fight on top of that, it actually wins you an audience. That's been proven over the years.

'I got that from church, where you'd always have to respect your elders.

'My mother used to take me there and it's a trait that has been instilled in me since I was a kid.

'I doted on my mother, she made such an impression on me and no words are enough to describe what a woman she was.

'I was born to love, but the environment I was in was unkind. You had to toughen up, you had to get some teeth. If you don't, move to the side and hide.

'When I went to school, there was cookery, drama and music and I wasn't interested in that. I always thought it was more important to protect the children who were being bullied.

'I got my mental toughness from fighting and the point of the matter is that I couldn't help being protective of people who are weaker than me. I'm glad, it's turned out well for me.

'If only I had known at the time that if I had took drama and music, I could have become an even bigger star, as an actor or singer.

'Even with cooking, those guys are like rock stars on television now. I've stayed in character right the way through my life; it's not always about doing something magical.

'I read somewhere that a person has received an honour for sweeping the streets for 60 years and he did by that staying in character. When you do that, wonderful things happen.

'My father told me to go and live with my mother, otherwise I would end up going to prison. That changed my life.

'I went to live in the Bronx when I was 16 and, by that time, I'd made so many mistakes that I was very grown up, in the respect of I knew I had to start living my life in the right way.

'The right way was not getting suspended from school, not to shoplift, not to fight but to choose a course of action and stick to it. I didn't have any distractions there.

'I became obsessed with learning how to box and that's the key to making it in a competitive environment such as sport. That's the sign of a potential champion.

'When doing that, you will always come across a little bit queer, as in funny or odd, but that can help you to succeed in the field that you are in. The amount of beatings I took as a kid, from my brothers and in the street, made me tough and everything else is conditioning of the body and mind.

'I was involved in three or four fights a week, minimum, from the ages of nine to 14, which made me able to take punishment. I used that to my benefit.'

For all of his amateur fights, Eubank performed his trademark leap over the top rope. He remained in the US after he turned professional aged 19.

Eubank had already boxed at New York's iconic Madison Square Garden in the famed Golden Gloves national tournament a year earlier, losing to Ron Essett – whom he later beat as a pro – in the semi-finals.

It was 1984, the same year he won the regional Golden Gloves at middleweight to set up the Essett clash, having also claimed Spanish Golden Gloves honours that year.

The first few months of 1985 proved to be Eubank's last as an unpaid fighter but he still picked up a gold medal in the US nationals and New Jersey's Golden Gloves, down a division at super welter.

His pro bow came in October of that year, with his first five bouts taking place in Atlantic City, all four-round points wins, to little fanfare.

Eubank came back to England in 1988 and adopted Brighton – a town where he later bought the title Lordship of the Manor for £45,000 – as his new home. He then met Ronnie Davies, who would train him until the end of his career, and first wife Karron, who soon gave birth to their first child, future boxer Chris Jr.

Becoming a family man gave Eubank more mouths to feed and, in the ring, he'd started to make a name for himself since his move across the pond.

In 1989, Eubank was 11-0 and only one man, Winston Burnett over six, had taken him the distance since his relocation to the UK.

He said, 'Adonis Torres was my first manager and he could see that my personality was gentle and that I'd always explain myself to people. The sparring in that place was more than real. I was there seven days a week for three years and I outlasted everyone. It was a baptism.

'I started doing well, back when you had to win tournaments in your own gym just to get a fight. I couldn't punch but I had quick hands and could move my feet.

'It took me years to learn how to punch correctly but I got them all down in the end. I vaulted the ropes for all of my amateur fights as well, as a means of standing out from the crowd.

'No one had a style like me. I was far ahead of my time in terms of movement and that put me in a different league.

'You have to serve your apprenticeship and, for that particular fight at the Garden, I asked for the universe to give me a sign.

'There was nothing. I was poor in every regard and I remember losing to this particular fellow and learning two things.

'In the second round, I bit this guy on the shoulder and it was disgusting. I was ashamed of myself and, from there, my conduct was impeccable.

'The other thing was that I sobbed and cried that I'd been beaten, which was the sign that I'd been looking for but didn't realise. I cared so much that I knew that I'd get there.

'I had the will to win, but it's hard to follow the path. It doesn't matter where you are or what the competition is, if you want to make it, get everything else out of your mind.

'If you have a girlfriend and she's taking up ten per cent of your mind, you only have 90 per cent to put towards the boxing.

'If you like going out with your friends to nightclubs, there's another 15 per cent so you're left with 75 per cent for the boxing.

'What I did was shut every single other thing out of my life and put 100 per cent into learning my craft. That's what saw me through.

'If you want to be exceptional, than you have to live exceptionally. In the boiling pot, with the pressure on, you stand there and take it. This is the bed you have made, you sleep in it.

'I came back over to the United Kingdom with everyone telling me I was weird because I had this focus, to win respect through boxing. Everyone respects someone who can fight.'

The year 1989 would see Eubank paired with Anthony Logan, the first time he'd been an underdog as a pro.

Logan had caused Nigel Benn problems a year earlier, dropping him before he was knocked out himself in the second round.

Four months later, Eubank had to go eight rounds for the first time to beat Logan on points in a fight that was supposed to 'shut up' the already outspoken new kid on the block.

A ten-round points win over the defensively sound American gatekeeper Randy Smith also caught the eye, but it wasn't in boxing surroundings that his big break came along.

He first met promoter Barry Hearn at the 1989 World Snooker Championships and, together, they would catapult Eubank to stardom.

Eubank said, 'When I came back to the UK, Ray Cattouse [former British champion] tried training me.

'When I signed for Barry, a guy called Darkie Smith tried training me, but I wasn't listening. If you ask him, Ronnie will tell you himself that I taught him more than he taught me.

'I remember Herol Graham punching me to pieces for two weeks in sparring without me landing once on him.

'I completely changed my boxing manner after that to a more patient, timed approach rather than my rush-rush style.

'I watched Michael Watson beat Nigel in 1989 and that taught me how to cover up correctly. Unlike Nigel, I wasn't fed durable patsies on the way up for a Porsche or Ferrari.

'I had to scrape my way. I fought guys like Eric Holland, James Canty and Michael Justin, who couldn't get fights because their records were deceiving. I had no money, nothing.

'Anthony Logan was a world-class fighter and ranked number 16 with the WBC, and I was a relative novice after just 11 fights.

'I believed I could beat him and I did so convincingly. When it's fight time, another side of me comes out. If you watch the fight, my arms and elbows are flared out in a novicey stance.

'When I went on to spar with Herol, he did mostly body sparring and that taught me to tuck my arms in closer to my ribs, which later benefited me greatly against Nigel.

'Although I believed it then, I doubt I'd have beaten Nigel at the time I fought Anthony, but I was the one who did all of the improving, whereas he just stayed the same.'

Whether that is true or not, Eubank had been calling Benn's name loudly since his tenth fight and even more so when his rival captured the WBO world title in 1990.

Eubank versus Logan had been chief support to another Commonwealth title defence by Benn, a first-round TKO of Michael Chilambe.

The hard-hitting Dark Destroyer then became a global force by upsetting Doug DeWitt in eight for WBO honours, doing so impressively away from home in America.

Eubank was trying to bypass the domestic scene completely, so had to bide his time before he was considered a worthy challenger. His new-found allegiance with Hearn helped.

He built up his world ranking through a WBC bauble, claiming their international title by stopping Hugo Antonio Corti in the eighth.

Two quickfire defences, both won inside the distance, against Eduardo Domingo Contras and Kid Milo, were nothing compared to the one-round demolition that came next.

Reginaldo Dos Santos was knocked senseless in just 20 seconds, including the full count, taking Eubank to 24-0.

Benn had cracked America after retaining his title against fellow feared puncher Iran Barkley via the three-knockdown rule, with their fight less than a round old.

Graham was picked to take on full WBC champion Julian Jackson, leaving Hearn to try and entice Benn back home to defend against his man.

Benn and his promoter, Bob Arum, were attracted by an offer that would reportedly see him earn four times more than Eubank – about £400,000.

Hearn was surprised that Arum agreed at all, let alone not ask for a rematch clause or stake in Eubank should the title change hands.

A large chunk of Matchroom Sport's capital was on the line, along with the belt. A grudge match sells, though, and it was clear that Benn couldn't stand the sight of Eubank.

More talking was done in the ring at Birmingham's National Exhibition Centre in November 1990, after Eubank had his ring entrance sabotaged.

Tina Turner's 'Simply the Best' suddenly stopped playing en route, but he ignored the absence of his theme music and leapt over the top rope as usual.

When the action started, Eubank had his mettle tested like never before, and the sturdy chin he became famous for was established by his resistance to the blows he took from Benn.

He was shaken by a loaded right uppercut to the chin as they came away from a clench, with Benn like a bull at a gate.

The impact of the blow was so painful that Eubank bit his tongue, causing a huge gash that he hid from his corner so as not to get the ring doctor involved. This was now a war. Back came Eubank with a ferocious attack that swelled Benn's eye shut by the fifth. Both warriors were laying it all on the line.

Eubank hit the canvas in the eighth, vigorously protesting it was a slip after taking an overhand right to the top of the head.

Down went Eubank again in the ninth, but it wasn't a telling blow as it strayed low, hitting him on the backside.

What it did, though, was lull Benn into a false sense of security, bringing down his own defences, which saw him walk straight on to a left hook that sent him tottering backwards.

A right hand over the top from Eubank followed as the corners started getting ready for the end of the round.

Eubank unloaded with wild hooks as the clock ticked away until referee Richard Steele stepped in to stop the fight. There were just five seconds of the round left.

Eubank turned around and screamed in delight, bashing his gloves together with his entire body tense, rippling with muscles. He'd reached the promised land.

He said, 'It's not a matter of how hard it was to become a world champion, it's about how desperate I was to be respected.

'There was no punch hard enough – and, believe me, he did hit them – that would have stopped me that night.

'It was my way of honouring the seven years I'd spent in the gym to get there with no girlfriends, no nightclubs and often in solitude.

'I'd train with injuries and, when other guys were taking days off for birthdays and Christmas, I'd still be working hard. I treated the gym like it was a church. I worshipped there every day.

'Me and Nigel were like two bulls and all bulls want to be the kingpin. He has that, he lives in that mode, he's angry. He was born that way.

'Nigel probably beat 80 per cent of his opponents before he got into the ring by intimidation. He had a way of making it a personal battle. With me, it's not personal, it's always objective.

'It just proves that manners, consideration, being kind to others and being objective about the things you want to do in your life, not saying things you'll later regret, can prevail.

'If you're humble, you can't really get knocked down, because there's nowhere to fall. If you stand tall, you stand proud. I believe in being good.

'I thought a lot about Nigel's punching power and said to myself, "What are you going to do if you become concussed?"

'In that situation, your nervous system separates from your muscles and you don't have control of your body. I would have to correct that in seven seconds or be counted out. Over and above that, I was clever. When I got hit, I went with him. It was a vicious contest that was as real as anything you'll ever see.

'He hit me in the fourth and chopped a half-inch gash on my tongue. The pain was excruciating. I went down in the eighth, but that was a slip.

'I told the referee he got that wrong and he asked if I was OK. I just smiled and said to him, "I'm OK, let me fight." I came back and stopped Nigel, you cannot deny me that.

'I was blazing a trail from there, I was in unknown territory. Boxing has nothing to do with personality. They can't give it to the other guy because they like him more.'

Benn went back to the drawing board, signing with Hearn and staying in England. He severed his ties with Arum in the process and never competed Stateside again.

It was a homecoming of sorts when Eubank defended for the first time against Canadian Dan Sherry at the Brighton Convention Centre in February 1991.

It didn't look like the fight would last long when Sherry went down in the first, but the Commonwealth Games gold medallist had a few tricks up his sleeve.

Eubank was held, turned, messed around and generally hustled by the showboating Sherry, who gave him a real taste of his own medicine with the theatrics. One such incident turned the tide in the tenth when Sherry ended up standing directly behind Eubank, who threw his head backwards and butted him.

Three times he fell to the mat before a stool was brought into the ring, which he nearly slipped off as well. Seriously concussed and swallowing his own blood, the fight was over.

A technical decision was called for, with all three judges ordered to take two points away from Eubank, who was still declared the victor. Sherry has never forgotten it.

More controversy came in Eubank's second defence against Gary Stretch, a British champion going up a weight after a fall-out with promoter Frank Warren.

Poster boy Stretch had an eye for the ladies but got ugly slicing open Eubank, who was put over twice in the contest without a count, by the right eye with a punch.

It left Eubank up against it in the sixth, when he was told in no uncertain terms 'one more round' before the gash left him unable to continue.

The upper hand deserted Stretch, who had a point taken off for pushing and was still ahead on the scorecards when the finish came in that session.

Eubank fought for his life and forced a standing eight count, then pushed Stretch through the ropes. Referee Tony Orlando stepped in before Stretch could make it back.

Those less-than-convincing performances gave Eubank's critics hope that he would soon get his comeuppance and his next challenger, Michael Watson, was fancied to dethrone him.

Watson was the only other man to beat Benn in the pro ranks and was seen as the people's champion who could vanquish the dastardly villain in Eubank.

They would box twice in 1991, the second time for the WBO super middleweight title. Tragically, the rematch was a life-changing final fight for Watson. There was no real sign as to what was coming, particularly in the first fight. So often in the bout, Watson looked to have Eubank's number.

Eubank vs Watson I was, at times, pretty uneventful but notable for being remarkably close, evidenced by the margins on the scorecards.

One judge had it all square, 114-114, while the other two scored it 116-113 and 115-113 respectively, both in favour of Eubank. Watson shook his head and left the ring.

Benn was supposed to be laying in wait for the winner, but the public outcry for a Eubank–Watson sequel saw them meet again less than three months later.

Watson was again the darling of the fans in his efforts to topple their figure of disdain.

Eubank had vacated the WBO middleweight crown so that they could contest the organisation's belt at super middle, last held by Tommy Hearns.

Both combatants were visibly heavier as a result, but the speed of the action between them was much quicker than before.

By the tenth round, Eubank was well beaten and fully aware there was only one way to prevail. He went down in the 11th, caught by Watson and too exhausted to plant his feet.

But the story of the round had far from ended. After rising, Eubank put all of his might into an uppercut that caught Watson flush, sending him crashing into the ropes and to the floor.

He was saved by the bell and ushered into the corner, with the 60-second break before the start of the 12th nowhere near enough time to recover.

He went back out but, 29 seconds later, was stopped on his feet after a hail of blows from Eubank. Watson's corner, including coach Jimmy Tibbs, were initially incensed at referee Roy Francis' decision.

That was until Watson collapsed in Tibbs' arms and left Tottenham Hotspur's White Hart Lane stadium in an ambulance, his life saved by emergency brain surgery in hospital.

The ambulance had to be called as there wasn't one at the event, or even a paramedic. Doctors wearing dinner jackets were summoned after eight minutes had passed.

Another 20 minutes elapsed before Watson was treated in a neurosurgical unit. He wouldn't awake from a coma for 40 days, after six operations to remove a blood clot from his brain.

He was completely paralysed in intensive care for eight months before the longest of roads to rehabilitation and six years in a wheelchair.

The British Boxing Board of Control were sued for negligence and Watson was awarded damages of nearly £1 million. He received less than half that figure as the Board were not insured. It left the governing body facing financial ruin.

Watson has gone on to lead a relatively full life and harbours no ill will towards Eubank, who believes his former adversary is the true champion among men.

He said, 'My first time with Michael, I underestimated him. I won by majority [decision], which was because I was wagering with him. He wasn't a maverick in attitude, he didn't seem to have an edge. That tricked me into thinking, "This guy doesn't have what I have."

'He didn't have that pepper or pizazz, because he was well rounded and a gentleman. He wasn't a bad boy.

'I thought it would be easy for me but it turned out to be the hardest fight of my career. He beat me for a lot of it, but I still knew I'd won. The whole nation wanted us to do it again.

'In the rematch, I came back to the corner at the end of the first round and Ronnie said to me, "If he keeps up this pace, you'll stop him in six."

'The pace was maniacal. After six, I thought, "I can't beat this guy, he just won't stop." His punches were travelling four to six inches, so they had his body weight behind them.

'If you know your boxing, you'll appreciate that 98 per cent of all knockouts come from very short shots. I was getting this beating and, basically, I'd almost given up.

'I could have wet myself and not had any shame, that's how bad the beating was. The adrenalin had stopped pumping because I'd given up. That's what keeps you going.

'I got a lot of credit for getting up after being knocked down, when I was thinking that I couldn't win. It was a great fight.

'That's what I'm supposed to do. If you can get up, you do so really I don't deserve credit for that. If you can't, you don't.

'I didn't do it for the public, I'd have had to look myself in the eye afterwards. I'd have had to live with me. I had to get up.

'I yearn to be a warrior, I yearn to be a stand-up guy. Even if I couldn't win, I'd never give up and with that comes honour. It's a great accolade.

'Integrity is something that you do because it's the right thing, not because there's someone to account to. I knew I couldn't give up and walk out a loser.

'My dignity allowed me to continue and I became vengeful. He'd hurt me, physically and emotionally, and wanted to knock me out. If I saw any opening, if I could get him once, I'd be vindictive and he dropped me in the 11th. As soon as my knee hit the ground, I'd recovered.

'I'd never really been down before, apart from in the eighth [against Benn] but that was a slip, as you may remember. I got up at the count of two and just boxed on.

'I walked forward and threw everything at Michael and, unfortunately, one of these punches put him into a coma. That is the only regret of my career.

'He's gone on to inspire a nation. He's motivating people who don't think they can recover from their injuries, by walking a marathon and being there for charities. He humbles me.

'The objective of boxing is to score points by striking your opponents and the real conundrum for boxers is to incapacitate an opponent for ten seconds and not a lifetime.

'The fighters who think of boxing as a game are normally the ones who get taken out. It's not a sport, it's a way of life.

'The guy who thinks it's a game who goes in with me would find out, after a couple of rounds, that I would be trying to break his spirit. They didn't sign up for that.

'That's how I defeated a lot of guys, because boxing was life or death to me. People think I'm eccentric, but I can't be like a normal man. You must have the right attitude for the job. If you're asking a girl out for dinner, you're not going to say "Oi, come here." She'd call the police.

'Your life, dignity and future are on the line every time you get into the ring, so you ought to be protecting that. If you don't, you're in danger.

'You should never fight someone who doesn't care about his life. If he's willing to lose it, you're going to have to take it.

'As a boxer, I lost my instinct to finish that night. I was still skilful enough to outbox my opponents but, if I had to press a knockout, it just wasn't there.

'If I had to bludgeon someone, I wouldn't. If I had to stop a man clean, with one punch, then fine, but I didn't want to, even though I knew that's what I should be doing.'

Eubank was crushed by what happened to Watson and it became apparent in the performances that followed.

It wasn't just that Watson's plight happened at his hands, there was a fear that, with his own fighting style, the same thing could happen to him.

Of the six title defences that followed, only John Jarvis was removed by a brutal right hand that Eubank seemed almost apologetic to throw.

Thulani Malinga, Essett, Tony Thornton, Juan Carlos Gimenez and Lindell Holmes all lasted the distance with him.

Had he not forced the issue, it would have cost Eubank the belt when he next tackled European champion Ray Close, from Northern Ireland, in Scotland.

The 11th again proved to be telling, with Eubank behind on points only to score a vital knockdown with his trusty right uppercut.

Close somehow survived the count, a 30-second onslaught and the last round to hear the final bell, when the judges were called into play.

One had it a 115-115 stalemate, another 116-113 for Close and the third favouring Eubank by 116-112. All counted the knockdown, making the first official's card telling in a split draw.

Such indifferent displays were not the form required, not with Benn, up a weight and world champion for a second time as WBC ruler, again on the horizon.

The chance to unify their titles was appealing for Eubank, as was the payday. He was actually paid £150,000 less than Benn, but £850,000 was still a huge purse for him.

Hearn struck a deal with the American TV network Showtime, which largely financed the fight. It also meant he had to agree on terms with another promoter, the one and only Don King. They filled Manchester United's Old Trafford ground to the tune of 47,000 spectators in October 1993, as 18.5 million watched at home on ITV.

But their sequel didn't live up to the original, as both knew only too well what the other man could do. All through the 12 rounds, it seemed close.

The nearest thing to real drama was when Benn got knocked through the ropes. He was also docked a point for low blows, which would prove telling.

It still seemed as if Benn had come out on top after 12 rounds, as the bout had ended on a high for him and Eubank had been, by his lofty standards, lacklustre.

One judge had it 114-113 for Benn, another 115-113 for Eubank. The third had it a draw, which proved the result. Eubank kept his title, but didn't acquire Benn's.

He said, 'Me and Nigel have two minds which are miles apart, a street brain and a society brain. In the rematch, there was still a psychological game going on.

'I have a lot of fun with him and I wind him up something rotten. He kind of deserves that because he's so mean spirited.

'I had him where I wanted him, that's what I thought, but Nigel was on his game for the second contest and I just couldn't pin him down. I had the oxygen, but not the accuracy.

'My view is that he did do enough to beat me, even taking into account him hitting me low and losing a point. A fighter knows. It was divine intervention if I've ever seen it in my life.'

The spectacle was one of the finest hours of ITV's *Big Fight Live*, with Eubank signing a big-money £10 million deal with growing network Sky Sports the following year.

He'd squeezed in a unanimous points win over Graciano Rocchigiani in the challenger's home nation of Germany and saw Close off again in a rematch on a split decision.

Another patchy showing saw Eubank, almost typically, need a late salvo to get over the line, with a dazed Close clinging on for dear life after two right hands in the tenth.

One judge had it a borderline ridiculous 118-112 for Eubank, while Francis tallied 117-114 for Close. The third offered 115-114 for the champion.

His agreement with Sky took effect afterwards and he made four more title defences in 1994, with a solitary TKO win over Sam Storey in seven rounds.

Mauricio Amaral, Dan Schommer and fellow Brit Henry Wharton were all outpointed unanimously, the match with Schommer taking place in South Africa.

A third fight with Close was due to take place in 1995, but a new opponent was needed after he failed a brain scan. The man who got the call to replace him was Steve Collins.

Collins had succeeded Eubank as WBO middleweight champion and was following his path by going heavier. He got home advantage, too, with the show staged in Ireland.

Eubank was unbeaten in 43 pro contests heading into battle. He rode to the ring on a Harley Davidson motorcycle. Behind all of the bravado, though, he'd been rattled.

Word had got back to him that Collins had enlisted the help of a hypnotist, who had apparently taught him not to feel pain.

As Eubank made his entrance, Collins was motionless in his corner, listening to his headphones. A repeat of Watson's plight was all that ran through his rival's head.

Both men were on the floor, Eubank in the eighth and Collins in the tenth, but saw the final bell of a colossal encounter.

Eubank lived to regret not finishing the job when he had the chance, with the three judges scoring it 116-114, 115-111 and 114-113, all in favour in Collins.

Eubank's ten-year unbeaten record went with it as he tasted defeat as a pro for the first time. His 17 successful world title defences had set a British record.

A smarting Eubank returned to action with a couple of first-round knockouts, wiping out Bruno Ruben Godoy and Jose Ignacio Barruetabena.

A return with Collins happened in September 1995, but Eubank was again outsmarted. He'd struggled with the fast pace set and the brawling tactics Collins brought into play.

It was a lot closer than the first encounter, with Collins getting the nod on a split decision. Two judges went against Eubank, both 115-113, with one favouring him 115-114.

He said, 'Steve was magnificent, not because he was good, which was plain to see, but because he was like a locomotive. He showed commitment that I didn't know he had in him.

'The biggest room in the world is the room for improvement and had I known this, I would have adopted a different strategy.

'I lost the first fight with him because he got into my head, but he beat me comprehensively the second time. Fair play to him.

'There was a release when I lost for the first time. A lot of people thought I was superhuman but I'm not. I'm just a guy.

'I admire him, he's given me knowledge to pass on that where there's a will, there's a way. Everyone can be beaten, it's just a matter of mind. I fought him on St Patrick's weekend in Ireland. That takes courage, and I was over there again for the rematch. He was so determined, he had tears running down his face.

'I congratulate him. To do your winning, you have to do your losing. When you're on top, you're OK, but it's when you're not you find out whether you can cut the mustard.'

Eubank announced his retirement after coming up short for a second time against Collins, but most knew it wasn't for good.

Those defeats cost him not only the belt but a lucrative showdown with Roy Jones Jr, who was then the IBF super middleweight champion.

The year 1996 marked his comeback but only the one fight, a fifth-round stoppage over Luis Dionisio Barrera. Another TKO over Camilo Alarcon followed in 1997.

That October, Collins retired and vacated his title rather than defend against Joe Calzaghe, so Eubank stepped in at 11 days' notice.

The Sheffield Arena was buzzing with national pride on the night, as England had qualified for the 1998 World Cup that same evening.

Eubank climbed through the ropes at the age of 31 and initially looked spent when he was dropped all of 15 seconds into the bout. 'Good shot' was all he could say to Calzaghe.

Naseem Hamed was topping the bill and sat at ringside, with his constant comments at the top of his voice getting to Eubank, who told him to 'shut up' more than once.

He rode the storm and got inside to work the body of Calzaghe, who tried to rush him several more times. Eubank pumped his fists in the air and the crowd cheered him on.

Down he went again in the tenth, momentarily touching the canvas with both gloves after a short shot from Calzaghe.

Eubank saw the final bell but knew he'd been beaten on points, even if he'd gained more respect from the fans. Scores of 118-109, 116-111 and 118-110 all went against him.

It seemed like the end of the road for Eubank's world title aspirations, but a move up to cruiserweight brought two bruising battles against WBO champ Carl Thompson in 1998. The first went the distance, which was testament to Eubank's durability as he'd already clocked up 50 pro contests.

He'd gained nearly 20lbs in weight to take on a naturally bigger man in the champion, who was rocked more than once himself during a thrilling war.

It was Thompson who prevailed with all three judges but not by much, 114-113 with two of them and 116-113 with the other. A rematch was hastily arranged for three months later.

Eubank's body failed him this time. His left eye had caused him problems in the first meeting and by the ninth round of the return fight, it had completely swollen shut.

The ringside doctor took a long look at him at the end of the round before the referee called the fight off. It proved to be Eubank's swansong.

The real choker was that Eubank was ahead on points. Two had him ahead 87-84 at the time of the finish, while the third had it even at 86-86.

Eubank said, 'I came out of the corner for round one against Joe Calzaghe smiling. I was moving around and sizing up the terrain.

'All of a sudden, a huge shot that literally came out of nowhere knocked me over. A first-round knockdown had never happened to be before.

'As I picked myself up from the canvas and brushed myself down, I thought to myself, "You've got your work cut out tonight."

'Going down in the first, I knew I was going to have the determination beaten out of me for the first ten rounds, but, in the 11th and 12th, I'd be knocking on his door.

'I did – and he stood strong. I showed heart, which people started liking me for, but hadn't I shown that in the Watson fight? Strange, but wonderful.

'I saw his hand speed and I thought I'd be able to deal with that. Well, four punches to my one, you can't deal with it. I didn't know whether he could go in the trenches, though.

'He held on and he deserved to win. I still felt like I could fight, so I carried on until Carl Thompson came along. I lost both times, but got more credit from those watching.

'I wasn't really stopped, it was the doctor's decision, but you could see from my eye that it was pretty nasty. I only had two rounds left.

'I felt more relaxed, I was getting my shots off well on the inside and hitting him with beautiful right uppercuts and good left hooks.

'To his credit, he didn't go from the punches, so all I had to do was last the distance. I was hitting him much harder than the first time around.

'He couldn't catch me with his jab and I slipped most of his shots, then all of a sudden he gets me in the eye and it starts to throb.

'I'd never agree with the decision because I'd have fought him with both eyes closed. I'd paid my dues, it was time to move on. I didn't want to belittle myself for going on too long.'

When he was at the top of the game, Eubank was a handful for anyone, not just in the ring but as a sparring partner.

Andy Flute, who later challenged for the British middleweight title, did one session with Eubank in his prime and was present at Bar Sport.

Eubank said, 'In your first sparring session with a new partner, you have to show them who is the boss, so I'd put it on them for the first couple of sessions.

'In order to keep the sparring, Ronnie, the godfather, the pitbull, used to explain to them that the way to stay with me was never give me time to settle.

'Preventing me from doing lots of damage was necessary for them, but my thing was about learning. Once or twice a week, I'd keep them honest.

'The bigger point here is that when Ronnie told them how to deal with me, many of those fighters went on to become champions themselves.

'I spoke to Mike Tyson in a correctional facility in 1993 and I asked him what he thought the most important thing was to learn in boxing.

'He said, "You think it's sparring and running." Cus D'Amato, who taught him how to box, didn't believe in running, only sparring. The latter is most key.'

The name lives on with the emergence of Chris Eubank Jr, who was actively dissuaded by his family from taking up boxing.

Much has been made of the relationship between the two, with dad thought by many to be an overbearing figure of detriment to his son's career.

Along with his brother, Sebastian, Chris Jr was sent to America at the age of 16 to live with a guardian, Irene Hutton, so they could gain dual citizenship.

Chris spent almost his entire amateur career there and followed the Golden Gloves route, winning Nevada and Western States regional honours.

Billy Joe Saunders took his '0' on points for the British, Commonwealth and European belts, while his first world title shot against George Groves also ended in failure as he dropped a unanimous decision.

Even Davies being in his corner has yet to produce the desired effect, as he's not in full charge of the fighter's coaching. Eubank Sr does not agree with the critics, though.

He said, 'Junior is a monster; he's already showed how cold and mechanical he is. I still believe you'll see how good he really is in the not-too-distant future.

'I don't want him taking punches that he doesn't need to. It's important to respect your adversary and the half he has to give you. I know he can take a shot, but he doesn't have to prove this to me. They take their toll. Only a person like me can see this. There's no one better.

'He would go on and box even if I wasn't there, but I will never step aside from him in boxing. I'll always be by his side.

'There are people who think that I'm stealing his limelight, but I would never do that to my son. He's my baby. It's mindless to think otherwise.

'I looked at a picture, not too long ago, of me when I won the world championship from Nigel Benn in 1990. I didn't see any of my brothers, or my father, next to me.

'I'm not insinuating any of the people around me were strangers, but I so wish that my father was there. It was awful that he wasn't.

'Who else would you put next to Junior? Do you think anyone else would have the depth that I have? You need to be beaten to within inches of your life to have that depth.

'To entrust my son to someone else would make me very irresponsible. It's a cruel way to think and not intelligent.

'He told me once that, when he was a child, he thought it was a normal thing for people to come up to me and ask for autographs and pictures.

'He didn't realise I'd done all of these things in boxing and what I had to go through to get this respect. When he did, he wanted the same thing. He thinks he can do what I did.'

Eubank has endured his fair share of drama since hanging up the gloves, with bankruptcy and a divorce among the issues he has faced. He was also arrested in his truck for breaching the peace on an anti-war activism mission.

Eubank had previously been involved in a fatal collision that killed a building site worker, after losing control of his car.

He was convicted of driving without due care and attention, fined £250 plus £1,450 costs and had six penalty points added to his licence. He later married his manager, Claire Geary.

Other brushes with the law have involved him taking a beer lorry without the owner's consent, claiming it had caused him an unreasonable obstruction.

He knows what he likes and he likes what he knows. Very few opinions will sway Eubank from the course of behaviour he wishes to employ.

He said, 'I told my nephew the following and advised him to commit it to memory, which I will share with you.

'Don't make noise in haste and remember what peace there may be in silence. Go as far as possible without surrender and be on good terms with all persons.

'Speak the truth and listen to others, even the dumb and the ignorant for they too have a story. There will always be those greater and lesser than yourself.

'Enjoy your achievements, as well as your plans, keep interested in your own career, however humble it may be. Your possessions will be gained in the fortunes of time.

'Exercise caution in your business affairs, for the world is full of trickery, and let it lead to what virtue there is. Strive for high ideas and be yourself. Do not feign affection or be cynical about love, take kindly to counsel and nurture your strengths. Do not distress yourself through imagination.

'The idea is simply this – be calm, gentle and true. All we are is people, no matter what we've achieved. Get across a message to people that will benefit from this information.

'People don't just base my legacy on my ability, it's the lisp that I have and the jumpers, and the pretend monocle that I sometimes wear. It's the truck that I used to drive.

'It's the philosophy that I can recite at a snap, it's the maverick that I've been. All of these things combined make my image.

'Shakespeare once said, "The world is a stage and we are all actors." It's true, you are acting whether you know it or not.'

That was the journey around the wacky world of Chris Eubank, who is certainly in a league of his own and still with a touch of genius about him.

CHAPTER NINE

YOU ONLY GET OUT WHAT YOU PUT IN – STEVE COLLINS

MIXING in good company and being ready when opportunity knocked paid off for Steve Collins – then it was him calling the shots.

It was necessary to spend time in his company at Bar Sport hearing about how it all began, and how his journey progressed, to get a feel for who the man really is.

It didn't take long for him to tell the story of how he came to be a star, but it was one that had the crowd in the Premier Suite captivated.

Collins wasn't even originally billed to be there. He got the call to join Carl Frampton as an added attraction for this show in Cannock and there are always parallels between the two.

Collins was the first and only other boxer from Ireland to win world titles in two weight classes, but his times and circumstances were vastly different.

Most modern boxers will wear that 'protected' stigma with the old guard, but not many would bring the same suggestions to Collins' door.

It would take the harshest of critics to claim that 'the Celtic Warrior' hasn't done the hard yards to achieve what he has in boxing.

He left Ireland at the age of 21 still starry-eyed about the sport, having cleaned up in his homeland as an amateur to the tune of 26 national titles.

The third of four sons, his family were of boxing stock. His father, Paschal, was a former prize fighter and uncle Jack O'Rourke had been an Irish heavyweight champion in the 1960s.

Collins became a part of the Corinthians gym in Dublin from the age of eight and racked up an 82-8 amateur record.

Tragedy struck Collins at 17, when his dad died of a heart attack while out walking. It was him who had persuaded his son to get a trade to go with boxing.

He left school to start work as an apprentice electrician at the Guinness Brewery, where most of his relatives had worked.

For Collins, it just wasn't enough. He'd wanted to become a world champion since first lacing on the gloves and was willing to work as hard as anyone to get there.

That meant pastures new and moving to the United States, where he turned up at one of the best gyms going looking to learn from the best.

Marvin Hagler, then the most decorated middleweight in the world, had more than a hand in that, albeit unwittingly. A young Collins idolised the 'Marvelous One'.

That took him to Brockton, Massachusetts, and the fight club where Hagler honed his skills, which was run by the Petronelli brothers, Goody and Pat.

Goody took a shine to Collins and helped develop him as a force, which led to his professional debut in October 1986.

Irish-Americans meant dollars at the time, and the bill on which he first punched for pay was stacked with attractions of that persuasion.

Future film subject Mickey Ward also featured while Freddie Roach, who would go on to train many of the game's best, including Collins himself, was still boxing.

Collins took care of Julio Mercado by virtue of a third-round stoppage and, with that, he was up and running.

He said, 'I had a great childhood. My father had a good job, I went to a good school and we lived near Phoenix Park, which was like a lunatic asylum there was that much happening.

'There was a boxing gym in the area and we'd go there most nights. I had my first fight when I was eight years old and the buzz I got from it made me sure what I wanted to be.

'The amateurs were a great training ground for pro boxing; it's probably better now as it's more skilful and technical.

'But I always felt my style was more suited to being a pro and I'd sparred with a few of them. I'd committed myself to winning an amateur title first, though. It just took me a long time!

'I'm a late developer, so the same thing happened as a pro but, since I was a kid, I told everyone I was going to be a world champion.

'I went to the States because Hagler was someone I looked up to. He was a great champion and someone I could relate to.

'I wanted to go where he was, hoping that the people who prepared him to be a champion could do the same for me. I found out where he trained and took it from there.

'I got married and, shortly after, I was flying out. I didn't know anyone over there, we just checked into a hotel. Later on, I got an apartment and worked on the building sites.

'I was introduced to Goody and he told me to come down to the gym. I arrived, trained and did a bit of sparring with Hagler's [half] brother, Robbie Sims.

'I realised that it wasn't a spar; this guy was out to do a number on me. He couldn't. I turned out to be more of a handful than he expected and gave a good account of myself.

'I knew what was happening; they wanted to see if I was going to waste their time or be worth their while. They saw potential.

'I mixed in great company and I got the knowledge right, along with the talent. Hagler was still the world champion and I was an up-and-coming middleweight.

'I used to watch him sparring and on the bag, but he'd never spar with me. That upset me because all I wanted was to be able to tell everyone I'd sparred with Hagler.

'I didn't understand why until years later. Sometimes we'd have amateurs in the gym, who'd spend a week there to mix with professionals, which gave them a buzz.

'There was this one kid over, he was a talented amateur but cocky. I was feeling nasty as I'd been training hard and, at the time, hating it.

'I told Freddie, "I'm not going to spar him" because I'd have probably knocked him out, which was wrong as I was ahead of him, as a top pro. That would have made me a bully.

'I made a decision and, once upon a time, I was the cocky kid in the gym and Hagler was the top pro. He would have badly beaten me up.

'My pro debut was great. It was televised on ESPN, so it was like being in a movie. It was my first experience of the big time.'

Collins' grounding in the US saw him go under the radar back in the UK, but it was a win over a fellow Irishman that really put him on the map early on.

The Irish middleweight title was on the line when he took on Sam Storey, which sold thousands of seats at the Boston Garden.

Both were unbeaten when they stepped through the ropes in 1988 and weren't about to surrender that status without a fight.

Collins was the clear winner after ten rounds and took a unanimous decision from the three judges. Scores of 100-93, 98-94 and 97-96 all went to Collins.

His status as an Irish-American meant he could box for US national titles, too, which happened in his 14th pro contest.

Kevin Watts was in the other corner, the defending champion who had defeated future world title challenger Tony Thornton to claim the strap.

A decent scrap ensued, which Collins won, but Watts was always dangerous, none more so than when he scored an 11th-round knockdown. Collins didn't panic and saw out the 12 rounds for the first time, getting him accustomed to the full distance. A unanimous decision was again the verdict, this time by scores of 118-109, 118-110 and 115-112.

Thornton was waiting in the wings for his first title defence and was a good scalp for Collins, who had to graft to get the victory.

One judge had it even at 114-114 but the other two went with Collins by margins of 117-110 and 116-112. It was another learning experience.

In early 1990, new WBA world middleweight champion Mike McCallum was looking for an opponent and Collins happily accepted the role.

Taking the belt from a great of his era was never going to be easy and the result proved true to type, with Collins well beaten at the final bell.

He was on the wrong end of unanimous verdicts, this time, and scores of 118-110 and 117-111 reflected the dominance of McCallum, who was on the top of his game.

Collins rebounded with five straight wins, only one going the distance, and spent the best part of two years chasing a rematch with McCallum.

The WBA eventually stripped McCallum of his crown for failing to defend for a second time against Collins, who was matched against Reggie Johnson instead.

McCallum countered with claims he declined a request to pay $50,000 for Collins to step aside, after he'd agreed to shell out $35,000 to the WBA to extend his mandatory date.

Collins versus Johnson took place in April 1992 and was a close-run battle, with the result – a majority decision win for Johnson – hotly disputed.

The crimson mask went to Collins as he was cut around both eyes come the end of the tenth, which he protested was a result of headbutts.

Southpaw Johnson wasn't penalised by referee Arthur Mercante, although both had been punished in the fifth for low blows, even though neither of Collins' two punches landed.

When it went to points, there was very little in it. One judge had it 114-114, a draw, while the other two scored it 115-113 and 115-114 respectively for Johnson.

This meant Collins would not get another world title shot without proving himself all over again. The only way back was through victories.

Trying to rebuild after two unsuccessful attempts at world glory, the last thing Collins needed was another setback on his record, particularly as he was coming down a level in his next fight to challenge for the European title.

The EBU bauble was almost irrelevant; it was the scalp of Sumbu Kalambay, a man further advanced in pursuit of the same goal, that was most important.

Kalambay had been the WBA world boss until McCallum unseated him in a rematch and was building a path towards former glories.

He'd reigned as European champion before outpointing McCallum in their first fight and Collins was his fifth defence, all in his adopted homeland of Italy. Brits John Ashton and Herol Graham had already lost over there.

Collins tried his luck in late 1992 and fared better, although he dropped a majority decision. Again, there were questions about how he could have lost after the beating he had dished out. Once more, he did.

The crowd had always been against him in these situations and this was no different. He was the away fighter and Kalambay was cuter.

Comparisons with the Johnson fight – which Collins still refuses to concede he lost fair and square – became apparent.

One judge had it a 116-116 draw, while the other had Kalambay up by a score of 117-114. The referee had it 116-114 for the home fighter, giving Kalambay victory. It was back to the drawing board for Collins.

He said, 'If you look at the pictures of me winning my first middleweight title, you can see how skinny I was back then.

'I fought for a world title in my 17th fight. I was the US champion and Michael Watson was supposed to fight McCallum, but he broke his nose in training.

'They were trying to find a substitute and I put my hand up and said, "I'll have a go." It might have been too early, but I learned more than beating ten mediocre opponents.

'I wasn't at my best in 1990. I met McCallum on the way up. He was 33, I was 26 and still learning. Guys like Sugar Ray Leonard wouldn't go near him because he was so slick.

'McCallum was the smartest I've ever been in with and had the best jab. He had the ability to ride punches, get past it and land quality counters. Defensively, he was so cute.

'I had to use all my strength and determination to win some rounds, but it was great to share a ring with him and that experience did so much for my own career.

'When you are in the ring with a great champion like that and you're giving it your best shot, they'll do something and you'll be like, "That was great, show me how you did that!"

'I didn't get a beating, I got educated, and I knew nobody from there was going to show me things like McCallum did. I gained experience and confidence.

'You see so many great amateurs turn pro who are like cash cows, who have to keep on winning to sell out arenas, so they bring in guys [for them] to roll over.

'On paper, he's a superstar but he hasn't had the education; they've been wrapped in cotton wool and haven't had the chance to reach their full potential.

'It works in reverse, too, when people don't look good because of their record when, in reality, they are because they've been thrown in at the deep end.

'British boxing has changed and they've got trainers, agents, solicitors, accountants. Everything now is much more professional, so good fighters go into it with their eyes open.

'It's a new era and the standard has definitely gone up. The world is definitely a different place to when I was boxing.

'I got another shot at the WBA title against Johnson, but there were so many issues in my personal life at that point.

'I took the fight for the money, which is a wrong reason, but I still think I won it. It was on a Don King show; in fact I think I'm still the only one he's ever paid in advance!

'We got an agreement early that the money had to be lodged, then automatically transferred to me when the bell rang.

'When you win it's great, but when you lose all you can do is try and find another level and dig down deeper next time.

'Things had not gone well but I was never broken or distraught. I knew I still had the potential to be a world champion, however long it took me.

'I was very upset about the Johnson result. Myself and everyone present believed I had won but, due to the politics of the sport, I didn't get the decision I should have.

'I thought I'd beaten Kalambay, too. He had beaten some of the best fighters around and was, undoubtedly, a world-level opponent. He was a hero in Italy.'

Collins' time in the US was drawing to a close. The riches he felt were befitting, even though he had yet to become a world champion, hadn't come his way and he had a family to support.

An 18-month period that included the setbacks against Johnson and Kalambay had come under the management of Barney Eastwood. By late 1992, others were courting Collins.

Barry Hearn won the race to guide him in 1993, by which time Collins was bouncing between Dublin and Belfast. Hearn had him move to Romford, Essex, to train.

The first of two encounters with Johnny Melfah, which both ended in TKO wins, was back in Britain. Ian Strudwick was then dispatched in seven.

The WBA penta-continental title may not have been all that meaningful, but it represented a return to 12-round action for Collins. He knocked out South African champion Gerhard Botes in the seventh.

A ninth-round stoppage of Wayne Ellis took Collins into 1994, which was a make-or-break year. Collins was so fed up with waiting for another world title shot he considered quitting.

Melfah lasted four rounds, a round longer than in their first fight, in a rematch that January and the eight-round points win over Paul Wesley that followed was little more than a keep-busy affair.

Turning 30 that summer, Collins had done his rebuilding and wasn't going to hang around forever. Hearn had to and eventually did deliver.

Collins had become the top contender for the WBO world title, but making the fight was not going to be easy. Englishman Chris Pyatt, the champion, had been and gone with Hearn.

Pyatt was now with Frank Warren, who promoted the match. It took place under his banner, at the Ponds Forge Arena in Sheffield on 11 May 1994.

There would have been nowhere for Collins to go had he lost. This time, he wasn't going to. Pyatt, under pressure, folded in five and there was a changing of the guard.

Collins was determined to defend his newly won crown as quickly as possible. He wasn't even back in the dressing room before Hearn started talking about what was next.

The winner of the Vinny Pazienza vs Roberto Duran fight, which took place the following month, was mentioned. Collins, in his post-fight interview, quipped that he'd fight them both.

A match was made in Hong Kong for October, when he would defend against American Lonny Beasley. In the end, the whole show was called off.

The rest of the year passed with no more action and, come 1995, Collins realised middleweight was no longer for him.

He'd always believed his power would travel up with him to super middle and, in his thirties, making the 160lb limit was becoming more and more difficult.

In the end, he would relinquish his world title without making a defence. But again, he would have to wait for opportunity to knock.

With Ray Close ruled out of a WBO title challenge at the higher weight, due to failing a brain scan, Collins was called up. The champion was Chris Eubank – and the fight was in Ireland.

Collins said, 'I enjoyed my stay in America, but the change came because I had kids. I saw what was happening in their society and I thought it wasn't a place to bring up children.

'I was doing good views but, financially, the money wasn't there. I parted with Eastwood on amicable terms. I wanted to further my career. I was recognised as someone who was definitely a world-class fighter but, when I moved back to the UK, it was almost like I had to start my career all over again.

'I was boxing to kill time on somebody else's night, while the television stations were waiting to go live with the main event, in front of a couple of hundred disinterested people.

'There was a lot of animosity when we got Pyatt, but it wasn't coming from me. He was a lovely guy, we were friends and we only parted ways for the fight.

'It did seem to me that, after everything that had happened to me before, I had to knock Pyatt out to win. When that happened, I was so happy I felt like crying.

'I knew if I got him, he'd go, and, if we traded, I'd been hit on the chin by harder punchers than him. He wasn't a bona fide middleweight; he was too small and that's why he lost.

'He pushed me away after the fight, when I tried to embrace him. I told him not to be like that, not to get caught up in the game the promoters were playing.

'Becoming a world champion was the job done, you've made it then. The hard part was the 20 years it took to get there and the time I had trying to maintain it.

'I'm lucky, really, because I'm sure there are better fighters than me that haven't achieved what I have. There's some luck involved, with being in the right place at the right time.

'I was never really a middleweight. I struggled so hard to make the weight, I just didn't have my natural strength because I didn't have the energy.

'All of a sudden, I got this opportunity to step up another eight pounds for the biggest fight that was available for me. Eubank was the best thing that happened to boxing in my time.'

Eubank's aura of invincibility had not yet been broken and he was still unbeaten – draws against Close and Nigel Benn were the only fights he'd failed to win – after 43 pro contests.

Only a cock-eyed optimist would have bet against him beating a late replacement in Collins, but the challenger had a game plan – and this one was like no other.

Hypnotherapist Tony Quinn deserves some of the credit, but nowhere near as much as Collins, for getting into Eubank's head.

Quinn had apparently trained Collins mentally to feel no pain and it was something even a man of Eubank's intelligence could not rationalise easily.

Eubank had been embroiled in mind games before, but this was new ground for the old warrior. It was clear before he got in the ring that he was up against it.

Collins emerged at the Green Glens Arena in Cork with his hood up, eyes closed and headphones on, the Rocky theme tune that heralded his arrival playing through them.

The two touched gloves and went to work in a bout that was not short on thrills and spills. Both men visited the canvas, but saw the final bell.

Eubank was down from a straight shot to the body towards the end of the eighth round before Collins was floored by a right hand in the tenth.

They weren't worlds apart, but the judges were unanimously in favour of Collins by margins of 115-111, 116-114 and 114-113. He was now, like Eubank, a two-weight world champion.

Eubank felt he'd been hoodwinked out of both his belt and his '0', and was desperate for revenge. Hence, there was a rematch before 1995 was out.

He had to return to Ireland, with their sequel taking place at the Gaelic games stadium of Pairc Ui Chaoimh, again back in Cork.

Collins again tried to bamboozle him with tactics, setting a fast pace and taking to wild brawling that Eubank was unaccustomed to.

Points once more ruled and it was a thinner margin than the first time, with a split decision. One judge had it 115-114 for Eubank, the other two 115-113 for Collins as he retained.

He said, 'I knew Chris for years before as we'd sparred together, when he was a welterweight and I was a middleweight.

'He was a skilful guy, but I was just too big for him. I was stronger, so it probably wasn't a fair fight. When he stood there and traded punches, I knew I'd come off better.

'I was still big at the weight and he was small, so I didn't have any doubts that I could knock him out. That didn't happen, in the end, but I found ways to win.

'This was at super middle and, once again, because someone was injured. I was in the gym skipping when I got the call.

'It was in Ireland, just after St Patrick's Day. It was like a movie script, it was corny. You have to give Chris credit; he's fearless and when you whack him, he comes straight back.

'I watched his fights and just thought to myself, "He's doing a lot wrong and getting away with it." I planned everything, from the press conference to standing in the ring facing him.

'We fooled the world. Back then, people didn't accept the way I approached it. A lot of people called the way I was going on arrogance.

'Before the weigh-in, we were in a little room at the back. Eubank walked in and I'm there skipping, trying to lose the last bit of weight before we went to the scales.

'He made a little comment, "very unprofessional", or something like that. I walked up, got nose to nose with him and told him, "I'm the new champ, I'm going to win."

'He looked at me like I had ten heads and I just kept telling him that I was going to win. I did it so many times it became a mantra. I looked like a lunatic, he backed off a bit and I could see that I'd scared him. I claimed I'd been hypnotised and Tony had done it to me.

'Tony told everyone I would punch harder, be faster, stronger and that I wouldn't feel pain or bleed if I got cut. The most interested in all this was Eubank. He wanted out.

'I ignored everything that was going on when I went to the ring or when he made his way in. I could feel it, through the ropes, but Eubank thought I was oblivious and it got to him.

'He caught me with a right hand in the first round and hurt me. Every time he hit me it hurt. Drama over, fight on, but it was probably the best planned fight of my career.

'I think it was the best performance of my career, but it might not have been enough. It could have been "and still" but instead I heard "and the new". It really was a dream come true.

'When it was over, I couldn't have a minute to myself. I was so overwhelmed by the people, I just wanted to escape. I could only really enjoy that night after I retired.

'In the second fight, I changed my style completely. I was very awkward. I didn't want him to expect the same thing. On both occasions, I showed I was a true champion.

'I still feel like I won the second fight more convincingly than the first one. When they announced it was a split, I wondered what was going on.'

With Eubank now seen off for good, Collins could move on. Unifying world titles in an exciting clash with WBC title holder Nigel Benn was Plan A.

Benn was invited as a guest to watch Collins box at the Point in Dublin against Cornelius Carr, which would go the full 12 rounds. Spirited Englishman Carr put up a fight but finished well beaten by Collins. Unanimously, the scores were 117-111 and 116-112 twice.

At the start of 1996, both would go their separate ways for title defences, seven days apart from each other. Benn went first, then Collins.

Benn would lose his belt to Thulani Malinga, while Collins beat Neville Brown. Now it was Collins in the driving seat for negotiations, should they meet.

He still had the greatest respect for huge underdog Brown, the recently crowned British champion who was thrust on to the world stage at the Green Glens Arena no less.

Brown was on the floor in the first round but showed great heart to get up and hang in there until the 11th, when he was clobbered twice again for the finish.

He would meet Collins again at Bar Sport, where even Brown, from his table in the audience, was taken aback by the compliments he received.

Their meeting was always a warm-up for Benn, though. Collins and him met in July of that year at the Nynex Arena in Manchester.

It would prove an anti-climax, with Benn injuring his right ankle when falling awkwardly after missing wildly with an overhand right.

The pain grew and Benn eventually turned away in round four in what looked very much like a surrender. The referee intervened, declaring Collins the winner by stoppage.

With such an unsatisfactory finish, a return had to happen and it did that November, at the same venue. There could be no excuses this time.

Benn looked every bit a shot fighter. He unloaded all of what was once an unstoppable arsenal at Collins who, six rounds later, still wasn't seriously troubled.

Before the bell went for the seventh, Benn was pulled out, with no real complaints from him or his corner. The Dark Destroyer was no more. He'd retired, in more ways than one.

Collins said, 'I first came across Nigel when I was in the States. I'd been promised a fight with Iran Barkley and, all of a sudden, I was asked to step aside so he could fight this Brit.

'Benn was the WBO middleweight champion and had smashed Doug DeWitt to become a world champion for the first time. He wiped Barkley out inside a round.

'All of it was unheard of. British fighters normally came over to America and got beat. I should know, I was over there.

'Nigel wiped that slate clean, but I never got the chance to fight him until I was a world champion myself. He hits very hard and, when I came forward, I didn't know what to expect.

'I tell everyone this, punchers are lazy. He got me with a left hook and I was gone at one point, and he looked at me thinking, "How is he still here?"

'He thought he couldn't hurt me, even though he did, and that gave me an edge. He thought I was too busy for him. From there, both fights were over.

'He was actually more dangerous when he was hurt. He would throw punches blind so when I had him on the ropes, I was very cautious. I just hit and slipped.

'It all came together. I'm no better than Nigel, but wars are won by planning and I'd planned a smarter fight that worked better than his.

'The old Nigel was gone, really. I'd missed my chance to pit my wits against that guy. I felt like the public hadn't got their money's worth, with four and then six rounds.

'I'd had a couple of defences before that. Neville was never a super middle, but was tough enough to trade punches for 11 rounds. He kept coming but he was too small for me.

'I've stopped guys who are far bigger and stronger than him, but he had the biggest heart of anyone I've been in there with.

'Some fighters never get the breaks that they deserve and Neville is one of the guys I love in the game. I've got a lot of respect for him and when I see him he always brightens me up.

'My most favourite people on this planet are boxers, but not all the best ones make it to the top. Neville is one of them.'

Eubank and Benn had been conquered, beaten twice by the man of the moment. There wasn't much left for Collins to do against anyone this side of the pond.

Collins desperately chased a fight with US superstar Roy Jones Jr. It was what he wanted for years, but it still didn't look any closer.

Benn had bowed out against him, but it also proved to be Collins' last night in anything approaching his prime on the big stage.

Two title defences followed. European champion Frederic Seillier began 1997 but a lack of motivation wasn't punished as the Frenchman was halted in five by a cut to his right eye.

By then, Collins was so frustrated with Jones he claimed he was going to knock on his door and challenge him to a fight on the street, then and there. Even that call wasn't answered.

Collins did get an American challenger that July in Glasgow but, instead of Jones, it was a fireman from Kansas City, Craig Cummings, replacing the unheralded Syrian Anwar Oshana.

Jones looked to have left him behind for good by going up to light-heavyweight, and it was hard for him to get up for Cummings, who was only ranked at world level by the WBO.

Collins was reminded to take boxing seriously again in the first round, when he was floored by his challenger, only to send Cummings to the canvas before the opening session was out.

It made him mad and Cummings was done for in the third round, with Collins still feeling embarrassed after being knocked down. Desire had reached its lowest ebb.

Later that year, it looked to all intents and purposes like Collins versus Joe Calzaghe was about to become a reality.

It got to the point where Collins was summoned to a cafe in London, where it was expected a head-to-head press conference would take place.

Collins arrived, hung around for a while and shortly left, disappearing into Leicester Square. Calzaghe and Warren, who had him contracted to fight on 6 September, were furious.

It was clear Collins wasn't keen on facing Calzaghe and certainly not in the less-than-salubrious Kingsway Leisure Centre in Widnes.

He eventually agreed to take on Calzaghe in October at the Sheffield Arena, but the hunger for anything less than career-defining tests had clearly gone. He cited injury and retired, vacating the WBO title at a second weight in the process. Calzaghe outpointed Eubank for the belt instead.

A comeback looked to be on in 1999, when he turned up across the ring from Jones Jr after he had easily dispatched Richard Frazier by second-round stoppage.

Jones Jr countered accusations he was ducking Collins by claiming he'd offered $3 million for a contest with the Irishman, who said he'd 'fight Mike Tyson' for that money.

Calzaghe reared his head again, too, when it became apparent from previous agreements that he was first in line to take on Collins should he come out of retirement.

After much toing and froing, Collins accepted this and started to train for the prospect but, understandably, wanted a warm-up bout first.

It was to come on the undercard of Calzaghe's world title defence against Rick Thornberry in June 1999, with the two then set to clash in the autumn.

Some weeks before, Collins stepped into the training ring with Howard Eastman for a sparring session, which frightened the life out of everybody.

Both had been told to take it easy, but Collins collapsed face down on the canvas and was taken to hospital, where tests and a brain scan were carried out. Both found nothing.

Collins took it as a sign boxing had become too dangerous for him and he hung up the gloves for a second time. He'd come out of retirement, ultimately, for nothing.

He said, 'The reason my drive to carry on boxing went was because there was no more big names out there for me. There was only Jones and a couple of kids that no one knew about.

'There was Calzaghe; he went on to become one of the best champions Britain ever had but he was just an up-and-coming guy in 1997. Joe didn't become a big name until a couple of years after I retired. He didn't offer me the fight then so why should I have when I was the name?

'The fight didn't appeal to me. He didn't bring reputation or a title, so there was no money in it. And at a 2,000-capacity arena? I was getting more than that at my weigh-ins.

'Jones is the one I've always wanted. I've told a few people he's scared of me. He doesn't want the fight, then or now. I'd take it tomorrow, even after all of this time.

'When I got in the ring with him, he ran like a child. I knew then he wasn't interested and would never be interested in giving me the only fight that would make me return to the ring.

'Looking at the earlier part of the 1990s, it was a wonderful time, to be in the mix when super middleweights from the UK were the best in the world. What a great era to be involved in.

'It takes a long time to get out of the habit of boxing. It's like I explain to people, from my first fight to my last was a period of 25 years.

'So that's a quarter of a century, non-stop, where I had to go on a diet and to the gym in the cold of winter to get punched in the head. That's long enough.'

Despite his closing comments, Collins still won't let you rule out him versus Jones Jr becoming a reality. Both may have called it a day, but he'd never say never.

CHAPTER TEN

UNBEATABLE TO THE LAST –
JOE CALZAGHE

IT was retaining his '0' while the injuries piled up that meant more to Joe Calzaghe than amassing one of the longest undefeated streaks in boxing history.

The reality is that one of the pound-for-pound greats of the noughties notched some of his best victories while carrying problems that would have affected anyone's performance.

Even some of his greatest wins – over the likes of Jeff Lacy, Mikkel Kessler, Bernard Hopkins and Roy Jones Jr – came when the Welsh dragon was less than 100 per cent.

Calzaghe's finest hour came when he was performing through gritted teeth, seeming to always be hurt, but still outpointing Kessler in front of over 50,000 fellow Welsh folk.

He said goodbye to the super middleweight division he'd called home for 14 years that night as the main man, holding the WBO, WBA 'super' and WBC world titles.

Making the weight was as troublesome as injuries by that point, and he stepped up to light-heavy for the twilight of his career. A year and two fights later, he'd done all he wanted.

Calzaghe may not have ruled with nearly as many exploits at 175lbs, but there's no denying the longevity of the reign he enjoyed at 168lbs. The Pride of Wales was a world super middleweight champion for ten consecutive years, starting with a coming-of-age victory over a true gatekeeper, Chris Eubank, in 1997.

Calzaghe's mark of 21 world title defences is the fourth highest in boxing history, above the 20 by Hopkins and Larry Holmes at middleweight and heavyweight respectively.

Only Ricardo Lopez, Wladimir Klitschko, Dariusz Michalczewski (all 23) and Joe Louis (25) have made more defences of a world title.

Calzaghe retired unbeaten with a 46-0 pro record, so missing out on the chance to beat Rocky Marciano's then-unparalleled 49 victories with no defeats.

Floyd Mayweather Jr, who beat the record by going to 50-0, was 39 bouts into his legacy when Calzaghe hung up the gloves, so he'd have definitely got there first had he boxed on.

It was more than eight years later when Calzaghe visited Bar Sport, where one of his challengers, fellow former world champion Richie Woodhall, posed the questions to him.

He was joined by his father, Enzo, who led him to his greatest glories as coach. It was the last time the Premier Suite got to see Joe's dad before he died in 2018.

Enzo went from being a boxing fan with little experience of the sport to leading one of the best fighters ever, earning him the *Ring* magazine's Trainer of the Year award in 2007.

Both had their critics, with some believing Joe was protected in a poor division and others of the opinion that Enzo was only in the corner because of who his son was.

Joe's promoter and manager at the time, Frank Warren, went on the record in 1999 suggesting a parting of the ways. His plea fell on deaf ears.

The Calzaghes knew of this and still didn't care, going on to achieve all of their goals. At the end of it all, that stance is unlikely to change.

Joe said, 'Father-and-son relationships rarely work in any sport, and for my dad, who has never boxed, to lead me was special. He was my trainer, my dad and my best friend.

'He took over when I was 17. I'd lost nine fights with my last coach when I was an amateur and I didn't lose in 20 years after. We were family but we could distance ourselves at work.

'If it wasn't for him, I'd have never boxed in the first place, so he should be rightly proud of what he created at the end of it.

'I was bothered about keeping my "0". I could have been 50-1, but I'd have still had that one [loss]. It wasn't worth the risk. It's every boxer's dream to retire undefeated.

'Boxing is a sport but it's your health and your family that come first. Even my children didn't want me to fight again. They were crying for me before fights sometimes.

'Everyone should retire on their own terms. Boxing has provided me with some wonderful times and amazing experiences. It's given me a life I could have never had otherwise.

'I'm so proud I was able to leave my mark on the sport. I did everything that I wanted to do. I'm lucky, when you look at some other fighters.

'I thought about carrying on and trying to beat the record, but my injuries were too bad. I remember speaking to Emanuel Steward [the famous late trainer and TV analyst].

'I told him I was thinking of retiring, how I was hurting, and he said, "If you don't appreciate what you've done now, you won't in the years to come either."

'To hear that from a great man like him, I knew it was my time to bow out. When you're not boxing at your best, I listened to my body and the people around me. You can't fight forever.

'It was difficult, just boredom more than anything when all you've done is box. I'm sure people thought I was coming back. Being retired is one thing, staying retired is another.

'There's a load of reasons why I didn't. My hands were packed in [damaged] so I couldn't train properly at the end of my career. If I'm honest, the hunger had gone with it.

'People didn't realise how hard it was for me, the fact that I was able to fight with the injuries. At one point, I couldn't even shadow box. My determination got me through.

'It's an explosive sport, there's so much emotion and, when that's gone, there's a void in your life. Eventually, you find other things to do and just be proud you actually did that.

'After 27 years of boxing, it was the right time to get out. I'm happy I retired when I did. It's not nice to see fighters still going when they shouldn't be.'

The Calzaghe name is written into the history of their native Italy, where most of the elder clan were born and raised in Bancali, a hamlet of Sassari on the island of Sardinia.

Enzo flew the nest to foreign climes, deciding to travel across Europe after completing his national service as a teenager.

His travels took him from place to place by any means possible, quite often hitchhiking, until he arrived on the south coast of England in Bournemouth.

Relatives ran a restaurant, where Enzo worked and lived. Tiring of the experience, he wanted to go back to his roots as soon as he'd earned enough money to do so.

When it came to pass, the adventurer in him surfaced again. At Southampton train station, the tannoy announced a service to Cardiff, and it was there he went instead.

That journey would change his life. Romance called with future wife Jackie at a Wimpy restaurant in the city and they were married all of four weeks later.

Baby Joseph William was born in March 1972 and was taken back to Sardinia more than once, as well as spending time with Jackie's mother-in-law in London. All of this occurred while Enzo was chasing his dream of making a living as a bass guitarist, which took him away from home wherever they were.

The village of Pentwynmawr was a poignant outpost, close to the Welsh town of Newbridge, which has become more synonymous with the Calzaghe name than anywhere in Italy.

Such are their exploits that Joe was made an MBE in 2003, then a CBE during his swansong year of 2008. Come 2010, Enzo was also made an MBE.

Enzo received his accolade in Wales through one of the Queen's local representatives, as he would have had to become a British citizen to do so at Buckingham Palace.

It was another reward for his services to boxing, which began in 1981 when Enzo got involved with Newbridge Boxing Club, then run by Paul Williams.

The tin sheet-clad gym was situated next to the local rugby club and was a place of learning for the Calzaghes, Enzo as a trainer and Joe as a fighter.

Williams retired in 1990, handing over the reins to Enzo during a year where Joe would lose for the last time. It was his tenth as an amateur, with 100 wins redressing the balance.

Those 12 months saw Joe beaten by Romania's Adrian Opreda at the European Junior Championships, after he was downed by Michael Smyth in the Welsh ABA final.

The disappointment of defeat was something Joe would never experience again, as he went on a run of tremendous success.

He'd already picked up four schoolboy ABA titles, but the senior ABA prize he won in 1991 was the start of something special.

Trevor French was seen off in the welter decider before Calzaghe jumped up to super welter in 1992 to repeat the feat, at the expense of fellow future world champion Glenn Catley.

He looked a shoo-in to go to the 1992 Olympic Games but, ultimately, it was Robin Reid who was picked at super welter for Great Britain. The two have been rivals ever since.

The Calzaghes believe this was because of opposition from within their own ABA committee in Wales, stemming from Joe withdrawing from an event in Norway through injury.

They were so enraged that Joe nearly turned pro there and then, but there was still a point to be made in his final year as an amateur before doing so.

The 1993 senior ABA competition saw him go up again to middleweight, where he made it a hat-trick of titles after ousting Darren Dorrington in the final.

It made Calzaghe the first man to win senior ABA titles at three different weights in successive years for 65 years, his predecessor being Fred Webster from 1926 to 1928.

Calzaghe said, 'My dad was a musician, so he was away a lot. He was a boxing fan, too, but we liked football as well. Being from an Italian family, we were all Juventus fans.

'I wanted to be either a boxer or a footballer, but my hands were a lot faster than my feet. We soon realised that when my dad bought me a speedball when I was five.

'I remember being left shivering on the substitutes' bench at a football match in the winter, not scoring any goals, then I went to the boxing gym and started beating people up.

'When I had to concentrate on one or the other, it was a logical choice. Boxing was my destiny and where I was worth something.

'I started boxing when I was nine years old. I wouldn't say I had a bad upbringing, but we weren't rich either. Everything was hard, nothing was given to me on a silver spoon.

'I had my first fight when I was ten, which I lost. I was robbed, by the way. The lad who beat me on a majority, his father was one of the judges. I beat the guy five times afterwards.

'Ever since I was young, I'd train like a professional, going on six-mile runs every morning. I developed my stamina at an early age.

'I didn't like school at all. I was bullied and didn't have a good time. Boxing was my escapism and the ring was where I felt best.

'Boxing has always been my job. I've only worked about three or four days in my life. I was at my mum's cake factory for about a day and a half.

'I asked to go to the toilet and ended up jumping on the bus to Newbridge. My mum wasn't happy. I told her, "Don't worry, I'm going to be a world champion, I'll look after you."

'Ever since I won my first amateur title, I wanted to be a champion. I loved winning. The hard work to do that came in that shack, Newbridge Boxing Club, and it got me to the top.

'It's been demolished now. Everything I've achieved started in that humble gym, which was taken down in a matter of minutes. The new club is just a mile away, though.

'It's a bit of a joke I never went to the Olympics. I was gutted about it. It was clear that I didn't get in the team because my face didn't fit. I was the best in Britain.

'I remember dad coming in from the selection meeting and I could tell from his face that I'd not been picked. That was a terrible low point. Dad was upset, I was upset, but it just wasn't meant to happen. Even then, I was in no rush to turn professional. There were still things I wanted to do.

'No one from Wales had ever won three senior ABA titles at three weights and, seeing as I wasn't going to the Olympics, that was something no one could take away from me.

'I did it at welterweight, super welter and middleweight, beating and stopping future world champions on the way. The only thing that was missing was going to the Olympics.'

Being an Olympian would have only added to Calzaghe's appeal when he decided to punch for pay, but there were still plenty of takers for a highly decorated amateur.

He was regarded as a puncher, even then. In the two years before he made the switch, only Dorrington had seen the final bell and he'd been down three times.

Calzaghe's early pro opponents fell in rapid time, with eight first-round TKOs recorded in his first 11 contests. In one, though, he'd been taken eight rounds.

He was a clear winner on points against Bobbie Joe Edwards, but got an early lesson about throwing the kitchen sink at someone who is going nowhere.

The British title came along in his 16th pro fight as Calzaghe overwhelmed Stephen Wilson for an eighth-round stoppage. Bigger things were already in Calzaghe's mind.

He would only defend the belt once, disposing of Mark Delaney in five. It felt even better silencing the crowd, who had heckled him with anti-Welsh jibes all night.

A split with managers Mickey Duff and Terry Lawless was on the horizon, too, and became a reality when Warren came calling at the end of 1996.

A breakthrough 1997 saw Calzaghe get ready for a world title shot with a further three outings, all TKO wins. He'd reached 22-0, with 21 of those fights ending inside the distance.

A match had been made with WBO super middleweight champion Steve Collins, who pulled out at late notice and retired instead. That has never sat well with Calzaghe, who also never forgot Collins' quip that 'he couldn't fill a parish church'. History has proved him wrong.

None of this mattered to Warren, who needed to make another fight with a creditable new opponent and fast. The call went to a man who needed no introduction.

Chris Eubank was rebuilding after his invincible aura had been shattered by two defeats to Collins, who had also done the double over Nigel Benn. He had such a history with the belt.

Fight-fit and ready to go, Eubank stepped in for bout number 50 of his illustrious career determined to put a big dent in Calzaghe's momentum.

The entire Sheffield Arena was in a state of shock when the ultra-durable Eubank was put on the floor from a left hand in the first round. It was all of 15 seconds into the 12 rounds.

Eubank was up at the count of two, smiling at Calzaghe and remarking, 'Good shot'. He'd go on to absorb the rest of his artillery and, like his relative Edwards, was still there at the end.

Calzaghe established an insurmountable lead on the scorecards, but faded fast in the second half of the fight. A late rally was required just to make sure.

The three judges unanimously agreed over the winner. All went for Calzaghe by margins of 118-110, 118-109 and 116-111. At the age of 25, Calzaghe had become a world champion.

He said, 'When I turned pro, I was told to calm down, because they didn't think a super middleweight could throw so many punches for 12 rounds. Everything I did was intense.

'I was a pretty hard puncher but looking back I should have looked to have gone the distance a bit more, because I was always hurting my hands.

'I've had injuries all through my career, ever since I was 13 years old. It got better when I started to use my speed as much as my power.

'I had the skills to be in range and still be elusive. I was too brave for my own good sometimes, but I was hard to hit.

'I always wanted to entertain and come forward. It was never really my intention to go the distance, although I always trained for it. I'm a southpaw, but I was never negative.

'The first time I went the distance [against Edwards], I was like, "Look at the size of this guy, he's a cruiser!" He just happened to be Eubank's cousin, too. I remember hitting him with the first shot of the night, an uppercut, my hand went and he just smiled. I knew it was going the eight rounds then.

'Winning a world title was always on my mind so, when I won the British title, I saw it as a stepping stone. Wilson was a good boxer and well schooled, but I got him out of there.

'The Lonsdale Belt is the most beautiful of all the belts, though, and what I was gutted with was that I only defended it once and had to relinquish it, again through injury.

'The early days were tough, I was on about £300 a week, but I got to 19 fights and 19 wins, with 18 TKOs, and I was British champion, but I could barely afford to pay my mortgage.

'I knew something wasn't quite right about that, so I spoke to Frank and he promised me three fights and then a world title shot, which he delivered.

'It was supposed to be against Collins, but he made a number of excuses and just didn't want to fight me. He pulled out about a week before.

'I thought Eubank was a harder fight. I was preparing for one style and then another but you know what you're getting with him. He's a hard, hard man.

'Eubank was on the undercard anyway, so he was in good shape and it was a massive opportunity for him. I used to love watching him, Collins and Benn.

'I remember going to a hotel for a press conference and Chris' Harley Davidson motorcycle was parked outside. I loved him, the way he carried himself. He was one of a kind.

'He came in and shook my hand, which was the hardest handshake I'd ever had, but I was young and cocky then, so I told him he was getting knocked out.

'He said he was going to take me to one place I'd never been and that was the trenches. I didn't even know what that was, but I did afterwards. It was the toughest night of my life.

'Come fight night, he's on the floor in the first round. It was the worst thing I could have ever done, because then I threw everything at him and he went nowhere.

'Four and five rounds go by, then six, and I'm absolutely shattered. After eight, I had nothing left. I was breathing heavily on my stool between rounds.

'In the tenth, a second wind came and I've never been so thankful of anything. In the last two rounds, I even managed to pick the pace up.

'There's no harder way to win a world title and it was the best experience I could have had. The determination I had to show to get through that set me up for the rest of my career.'

Now on the map as a global force, Calzaghe's plan was to pick up more of the belts at super middleweight. But that would not happen for a good number of years.

His first defence came in early 1998 and lasted less than three rounds. Branko Sobot wasn't even supposed to be his opponent, coming in after Tarick Salmaci refused to fight.

Second challenger Juan Carlos Gimenez Ferreyra had some pedigree but had failed in three previous world title attempts. He'd taken both Eubank and Benn the distance.

Ferreyra had never been stopped before, but was retired on his stool at the end of the ninth round. It wasn't earth-shattering, but Calzaghe had made a statement. He had the bit between his teeth again as the shoe went on to the other foot, with Reid in need of a world title shot. There was still bad blood between him and Calzaghe.

It wasn't just about the Olympics, where Reid won bronze after taking a place that Calzaghe considered to be rightfully his.

Reid had later refused to defend his WBC world title against Calzaghe, too, which led to Warren turning to Collins and the WBO crown.

They would settle their differences in the ring come 1999, with the end result splitting opinion. A hard-fought and palatable 12 rounds produced a split decision.

All three judges had it 116-111, one for Reid and two for Calzaghe. There would be no rematch, despite many seeing what happened differently.

Calzaghe would make one more defence before the end of the year and predicted, as with Sobot, that Rick Thornberry would be out of there in three. All the third round was notable for this time was Calzaghe again hurting his hand, after he'd dropped Thornberry in the second.

The lacklustre nature of his display, although he was a clear winner and never in any danger of losing, gave the critics ammunition and cost him a debut in the United States that year.

Points margins of 120-107, 119-109 and 119-108 reflected his superiority, but didn't enhance his reputation. Then came the new millenium, along with a British showcase for Mike Tyson.

Tyson was to box in England for the first time, blasting out Julius Francis in just two rounds at the Manchester Arena. Calzaghe held a prominent spot on the bill.

His clash with David Starie was the only world title fight on the card and, again, he would complete the full 12 rounds to little fanfare.

Their dour encounter was screened in the US on Showtime and hardly set the world alight, with a bloodied Starie as negative as they come. Boos were heard by the halfway point.

The judges were all in agreement, but by differing margins. Scores of 120-108, 118-110 and 116-113 all went to Calzaghe.

In August 2000, Calzaghe would rediscover his punching power against the rising Omar Sheika. There was no love lost between those two, either.

They got Sheika at the fourth time of asking and his mouth came with him. He shouted at Calzaghe during the introductions and shoved him as the referee was giving his instructions.

Calzaghe made him pay when Sheika went for broke after four fruitless rounds of trying to make an impact, along with sustaining a cut by his right eye.

All Calzaghe did was block his work and then unload his own blows, with the referee stepping in with Sheika getting clobbered at will during an all-action fifth.

Calzaghe said, 'You beat Eubank and think you're going on to unify the titles, but the politics of boxing soon makes you realise it's not that easy.

'After Eubank, I made a defence and got a really bad wrist injury. There were even some worries about whether I could carry on fighting.

'I was having problems with my elbows and shoulders, too, and it was getting to me. I wasn't enjoying boxing any more.

'At that point in my career, had I earned the money to make me a multi-millionaire, I'd have retired. That's how bad it became.

'I told everyone Sobot wouldn't last three rounds with me and that's what happened. Like with Ferreyra, you can only beat what's put in front of you.

'I defeated Reid with one of my worst performances and I fractured my left hand after three rounds. I was awful that night.

'I was maybe over-confident going in there and, to give him credit, he fought the right fight for him but I wasn't lucky. I still won fair and square.

'No disrespect to Thornberry, he was a good opponent and took a lot of punishment, but I was hurt again. I showed what a champion I was by winning with my one good hand.

'I'd hardly sparred for the next two years, probably up to the point I fought Starie. I was only going at half pelt. It was frustrating.

'Me and Starie were on the same bill as Tyson, who had come over to England for the first time to box Julius.

'I stayed at the same hotel as Tyson, who had took over most of the top floor with his massive entourage. They had a gym downstairs, where I was, and no one really noticed me.

'I saw Mike and asked him for a picture. He was a bit rude and dad told him to smile. He looked like he was going to kill the pair of us.

'We came across him again later on and it was like talking to a different person. His personality had completely changed. I sat with him for ages. We discussed our promoters, I was with Frank and he was with Don King. Again, he switched. Pretty soon, he was on about how much he wanted to kill Don.

'I was just nodding and smiling, thinking this guy is absolutely nuts. He's a very strange, complicated sort of character.

'It was a clash of styles against Starie; he just waited for me and wanted to tie me up. That was the only way he could get through it.

'I had Sheika after that and he was big-headed, loud-mouthed and arrogant. I couldn't stand him. I really wanted to knock him out. He could punch, but this time I could spar. I was rusty and my timing was off, but I could spar. It came together in five. I was happy to be back to my best.'

Calzaghe had already taken part in three all-British world title affairs when he completed 2000 by facing Richie Woodhall.

Woodhall was another former WBC champion and one of Reid's successors, but there was no beef between him and Calzaghe. In fact, they were friends.

That continued past the fight and past their reunion at Bar Sport, which came nearly 16 years on from when they traded blows.

Calzaghe's seventh defence of the WBO belt might have ended early had Woodhall not soaked up a flush right hand in the opening minute of battle.

He was pegged back as Woodhall regrouped to up the pace and land the cleaner punches in the second, with his best work coming early on.

By the second half of the fight, Calzaghe had started to take control and went through the gears down the stretch.

A right hand over the top as both fighters traded bowled Woodhall over in the dying seconds of the ninth but, despite being bloodied, he heard the bell.

Calzaghe resumed his onslaught when the action restarted in the tenth as he pinned Woodhall on to the ropes and let his punches go.

He covered up, taking the blows until referee Roy Francis stepped in to spare him further punishment just 28 seconds into the session.

He said, 'There was never any falling out between me and Richie, business is business. Obviously, we had the same promoter so the fight was easy to make. I remember going to one of the press conferences and on the way home we stopped at the services. We saw Richie and his dad, Len, in the cafe.

'I was with my dad, too, and they were like "Hey, come over." It was mad, I was fighting the guy in a few weeks and we were sitting there having a cup of coffee and a sandwich!

'I had mixed feelings about all of it. Richie had lost his world title and that was a shame. It would have been better if we were both world champions and it was a unification bout.

'We got in there, it was a tough test. Richie put up a great fight and made it as hard as he could. He won some of the earlier rounds.

'Richie was technically good and caused me problems. I knew what I was in for and I'd trained extra hard for it. I was in great shape and I needed to be.

'It was strange, in a way, to go up against someone you respect so much and is, above all, a friend. But when we touched gloves and I looked into his eyes, I knew he wanted my title.'

Calzaghe had still to put up his crown against an unbeaten challenger, but 2001 brought with it the imposing figure of number one contender Mario Veit.

Both were 30-0 going into battle, but Calzaghe's 25 TKOs were far superior to Veit's 18. The 6ft 3in German looked beaten before he started, such were his nerves.

Veit, a former chef, cooked up a plan to box behind the jab but he was no match for Calzaghe, who cut him down to size in less than a round.

He sent Veit to the canvas twice before the referee's intervention. Calzaghe was cementing himself as British boxing's man of the moment. Even then, Warren was mooting a step up to light-heavy to take on Roy Jones Jr Stateside, but it would not come to pass until the swansong of his career.

That would have meant leaving super middle around six years earlier, along with relinquishing the WBO strap that hadn't yet become his mainstay.

The prospect of competing overseas was close, but it wouldn't be a trip across the pond. He got Denmark instead and had Tyson to thank for it, too.

Calzaghe's first defence outside Britain supported Iron Mike's scrap with Brian Nielsen as he took on an American, Will McIntyre, in Copenhagen.

Again, Calzaghe was explosive as he dropped McIntyre in the third and fourth rounds, with the end nigh after the latter. He looked awesome, but it wasn't much of a test.

Lining up former world champion Charles Brewer in 2002 seemed a step in the right direction. Indeed, taking on a more credible American almost seemed like an audition.

It was a tale of two halves, with Calzaghe in the ascendancy and determined to catch the eye early on, before Brewer called upon his guile to haul himself back in it.

Both men wobbled but never looked like folding. Brewer, who had to lose two pounds at the weigh-in, was not found wanting for durability or stamina, just the input to nick more rounds.

Calzaghe's hand was raised unanimously thanks to points scores of 119-109, 118-111 and 117-112 so it wasn't, by any means, close.

Two more title defences would complete 2002 and both were hampered by withdrawals.

First David Telesco pulled out three weeks before the fight due to a contractual dispute between his two managers.

In came the tough but outclassed Miguel Angel Jimenez, who was whitewashed over 12 rounds and docked a point for headbutts in the tenth. None of the three judges gave the challenger anything, with identical scores of 120-107.

Next up was Thomas Tate, who cried off, stating he had burst his eardrum. Tocker Pudwill was drafted in and blasted out in just two rounds, with Calzaghe left frustrated by a year that showed promise and delivered little.

A bout with former WBA world boss Byron Mitchell was struck in early 2003, but didn't happen until June due to two postponements.

It was short-lived but compelling when they finally went to war, with the second round proving to be an all-action shootout.

Calzaghe had never been down but was felled by a right hand after body shots. His response, seconds later after getting back up, was a left hook that sent Mitchell over.

He'd certainly made a beast angry in Calzaghe, who was now catching a dazed Mitchell at will. The referee jumped in after 18 punches without reply.

Viewers on Showtime were watching and, unlike what they had witnessed from Calzaghe before, thought it was good fun. The target was now Hopkins, but it wouldn't materialise yet.

In 2004, after Warren and Calzaghe both gave up hope of enticing Hopkins for the time being, IBF light-heavyweight champion Glen Johnson became another target.

In the meantime, Mger Mkrtchyan was Calzaghe's mandatory challenger and had to be dealt with, which came by TKO in the seventh of a rescheduled affair.

They would have clashed earlier had Calzaghe not had the flu, around the time when WBA super middleweight boss Anthony Mundine turned down a unification bout with him.

It was Calzaghe who put the belt up the first time a world title was contested in the city of Glasgow in Scotland, with their people watching him defend against Kabary Salem.

Victory equalled Eubank's 15 defences of the same crown, but caution was needed against a rough-house merchant like Salem, who in the opinion of many was a dirty fighter.

It had already got ugly at the weigh-in, where Calzaghe had grappled with Salem's trainer, Nettles Nasser, in a dispute over the scales.

It got uglier for Calzaghe when he was felled for the second time in his career in the fourth round, a loaded right hand sending him to the mat. The positive from it was that he'd again shown what an excellent chin he had.

Salem was just as tough and took a ton of shots from there until the finish, climbing off the canvas himself in the last round.

The fourth round should have been a 10-8 round for Salem but instead he was penalised for intentional headbutts. Calzaghe had a point taken off for the same offence in the 11th.

The winner wasn't in question, the judges tallying 118-107, 117-108 and 116-109 for Calzaghe. A bruising encounter, but nothing earth-shattering.

Antonio Tarver, holder of the WBC and WBA 'super' belts at light-heavy, was another potential adversary before 2005 arrived. Again, it didn't happen.

Calzaghe agreed to travel to Northern Ireland and give Brian Magee a shot at his title in Belfast, but that didn't come off either.

He fell foul of a WBO rule that forbade him from making a voluntary defence less than 60 days before an enforced bout – and his mandatory challenger insisted that stay in force.

Who was Calzaghe ordered to fight? Mario Veit, who he'd blown away in 112 seconds four years earlier. He'd have to go to his opponent's backyard of Germany, too.

They'd won the purse bids and that was that, but Calzaghe was furious and vowed to make Veit pay, which he did, this time with a sixth-round stoppage after a sustained beatdown.

Nothing was happening again for Calzaghe, who put a frustrating 2005 to bed with a whitewash points win over Evans Ashira.

Two verdicts of 120-108, plus one of 120-107, made it barely a contest. To make matters worse, Calzaghe hurt his left hand again on the rock-hard Kenyan's head.

He said, 'Veit was 6ft 4in and 30-0 [going into the first fight], like me. He was untested but well-schooled and extremely fit, so I was expecting to have it harder. It turned out to be easy.

'I had to win well against McIntyre, because my first time on a Tyson bill was one of my worst performances, against Starie. He was gone from round three, I could see it in his eyes.

'I beat Brewer when he was at his best, he'd trained for four months solid to face me. I had to dig really deep to win; we both proved we were true warriors.

'I started to have problems with my left hand again in the Jimenez fight. I hurt it hitting his head! He was a tough man, I realised that after three or four rounds.

'Pudwill was what it was, but I love knocking people out. I rushed at him too much, but that's being extra-critical of myself. I needed to move up a level.

'For a different reason, Mitchell was probably one of my proudest wins. I'd never been dropped anywhere, as an amateur or even in sparring.

'I was put down, without ever really knowing anything about it, and all I could hear was the count from the referee.

'I got dropped by a big puncher, got up and carried on. You react on instinct, because you don't know what will happen when you get hurt. I showed what a champion is all about.

'I tried to box Mkrtchyan. I could see he was tiring and I knew I'd finish him off. When you know you're going to win, what do you really learn?

'It was clear I needed to be more active after I'd been in with Salem. I needed to show I was better than that, and I knew it might be another defence at super middle.

'It had been suggested to me that I should give up my title and move to light-heavy, but I didn't want to give up something I'd worked all of my life for.

'Television didn't want the rematch with Veit, obviously, as I'd knocked him out in one round before. I had to go to Germany and knock him out in six instead.

'I thought I was going to stop Ashira. If my left hand was there, I could have kept the pace. He would have pulled out, or I'd have knocked him out in four or five rounds.

'Frank couldn't deliver that big fight I was looking for at light-heavy, but it did eventually happen at super middle. We'd chased Lacy for a long time to get there.'

Calzaghe became highly motivated again after finally getting that unification fight with Lacy, the IBF champion, in 2006.

They should have met earlier, but the original date could not be met by Calzaghe due to a broken metacarpal in his left hand sustained against Ashira.

Warren rescheduled it for four months later, and Calzaghe could not let either the fans or Lacy down again. Had he pulled out, Calzaghe versus Lacy might not have happened.

Lacy was unbeaten after 21 pro contests, with 17 stoppages, but had just over half of the experience of Calzaghe, who moved to 40-0 (31 TKOs) with the nod over Ashira.

The general consensus was that Calzaghe wouldn't get past Lacy, regardless of whether he was injured or not. A good number of people had written him off.

They were made to eat their words as Calzaghe dominated from start to finish, even with his injured left hand swelling from further combat.

Lacy, who bled from both eyes and his nose, was battered over the distance and went down in the 12th and final round, although he somehow survived to the final bell.

Calzaghe coasted to victory, the only blot on his copybook coming when he was deducted a point in the 11th for holding Lacy in a headlock.

Two judges had it 119-107, while the other scored it 119-105. Had Calzaghe not committed that cheeky act, he'd have won by a shut-out score.

Enzo had told his son all along that he would beat Lacy at a canter and he turned out to be absolutely right. At long last, Calzaghe had started to clean up the division.

He said, 'My dad talked me into fighting [Lacy]. I was the underdog, which was hard for me as that was a first. About 90 per cent of the press thought I was going to get knocked out.

'Lacy came over for one reason – they thought I was shot. His camp reckoned I'd be easy pickings. It had been nearly nine years before I even got a unification fight.

'Everything I'd have ever done would have gone out of the window had I lost. Instead, I won every round. I wished it had gone 15!

'About two weeks before, I went to Harley Street about my hand and had injections. The doctor told me to rest it for a month.

'I couldn't spar for a few weeks, so I wanted to postpone it again. My dad gave me one of his inspirational speeches; there were a few choice comments thrown in there!

'He told me it was going to be one of my easiest nights and that this guy was too slow and I was much faster. Of course, I trusted him. No matter what, he was proud of me.

'As soon as we had that conversation, my mind was made up that I was going to fight as planned. It was surreal. From there, I felt it was my time, so I stayed calm.

'He moved about four or five times to throw one punch. I could throw four or five punches in that time. That's how we worked it out. He was loading up, I'd duck and he'd miss.

'I managed to put on a boxing clinic and I was so relaxed about it. Lacy was expecting me to slow down and I never did. Personally, it was my favourite win. I performed to my best.'

With the hunger for success now back inside him, Calzaghe wanted more belts. In the meantime, it was back to defences.

Sakio Bika was nicknamed 'the Scorpion', because he was stung by one at the age of 13. He was more like a human octopus, such was the way he flailed over his opponents.

Calzaghe got sucked in and brawled too much at close quarters, but still boxed well enough to win unanimously by scores of 117-110 twice and 116-111.

Kessler had become the only other double world super middleweight champion, in possession of the WBA 'super' and WBC titles going into 2007.

Talks began about the prospect of four belts going to one man, but Calzaghe would make his Millennium Stadium debut first.

The home of the Wales national football team in Cardiff was relatively new, so Warren was keen to test out the arena first and Calzaghe needed a warm-up.

Peter Manfredo Jr possessed name value due to his exploits on American television with reality boxing show *The Contender*, and had a legend, Sugar Ray Leonard, in his corner.

He came into the frame because American broadcasters HBO, after screening the Bika clash, were not willing to show Calzaghe versus the IBF mandatory, Robert Stieglitz.

Calzaghe had to vacate the IBF title to fight Manfredo, with just the WBO crown on the line, in front of 35,000 fans.

He was no match for Calzaghe, who equalled Holmes and Hopkins' record of 20 successful title defences with an easy, if arguably too quick, third-round stoppage.

The next month, Calzaghe got his super fight. There was talk of it happening in Kessler's backyard of Denmark, but Wales ended up getting the nod.

The attraction of a phenomenal live gate swung home advantage and, indeed, bigger numbers poured into the Millennium Stadium this time.

They were treated to a 12-round war in which both men put it all on the line, but workrate was key. Calzaghe threw a staggering 1,010 punches, compared to Kessler's 585.

The great Dane was often more accurate and hurtful, but he couldn't cope with the volume of blows from Calzaghe. Viewers were equally enthralled on HBO and Setanta Sports.

It was by no means easy, but there was a clear winner. Once again, Calzaghe's hand was raised by two 116-112 margins, the other having it 117-111.

He said, 'I'd been WBO champion for nine years and I didn't want any more mandatory defences. Kessler was the only thing on my radar.

'After beating Lacy, I had Bika, who no one wants to fight. He's got the hardest head in the world and his elbows hurt just as much.

'It looked like I'd been battered, which I had, just not by fists. It was horrible. Manfredo was a good pay-day but, no offence, that was about it.

'Me and Kessler were head and shoulders above anything else in the division. The combination of wins between us was something like 84-0.

'I had walked around the stadium earlier on in the night, with my hat on so no one would recognise me, just to get a sense of what it was like out there.

'It was massive, more of a football crowd and atmosphere, and the roof of the stadium really keeps the noise in.

'When I was doing badly, all I could hear was "Denmark, Denmark" from the crowd. When things were going better, I could feel the roar going through my body. It was incredible.

'There was massive pressure on me and respect between the two of us. Me and Mikkel are friends. He was probably the best I've boxed.

'To me, he had the whole package. I'd studied him, so I knew what he was all about before we went in. He was convinced he'd win, he was undefeated and I was an ageing champion.

'It wasn't an easy fight, for a lot of it. The first round was pretty even, I won the second and third and he won the fourth and fifth.

'The first few rounds were close, then I adapted to him. I used my jab. I was edging it, but it was tight. I was forcing it, the atmosphere wasn't getting to me, but I was trying too hard.

'Kessler thought I was going to attack him and I did. He was expecting me to come forward and was counter punching. He slowed me down with a big uppercut in the fourth.

'I was 35 at the time, and he hits hard, I can confirm that. When he caught me, there was a time that I didn't know where I was.

'In the middle of the fight, I had to change my style to accommodate for his. Regardless of [the fight] being close, his punches had an effect.

'I got read the riot act from my dad in the corner, as you can imagine, along with a few slaps that I didn't really need! I stayed with it and hurt him with a body shot in the eighth.

'He was holding on, pushing me away and, from there, he was a little more cautious about going on the attack. I called on my southpaw skills, along with the feints, and outboxed him.

'He was trying to knock me out, so I had to be switched on to the last second. I had good rounds in 10, 11 and 12, so I knew I'd won and I was pleased to hear the final bell.

'It was my crowning moment and, as it turned out, my last fight in Britain. It was great occasion for me and my family.'

Not only did Calzaghe sign off in style on British soil, Warren finally delivered on his promise to get him that big fight in America in 2008.

Calzaghe's popularity had reached its peak, evidenced by him winning the BBC Sports Personality of the Year award for 2007.

Knowing he was coming towards the end, he would pursue the two names he'd always wanted to share a ring with – Hopkins and Jones Jr. Over seven months, he got them both.

Hopkins, whose aforementioned record for defences had been surpassed when Calzaghe vanquished Kessler, was the first in line as Calzaghe finally went up to light-heavy.

He'd unified weights before and had proved to be pound-for-pound one of the best, but Hopkins was 43 by then and defending the *Ring* magazine title.

Calzaghe didn't care a great deal for belts at that stage, but it had been a long-standing ambition of his to box in Las Vegas. That desire would be fulfilled with this one.

Both were veterans but still possessed the relevance to garner a lot of attention. Hopkins sent it into hyperbole by allegedly claiming 'he would never let a white man beat him'.

That looked a decent bet when Calzaghe was put down in the first round by a right hand. As before, he took it well and answered in kind.

It continued to be Hopkins early on, but the key weapon that had dropped his opponent was starting to find its target less and less.

Calzaghe, who was approaching his 36th birthday, got the hang of blocking the shot that had felled him and, as with Kessler before that, outpunched a man over seven years his senior.

The punch statistics told a story of their own over the distance, with Calzaghe landing more on Hopkins than any other opponent before him without really forcing the finish.

That led to a split decision, with the often-controversial judge Adalaide Byrd leaning narrowly towards Hopkins by a 114-113 margin.

She would be overruled by scores of 116-111 and 115-112, both from fellow American judges, which went to Calzaghe. Calzaghe had finally got to Hopkins and beaten him, too.

He said, 'I started boxing in working men's clubs and leisure centres, so to go to Vegas was another dream for me.

'I'd struggled to make the weight badly for a while before, so I knew I could never make super middle again. It was clear I only had a couple of fights left in me.

'I'd achieved everything I wanted to achieve at super middle, after ten years as a champion and then winning all of the belts.

'I spoke to Frank and he asked me who I wanted from the division above and I told him Hopkins. He wouldn't come over here, so I went to America.

'I went over and bought my own ticket to watch Ricky Hatton versus Floyd Mayweather, just to see if I could bump into Hopkins.

'He was a legend there and still is now. He was one of the best fighters in the world, too, at this point. It's a lot for a Brit to go over there and beat someone like that.

'I'd never been down in the first round before. I fell into him and he caught me with a good right hand. I was more proud with how I got up from it.

'I let my combinations go and felt like I was outworking him. It was a messy fight; Hopkins is so awkward and has all of the tricks. I just kept punching and my fitness told in the end.

'He had a style that didn't mesh with mine and he was allowed to get away with a lot. He needed to rest far too often during rounds.

'When I heard it was a split, I thought it was me who was getting robbed. Everything was against me and I still won. The Americans gave it to me.'

Hopkins will still probably never entertain the notion that he lost fair and square, but Calzaghe's US star had been made. Trouble was it wouldn't be in the sky for long.

Calzaghe knew in his heart of hearts there was a swansong across the pond to take part in before the fat lady started singing. The only man left he wanted to join him in that was Jones.

Before it could transpire, time under Warren's decade-long management would come to an end. Allegations of 'total disloyalty' were made, even if respect of his skills remained.

They split in 2008 and ended up in court over their differences, with Calzaghe determined to promote himself from there. It was never a long-term plan to carry on fighting.

Joe and Enzo made the agreement with Jones that Warren, for a number of reasons, couldn't. Calzaghe and Jones would fight under the lights of Madison Square Garden in New York.

It was another dream come true to box at MSG, but he couldn't lose to Jones in the process. Getting to 46-0 was the end game.

The showdown had been postponed for a couple of months, with Calzaghe's right hand troubling him. His southpaw left had been through enough.

Deja vu of a less-than-desirable kind came along again in the first round when Jones, 39 himself at the time, mustered some of his old power to drop Calzaghe.

It felt like an exhibition to some when Jones struck with a straight left, but Calzaghe shook it off and stayed close to again score with the better blows over the course of the fight.

The cards were called for and were all identical, 118-109 to Calzaghe. What had looked to be an encounter fraught with danger had barely ended up a contest.

He said, 'I was cutting corners and getting injured all of the time, but I still decided to fight Roy. It was emotional going in, knowing it was my last fight. I could have fought him at the Millennium Stadium but, to me, to get to finish off at Madison Square Garden, against a legend, was perfect.

'I was walking around thinking "wow" and to be in that ring was quite humbling. I went down in the first round but, from the second, I was dropping my hands and enjoying myself.

'I wouldn't disrespect Roy to claim that I kept him up, but I wanted to do the 12 rounds. I didn't look for the knockout; it was my final time and I wanted to see the finish.

'You are only as good as your last two fights – and I'm pretty happy with mine. I didn't want an unhappy ending for me.'

It became official in 2009 that Calzaghe had called time. His 2014 call into the International Boxing Hall of Fame might not have happened, had he not played through the pain.

CHAPTER ELEVEN

THE COBRA MAY BE NO SAINT – CARL FROCH AND GEORGE GROVES

NO one was ever going to be able to take away the spectacle that Carl Froch and George Groves put on at Wembley Stadium after they called time.

Even if the big fight in Las Vegas had happened for Froch, which Groves, ironically, experienced instead, there would have been nowhere near the 80,000 who attended that night.

It might have meant more money, but men with millions in the bank wouldn't necessarily be overly concerned about that anyway.

The return was, in every way, a grudge match and the hatred between the two meant Froch was at his best the second time around.

Look back now and who was left for Froch after that? No one wanted to see a sequel with Andre Ward, while Julio Cesar

Chavez Jr was facing a rebuilding process after a second loss. Mikkel Kessler had already retired, even if he's been in two minds about it since. Hearing that is the nearest Froch has come to changing his.

Only James DeGale was really calling Froch out, which at the age of 38 would have made him the old lion against the young cub.

Froch had been outpointed twice before – the only losses of his pro career – by Kessler and Ward. He'd gotten revenge over the former, but styles would never mesh with the latter.

That exhilarating Wembley experience on 31 May 2014 was big enough to be his last abiding memory of the ring. He never thought it would be topped – but it was.

When Anthony Joshua beat Wladimir Klitschko in 2017, there were 90,000 spectators at Wembley, setting a new post-war attendance record for a boxing show.

Although the precedent they set was later surpassed, it didn't detract from what was a memorable event. After the controversial finish in their first fight, this time there was no room for doubt. Froch left Groves crumpled on the floor from a peach of a right hand in the eighth round, which ended their feud once and for all.

'The Cobra' was no more for competitive action, even if it took him a year to make up his mind for sure. When it came to D-Day for him, it was game over.

Hanging up his gloves was in the back of his mind when Froch visited Bar Sport in 2015 and he was talking more about acting and appearing on television than fighting.

He officially retired less than a month later, after joining Sky Sports full time as a boxing pundit. Everyone who had listened to him in the Premier Suite beforehand wasn't surprised.

Froch said, 'So many athletes go through their career and never get that defining moment. No one will ever take that away from me, it's impossible.

'I've never gone through my life thinking about what I was going to earn; money doesn't motivate me. I've always enjoyed the sport.

'I've earned massive purses but, as a fighter, I've never done anything that's not genuine. I look back on what I have done with great satisfaction and pride.

'The only time I've got itchy feet is when Kessler was on about coming out of retirement and I was thinking, "We've got a fight each, one-one."

'He sent me a personal message and I thought about it, but it didn't last long. I got up and actually did a run one morning. I got halfway around and then walked back.

'My back was hurting and my Achilles tendon was sore. I just thought, "I'm getting too old for this." I'm happily retired.

'I'm a pundit, a co-commentator, I play a lot of poker online and I'm project-managing and investing in property and I've got kids. I'm more busy now than when I was boxing.

'I retired a champion and I'm now living the rest of my life as a champion. I'm a very happy man each day and every night when my head hits the pillow.'

Groves still had plenty left at the time and never even contemplated that his career might have come to an end, even if there were more bumps in the road.

It's testament to 'Saint George' that he came up short twice against Froch for the world title – and then also Badou Jack – yet still reached the top.

The road back was a long one and when he came to Bar Sport, he was the WBA 'super' champion and the number one super middleweight in the world with the *Ring* magazine.

The visit to Cannock came four days shy of Groves' 30th birthday. He was the elder statesman of the division, a ten-year pro.

Callum Smith would later rip his title away, but not even he could change the fact that Groves had been a world champion. Nobody can.

Groves would not see past 30 as an active fighter, announcing that he was hanging up his gloves soon after the defeat to Smith.

Smith was the third Englishman he'd contested the WBA crown with, having previously outpointed Chris Eubank Jr after halting Jamie Cox in four rounds.

His showdown with Smith was a World Boxing Super Series final and was contested in Jeddah, Saudi Arabia.

Groves, who had been out for eight months after undergoing shoulder surgery, boxed reasonably well but was counted out shortly after taking a big left hook in the seventh.

There were four judges, instead of the usual three, who had Groves up between them. In the heat of the post-fight interview, he initially ruled out retirement.

You can always trust DeGale to pipe up in these situations, but Groves walked away having beaten him twice, amateur and pro. That will bother 'Chunky' for quite some time.

Groves eventually announced his retirement with a written speech, video montage and image on Instagram, which was simply titled 'thank you for the memories'.

The footage contained poignant words from the Green Day song 'The Time of Your Life'. Some of the lyrics could not have described his fighting days any better.

'It's something unpredictable, but in the end is right, I hope you had the time of your life.' The pick of Groves' heartfelt personal thoughts, at an emotional time, backed this up.

He said, 'Some of you might think it's odd that I'm choosing this time to retire. I'm still young, fit and healthy and there are still some big fights out there for me.

'Over the years, I've seen and sadly known the dangers of the sport and I want to, respectfully, bow out while I'm at the top of my game.

'I've learned that doesn't always mean coming off the back of a win. I've boxed at the highest level, I've been a champion and I'll be leaving the sport relatively intact.

'I knew the desire to fight again had left me. Retiring at 30 was a suggestion I first heard ten years ago. I thought it was a good idea then and I still do now.

'I have a young family at home, and it's time to spend some of my better days with them. I'm also planning to follow my new interest of motivational speaking.

'Boxing has been my life. I would like to thank everyone who has shown me love and support. In my darkest and hardest times, their energy and enthusiasm kept me focussed.'

A wave of media interest followed Groves' news and Froch, when quizzed on the matter, wasn't exactly in eulogy mode.

He said, 'I won't miss George Groves and I'm not sure British boxing will miss him, these days at least. There was nothing left out there for him.

'He will be remembered for all of those mind games and smart words he came out with but, I have to be honest, I never found him funny or clever.

'On the flipside of that, I can't deny that Groves made a massive, positive impact on the end of my career. We were another pairing that brought the country together.

'Between us, we filled Wembley and raised the bar for the next generation, led by Anthony Joshua, of course, to box there.

'Groves helped me to finish my own career in the best way possible, so now it's his turn to call it a day. Fair play to him.'

Groves' curtain call was coming up to five years after he faced Froch for the second time. Over that period, he showed how much becoming a world champion really meant to him.

Rewind to 2014 and Froch was still sitting on the fence when Groves returned to action for the European and WBC silver belts four months later.

Groves showed he was a cut above Christopher Rebrasse at Wembley Arena, winning unanimously on points with scores of 118-110 (twice) and 117-111.

The dynamite in his fists returned in flashes when he put up the WBC silver title with Denis Douglin, who was trained by his mother, Saphya. 'The Momma's Boy' was finished in seven.

Badou Jack won the WBC crown from Anthony Dirrell in 2015 and Groves was mandatory challenger, with the two meeting at the MGM Grand in Vegas on 12 September that year.

Groves took the fight to Jack in the first round but was wobbled by a straight right hand to the jaw. He took a knee and both gloves touched the floor.

He'd regrouped by the second and a technical tit-for-tat encounter ensued. From there until the final bell, neither man shied away, so there was plenty of entertainment value.

The scorecards saw a split decision recorded. The knockdown wasn't telling, with tallies of 116-111 and 115-112 for Jack, while the third judge had Groves up by a round, 114-113.

The beaten contender stormed out of the ring, feeling he had done enough to force a changing of the guard and knowing another rebuilding process was ahead.

It took all of 2016 for Groves to shuffle back into the pack and a third world title setback led to a third coach, with Shane McGuigan following Paddy Fitzpatrick and Adam Booth.

Groves returned against Andrea Di Luisa, who had the towel thrown in for him during the fifth, before claiming the WBA international strap against the grossly untested David Brophy, who was overwhelmed in four. Martin Murray, though, would be a much bigger test.

It was a make-or-break fight for both parties, but it was Groves who prevailed as the deserved winner over the four-time world title challenger. All three judges had it 118-110.

He finished the year with another defence of the WBA international title against Eduard Gutknecht. The tragic side of boxing would rear its ugly head again.

Groves had hammered away at a bloodied and swollen Gutknecht in the later rounds, but he heard the final bell. One-sided cards were 119-109 twice and 119-110 for Groves.

Gutknecht collapsed in the dressing room after the fight and slipped into a coma. He went on to suffer multiple strokes and was unable to walk or talk. The trauma got to Groves.

There was to be little time to get out of a fighting mindset. Just 19 days later, it was confirmed that Groves would fight the Russian Fedor Chudinov for the vacant WBA 'super' title.

Felix Sturm had dropped the belt through injury, after beating Chudinov to make it 'one-one' between the two. Groves, rated third by the WBA, was preferred over Stanislav Kashtanov.

Groves had to get his mind on the job, whatever had regrettably happened to Gutknecht, before he and Chudinov got it on.

The date, 27 May 2017, is one that Groves will never forget. This time, he would not be denied, no matter how hurt he was.

He broke his jaw in round three and was cut above the eye in the fourth, but Groves was walking through walls. He trapped Chudinov in the sixth and let fly, forcing the finish.

Frank Bruno springs most readily to mind when you think of an Englishman who had gone all around the houses before getting there, but Groves was finally a world champion.

He said, 'My first spar back, after getting chinned by Froch, was a few rounds against Gennady Golovkin. After two days, he broke my rib.

'I'd gone out to where he was [Big Bear, California], which was 8,000ft above sea level. I'd done a few hill sprints and got a bit sunburnt. I was still out of shape.

'Both of us were told to wear body belts, but I didn't think I needed one and lived to regret it. We were going home after that.

'Rebrasse was a good opponent, he took an awful lot of punches. I gave it a real good go, but I didn't manage to get him out of there.

'The WBC title was my target at that point, and Anthony Dirrell was the champion until he lost it to Jack. I got Douglin, in the meantime, and it was good to knock someone out.

'It might be nice to go out and watch boxing in Vegas, but it's a bit soulless fighting there. You're not really treated that well.

'I was trying to get into my changing room and had problems getting past the security guard, because I didn't have the right credentials. Their rules are the law.

'Jack was the only time where I felt like I'd blew it. If it hadn't been for that flash knockdown, I think I'd have got the win. That was the lowest point of my career.

'I'd had cabin fever, having been in America for two months before the fight, and I was desperate to get the job done and go home.

'When I boxed Jack, he was a nothing compared to the superstar he is now, so I felt like I'd let myself down. It wasn't a good feeling.

'Di Luisa was my first time under Shane and I think I boxed well. I felt sharp and dictated the pace from the get-go.

'Brophy was an unknown quantity, it was more comfortable than Di Luisa and the body shot that finished it I'd been working on with Shane.

'I knew what Murray was about, he's a skilful fighter and he was never going to let the occasion get to him. I landed big blows and hurt him, but he's gritty and that got him through.

'Nick Blackwell was already in a similar situation to Eduard after his fight with Chris Eubank Jr, and I'd pretty much done all of his sparring for that, so it was close to home.

'Then it happens to me and it's sad and tough to deal with. The best and most efficient way to be is emotionally detached from boxing, because it's a sport and a business.

'What happened with Eduard does frequently cross my mind, but I needed to carry on boxing. That said, I'm always going to struggle with his situation.

'It's a horrible thing and it's very distressing. I feel for him and his family. They don't blame me and to be relieved of that sort of guilt was a wonderful thing that they didn't need to do.

'I had to put it behind me, I had another world title shot. Winning the belt, at last, was the greatest feeling I could have in boxing. I was sick of feeling sorry for myself about the past.

'It was a long time coming and to go out and finally get one, rather than have to make excuses, made it all worthwhile. It was do-or-die stuff.

'Chudinov was easy to hit, but he was stronger than I thought. I found that out. He throws these weird punches, where his arms don't move much and his fists come over the top.

'He hit one in the third and I heard this crunch. I'd broken my jaw before, for England in Poland as an amateur, so I knew what it was. I left my gumshield in between rounds.

'We clashed heads in the fourth, which left me with blood coming into my eye, but it was now or never. I don't think I would have come again. Even if my body was up for carrying on, my brain wouldn't have been had I lost. It would have been the hardest thing I'd ever done.

'The best commentary I've ever had was on that fight – and it came from Froch. He was, actually, quite nice about me. I'd have never thought that.'

So even Froch was relatively happy when Groves' night came along. Any fighter who first laces on the gloves dreams of those glories and should respect anyone who gets there.

For Froch, that journey began when he was ten years old, growing up in the Colwick part of Nottingham and representing the Phoenix gym out of Gedling.

He displayed an aptitude for the sport but was Phoenix through and through, so drifted out of boxing for four years when his family relocated in his teens.

Not wanting to box for anyone else, the next time he fought competitively was when he was a man, but he soon raced to the country's top honours.

He picked up two senior ABA titles at the age of 21 and 23 respectively, going on to compete at the 2001 World Amateur Championships.

It was there where he became the first-ever Brit to medal at the tournament. Frankie Gavin would later become the first male to win gold.

Bronze at 75kg was his last great accolade before handing in the vest and headguard, with a great grounding and an 88-8 unpaid record to his name.

When the time came to punch for pay, a 24-year-old Froch turned over under the tutelage of Rob McCracken, who would remain in his corner for the rest of his career.

They took Mick Hennessy as their business manager and operated under the Panix Promotions banner, operated by Panos Eliades. His stable featured Froch, fellow new signing Matthew Thirlwall, David Walker, Lee Meager and Leo O'Reilly. They were dubbed 'the Real Class of 2002'.

Froch soon made a name for himself, stopping people for fun until Vage Kocharyan became the first to take him the eight-round distance in his ninth fight.

His first title shot came next as he halted Alan Page in seven to become the English champion. It led to a crack at Commonwealth boss Charles Adamu in 2004.

The never-stopped Ghanaian proved as tough as he looked and tried every trick in the book to try and drag Froch into the trenches, to no avail. He lasted the distance but relinquished the crown, establishing Froch as a domestic super middleweight force to be reckoned with after 12 bouts.

He retained in 11 rounds in his first defence against Canadian Mark Woolnough before putting up his crown, with the vacant British title also on the line, against Damon Hague.

A right hand finished Hague off inside a round, giving him both straps. He went on to win a Lonsdale Belt outright with wins over Matthew Barney, Brian Magee and Tony Dodson.

It was his last British title defence, against ageing former WBC world champion Robin Reid, that cemented Froch as the hot prospect going on to better things.

A battered Reid retired at the end of the fifth, leaving little doubt that Froch had arrived. He'd cleaned up domestically and seemed deserving of a jump straight up to world level.

Froch said, 'I was one of three brothers, I felt sorry for my mum! Lee was the oldest and Wayne the youngest. We were always beating each other up.

'I spent most of the time defending myself from my big brother, until me and Wayne used to gang up on him. Boys will be boys.

'I started boxing when I was ten, but I stopped for a while when I was 15 because my mum, Carol, became a licensee and got a pub in Newark. The gym was so far away from where I was living that I ended up having four years out. I was taking a break from the sport but I was missing it.

'When I was 19, I got back to Nottingham and carried on in the amateurs, but I knew my style was better suited to the pros. My hands were low and I threw punches from my hips.

'Most amateurs work off vertical forearms, going for the jab and then the left hook. I didn't enjoy fighting like that, even though I did well.

'I noticed it the most when I boxed for England, because it was all about scoring points against international opponents.

'I felt like I was being held back a lot. I just wanted to get stuck in and have a scrap, like I would later do as a professional.

'It was nice to come from the amateurs, where you have that team camaraderie, into a professional camp where there was a good group. I went with Rob, who has been my coach since day one, and I learned my trade at a gym in London. The hard rounds of sparring could be a nightmare.

'I had partners like Howard Eastman, a really heavy puncher, and Wayne Alexander when he was a British champion. It was always hard work.

'The amount of gym wars I had there, I'd love to watch some of the footage back. I really learned the rough and tough side of the business. Anything can and did go.

'It got me ready for what lay ahead in the pro game and I called on that when I had to go 12 rounds for the first time, against Adamu for the Commonwealth title.

'He was just a horrible, nasty fighter. He'd hold, headbutt, elbow you, whatever he could. By the eighth, I was almost out of breath.

'But then I put him down in that round and I thought to myself, "He bleeds, he can be hurt!" It gave me the strength to finish the fight strong.

'That was such a learning curve for me at that point in my career. It gave me that experience to go forward.

'I'm a bit of a traditionalist at heart, and the fact that I won the English, Commonwealth and then the British title is the way I thought it should be done.

'It was always my first goal to become a British champion and win a Lonsdale Belt outright. I defended it three times against decent names domestically. I achieved that quite easily.

'I had a tough night against Brian Magee, but I knocked him out in round 11. Reid was a name on my record that people could relate to, as he fought the Welsh guy, Joe Calzaghe.

'Let's also not forget that many people thought he beat Calzaghe, in a lot of people's heads, including my own, and didn't get the decision. It was a split and everyone thought he'd won.

'I'm not going to say I beat Reid at the top of his game; he was past his best and he wanted to get the British title off me before he retired.

'I was in Miami with Eastman for six weeks and getting the better of the spars between us. I wasn't getting hit and I was landing some good shots myself.

'He had a world title fight against Bernard Hopkins, which I watched and thought Howard did well [in]. I fancied my chances against Hopkins, that's how much confidence I'd got.'

When he'd made up his mind that he wanted to go after a world title, there was only one man he wanted – Calzaghe. He chased the division's kingpin until he went up a weight.

We'll always wonder what would have happened if the young and hungry Froch had tackled Calzaghe, who was close to retirement, in 2008.

Calzaghe, though, went up to light-heavy and relinquished the WBC super middle belt, with Froch first in line to challenge.

Froch's year had consisted of a fourth-round stoppage of late replacement Albert Rybacki, who had stepped in for Rubin Williams, when his chance came long in December.

They got Jean Pascal, who was also unbeaten, on home turf at the Nottingham Arena. Froch needed grit and determination, but managed to come out on top.

The joy that followed the unanimous points win, by easier-than-expected scores of 118-110, 117-111 and 116-112, was shared by everyone connected to Froch.

He said, 'I concentrated on getting myself into the prime position and it took two years to build my ranking enough to be mandatory.

'It took me, my manager Mick Hennessy and my coach Robert McCracken to Thailand for a WBC convention, to show our faces and put my name about.

'I was turning down opportunities for European and IBF title shots. I was even offered a fight with Antonio Tarver. I wanted to stick with the WBC and Calzaghe was their champion.

'That green and gold belt was the one I wanted and Calzaghe having it made me go after it even more. He was finally in a position to either fight me or vacate. He chose the latter.

'I don't know how he's got the cheek to even try and pipe up and criticise me, when I'd done it the old-fashioned way. He chose to fight a 43-year-old man, Hopkins, instead.

'It was supposed to be me and Denis Inkin for the vacant title, but he pulled out twice so in came Jean Pascal. It turned out to be an epic between two unbeaten warriors.

'Pascal was a tenacious man who had the attitude to match. He came over unbeaten thinking, "Who's this skinny kid? I'll take this."

'He gave me mouth at the press conference and the weigh-in, but I was so up for the fight. To get a chance at the best belt in the world, in front of my home town, was something else.

'I had a sore rib going into the ring, a few niggles in fact, but I always competed with injuries. I'd never pull out of a fight.

'We just had a 12-round tear-up. I should have boxed him more, to be honest, but I backed him up and started to believe I could beat him.

'We punched holes in each other until I, rightly, got the decision. That was the start of my world title journey.'

As an elated Froch celebrated in the ring, his trainer was keeping something from him that he couldn't hide any more. McCracken's mother, Christine, had died just days before.

Froch said, 'Rob being the man he is, I never had the slightest clue, not even by his demeanour. It was only when I had my glove lifted, after the fight, that he told me.

'He wasn't going to let that interfere with my dream shot at a world title. It was such a sad time for him, but he never let it show. He deserves so much respect for that.'

Doors should have been flung wide open for Froch from there. But the timing wasn't great, with terrestrial television again falling out of love with boxing.

He was keen to become a fighting champion, too, and was prepared to hit the road and prove it. Jermain Taylor's camp made contact and it was off to the United States in 2009.

He needed a scalp like Taylor to state that case, but he was no pushover. The first Olympic boxer from Arkansas was a dangerous customer and nearly took him out.

Taylor planted Froch on the canvas with a booming overhand right in the third and, going into the last, Froch was behind on two of the three judges' scorecards.

All had it 106-102, two for Taylor and one for Froch, who had to knock his opponent out to avoid a first pro defeat and a changing of the guard.

What the officials hadn't counted on was Froch's never-say-die attitude as he launched the latest of late salvos to maintain his grip on the WBC title.

Taylor shipped a bunch of punches and was dumped in the corner by a right hook to the jaw. He took more punishment before he was pulled out, right at the death. Time left in the contest? Fourteen seconds. That's how close Froch was to losing for the first time that night. He'd announced himself to America.

Three months later, in July 2009, Froch agreed a deal that would dominate his career for the next two years. He signed to take part in the 'Super Six' World Boxing Classic tournament.

The brainchild of American television company Showtime, the six-man competition would see the winner walk away with both the WBC and WBA world titles.

Froch joined Taylor, Kessler, Andre Dirrell, Arthur Abraham and Andre Ward in the line-up, first facing the unbeaten Dirrell back in Nottingham that October.

They had to box in the early hours British time to accommodate TV scheduling in the States, but 9,000 were still on hand at his home city's arena.

Froch again had to dig deep as he was dragged into the trenches, with Dirrell docked a point for holding. It went the distance and he won ugly on a split decision.

Two of the judges felt Froch was two rounds ahead at the final bell, 115-112 counting the deduction, with the other scoring 114-113 in favour of Dirrell.

It set up a match with Kessler, who had lost his WBA belt to Ward, in Denmark in 2010. It turned out to be a Fight of the Year contender and the start of a great rivalry.

A close contest was hard to call but, at the final bell, it was clear Kessler would get home advantage. Controversially, he got the nod from all three judges.

The scores were 116-112, 115-113 and 117-111 for Kessler, with Froch bemused at the manner in which his '0' had gone.

Perhaps the loss of his unblemished record after 26 pro bouts hurt him more than losing the belt but, this being tournament boxing, he would soon get the chance to bounce back.

The WBC strap was again vacated, due to Kessler's withdrawal with an eye injury, so Froch was given a lifeline against feared puncher Arthur Abraham in Helsinki, Finland.

With the Kessler defeat still fresh in his mind, Froch was taking no chances on foreign soil and handed Abraham a boxing lesson, winning convincingly on points.

It was so nearly a whitewash, with one score of 119-109 saving Abraham from a complete 12-round shut-out. His power had been completely negated.

Now with two Super Six wins out of three, Froch went back to the United States in 2011 for his semi-final against Glen Johnson.

Froch did what was necessary to see off Johnson, who was 42 at the time, by majority decision and never really left his comfort zone to do so.

The scores were 117-111 and 116-112 for Froch, with the other card level at 114-114. It put Froch into the decider with the chance to become a double world champion.

All that was left was Andre Ward. A Floyd Mayweather-esque southpaw at 168lb, the Olympic gold medallist was as aloof as they come.

He slipped and moved to frustrate Froch, who spent most of his time punching thin air. He was never out of it, but Ward was nicking the rounds.

Ward let his jab slide in the later rounds, though, which allowed Froch to come back into it, although it wasn't enough. Ward won unanimously.

Two scores of 115-113 reflected how Froch kept coming, but the third judge had Ward running away at 118-110. He remained the only man to beat Froch and not lose back to him.

Froch said, 'I won my first world title live on ITV, then the recession hit and they pulled out of boxing. There was nothing for me to do.

'I wasn't going to sit around looking at the belt on my mantelpiece. I wanted to be defending it. Four months later, I was back in there.

'We went to Connecticut for Jermain Taylor and I thought, "I fancy this." He had just beaten Jeff Lacy, one of Calzaghe's biggest wins, so I wanted to do a job on him.

'What a fight it was. It was the first time I was put on the seat of my pants in a professional ring. I told myself, "I might be down, but you won't be keeping me down!"

'I climbed off the canvas, looked at him, smiled "good shot" and came back. I started to hurt him from the ninth. I walked through a couple of big punches and kept pressing.

'There were 18 unanswered punches in the last round when I forced the stoppage. It was like three in one – he was out on his feet, the referee was jumping in and the towel followed.

'It was a conclusive finish and what a time for that to come. It was unbelievable. Then came the chance to be a part of the Super Six.

'I had Andre Dirrell first in Nottingham, which turned into a boring, horrible, awkward fight, but I won it, fair and square.

'We wanted to go to Denmark earlier to get ready for Kessler, but the planes were grounded because of a volcanic ash cloud. We should have postponed.

'But his promoters, Sauerland, sent a private jet and, like an idiot, I jumped on it and went over. It was the one time I didn't take my coach's advice.

'I had never taken weight off but this time I had to sit in a hot bath for four hours before the weigh-in. I felt exhausted and that told in the ring. I was drained by the fifth.

'I felt Kessler beat me fair and square. In his backyard against "the Great Dane" – he was treated like David Beckham over there – I knew I wouldn't get the decision.

'I was devastated but, with it being a tournament, I knew I would get the chance to win a world title back, which I did the very next time against Arthur Abraham.

'He was very much like Golovkin is now – a big puncher who was going around knocking everyone out. A lot of people thought I was going to lose again.

'But, like Golovkin, I just thought he was a small middleweight and I was a big super middle. He was with Sauerland, too, and I wasn't going to lose to them for a second time.

'I punched in bunches and used my amateur style of range and technique. It was almost a flawless victory, too easy, and I was WBC champion for the second time.

'It came down to me and Andre Ward, who is very effective at doing what he needs to do. He's got a fast jab and he's almost impossible to hit. To beat him, you have to knock him out.

'When I lost to Kessler, I had bumps and bruises and my nose was broken. We were both cut, my rib was sore and I could barely breathe.

'I gave him my belt with pride, from one warrior to another. I had lost to a proper man. With Ward, it barely felt like I had been in a fight. It was more like I had been pick-pocketed.

'The frustration of that was just awful but, after that, came the built-up pressure and the excitement to go on.'

The Super Six was over by 2012 and Froch was left with no world title and seemingly poor prospects, leading to a split with Hennessy.

Matchroom had started their monopoly of British boxing on Sky Sports, so siding with promoter Eddie Hearn seemed to be the only way to go.

Hearn planned to build him up again slowly, with a couple of keep-busy dates building back up to the big paydays Froch had become used to.

Froch had other ideas, insisting he wanted to fight the best men he hadn't already shared a ring with. After the IBF installed him as mandatory challenger, that meant Lucian Bute.

The champion had clocked up 30 straight wins and was a notable omission from the Super Six. He was an obvious target, with the belt and scalp he would represent.

A turn-up for the books followed when Bute folded in five, with Froch putting in one of his most devastating displays.

He looked like a man possessed as he got his licks in, walloping Bute with everything in his arsenal. There were no arguments when the finish came.

Coming back to the Nottingham Arena in such style meant a first title defence under those lights before 2012 was out, in what proved his swansong on the grounds.

American foe Yusaf Mack couldn't back up his mouth with action, after getting under Froch's skin by calling him 'a fake Calzaghe'. He was blasted out in less than three rounds.

It was as clean a win as Froch ever had after drug testers had knocked on his door at 6am two days before to take a random sample.

Negotiations were well under way for a rematch with Kessler in 2013, even though there was no bad blood between the two.

There was and still is respect. But Froch wanted to get his own back and capture a world title he had yet to win, with Kessler now the new WBA champion.

A multi-million purse saw Kessler agree to come to the UK, with the O2 Arena in London chosen for the May showdown.

Froch had never lost to anyone twice and got his nose in front early on, before weathering the storm as the advantage swung back and forth between the two.

He was wobbled in the 11th by a right hand from Kessler, for whom a big finish proved too little, too late. It was another terrific tussle, but there was no doubt Froch had won.

Scores of 118-110, 116-112 and 115-113 confirmed as much, as Froch got his revenge and the WBA crown. He would defend both of his belts against Groves that November.

Froch said, 'When I first went with Eddie, he wanted to get me a nice easy fight to get me back into it and put me on Sky Sports. It wasn't massive money they were putting up, either.

'I told him to get me Bute. I knew I'd beat him. In my mind, I was almost unbeaten. I didn't believe I had been beaten by Kessler and I don't know how anybody can get the better of Andre Ward; he's a nightmare. No one had ever beaten me up but, once again, I was the underdog. People were coming up to me saying, "good luck", and I could tell in their eyes they feared the worst.

'I wanted a comeback fight that made the public go, "Wow, this kid is brave." He was a very slick southpaw, but I knew he'd never be comfortable with a 12-round warrior.

'I knew, one way or another, I'd get him out of there. It just so happened that it came that early. I shell-shocked him and tore him apart from there. I was a world champion again.

'I took the play away from Mack straight away. The stoppage came a bit earlier than I thought it would. There was no malice; I hadn't really listened to what he'd said about me.

'You have to give the British Boxing Board of Control a diary of where you will be and at what times you are there, so the testers get a comprehensive note of your movements.

'I was about to go on an early run when there was a loud bang on my front door. Before that, it was at eight in the evening – and I missed *Coronation Street*!

'You do a test on fight night anyway – before or after. Both boxers are tested, win or lose, so there's no escape.

'I consider Mikkel a friend and we had a gentlemen's agreement that he would come to England and defend his title against me. We had to strike a deal, but he was true to his word.

'In the build-up, he made the mistake of telling me my arms were too long and he hates my jab. I worked on that the most from there.

'It felt really good to beat him, but the bad thing was I had to beat a nice gentleman like Mikkel and a real sportsman.

'He was in there to do business and he was trying to hurt me. A couple of times he did that but I got him more. I deserved to win and the decision was correct.

'I went for the stoppage late on, but he fought back and showed great heart. I was 100 per cent in the rematch, light on my feet and boxing to my best. Everyone enjoyed it.'

When the prospect of fighting Froch first reared its head, what Groves lacked was the experience of going where his nemesis had been at the highest level.

Up-and-comer with a good amateur pedigree behind him – like Froch, Groves was a two-time ABA champion – was more how he was perceived.

Despite claiming to be a shy youth, Groves was never far from the limelight due to his fighting skills. He actually started out as a kickboxer from the age of seven.

He was just 13 when he appeared on Eurosport broadcasts, winning four world junior titles and European honours using his feet.

Dad Donny had been an amateur boxer and son George followed in his father's footsteps when he walked through the doors at Dale Youth Boxing Club.

It was there he first met James DeGale, a rival more vociferous than even Froch, with a vendetta against him that may never end.

The first time they touched gloves was in the 2007 senior ABAs at middleweight, with DeGale expected to prevail as the more decorated boxer.

He was a back-to-back ABA champion and already a Commonwealth Games bronze medallist. Bear in mind, it was only the divisional stages when he took on Groves.

A majority decision went against DeGale and so began a rift that has never been healed, with Groves going on to win the national title at the expense of Marlon Reid in the final.

It came too late to stake a serious claim on DeGale's place at the 2008 Olympic Games. 'Chunky', two years older and with the edge in experience, later took gold in Beijing.

Groves hung around at home and claimed the 2008 senior ABA title, beating Karl Kirkham to secure his double. He ditched the vest and headguard later that year.

His pro debut saw him box over a long distance for a maiden affair, six three-minute rounds, with Kiril Psonko doing very well to last the distance with him.

The only man to do likewise in his next 11 paid outings was Belarus hardman Konstantin Makhanov, who took Groves to eight.

He'd won and defended the Commonwealth title in that timeframe, with Adamu again the man to beat. He was put down in the first and twice in the fourth before a sixth-round finish.

But it was Groves who was on the floor when he put the belt on the line against Kenny Anderson, getting up in the third to halt the Scot in the fifth of a bad-tempered affair.

Meanwhile, DeGale had become the British super middleweight champion and 2011 was the year for their sequel. The O2 Arena in London was packed to the rafters, expecting fireworks.

Groves produced a tactical masterclass to edge past DeGale, who came on strong in the later rounds, but the close nature of the finish meant no one could be sure who had won.

A majority decision was again the verdict, but this time after 12 rounds. Groves hadn't lost on the card of any judge, but it was wafer-thin stuff. Two had it 115-114, the other scored it a draw at 115-115.

DeGale was beside himself with despair, screaming 'what, what' exactly as he had done at the culmination of their battle in the amateurs. Groves was his bogeyman.

He went on a two-year run after that with six wins and five TKOs, only Glen Johnson lasting the pace with him in another Commonwealth title defence.

The first was his one and only defence of the newly won British title, silencing Paul Smith more emphatically than expected in two rounds.

Groves was 19 years younger than an ancient Johnson when they met, prevailing unanimously by two 120-107 scores and one of 119-109, with the veteran down in the 12th.

He picked up the WBA inter-continental strap in the last fight of that run, against Noe Gonzalez Alcoba inside five. He walked into the ring as Froch's mandatory five months later.

Groves said, 'I actually first went down to Dale Youth when I was seven, but they told me I was too young to fight and to go back when I was 11. That steered me into the direction of kickboxing, but I always planned to be a boxer. I started boxing when I was ten and when I was 13, I started to concentrate on boxing.

'Between then, I was doing both and there were times I'd be boxing in a schoolboy final on the Friday night and kickboxing for a British title the next day.

'I really enjoyed my days at Dale Youth, which was in the Grenfell Tower block which had the tragedy of the fire there. I was so sad to learn about that and was as shocked as anyone.

'I'd only been there a few days before that to see friends, so I was devastated. I've donated my gloves after fights since to raise money for the cause, which was the least I could do.

'When I first met DeGale, I was a growing lad going up the weights from super lightweight and he was a podgy lightheavyweight coming down, hence his "Chunky" nickname.

'We sparred together many times. Those sessions could get pretty heated. He always acted like he was special, but he could never push me around.

'There was a lot of pressure put on both of us when we both went to middleweight. I knew I had the technical ability to beat him, I just wasn't sure how to go about it.

'In the first fight, it's the little details that get forgotten that make it interesting. For instance, I'd boxed earlier on that night against Louis Reed, who was from our gym as well.

'While DeGale has his feet up, doing his bandages, watching my fight, I was in there slugging it out and still managed to beat him less than two hours later.

'I'd have loved to have boxed him again as an amateur, fresh this time, because he couldn't hack the pace when I put it on him in the last round.

'When I won, that's when the real pressure started but, unfortunately, I couldn't get into the elite set-up at England. I was always sort of in the reserve team.

'Sending DeGale to the 2008 Olympics was the right decision because he came home with the gold medal. I did want to wait for London 2012, but it was too far away for me.

'I wanted to win the ABAs again and turn pro, which I did. I got stuck into a new challenge, which I desperately needed.

'I sparred with Froch early on in my pro career and I was chuffed with how well I'd done. He said he'd help me if I ever needed it, funnily enough.

'Both me and DeGale won domestic titles in our ninth pro fight, but he turned over after me. It was his 11th when we met again, I'd had 12.

'To have that arena sold out for a domestic fight was unbelievable; it was setting a trend. We talk about rivalries but as time goes on in boxing, you run out of energy for that.

'It's made for a fascinating story and I never thought of it as over. No one has ever thought I was going to beat DeGale and I've done it twice.

'It's nice to have people on your side, but it's satisfying to upset the odds. Everyone was raving about him, but I had self-belief against an opponent I knew.

'It was a fight that I knew was always going to be thought of as close, because I was under instructions to nick rounds, which I did.

'When it went to points, I knew I'd done enough, but you never know. It felt good, more than usual, as it would do against him. I enjoyed that.'

The aforementioned sequences of events for Froch and Groves – which were long, punishing roads at times – brought the two together in 2013. For Groves, it was his first chance at the big time. For Froch, it was hassle he could do without and that told both in the build-up and early parts of the fight.

It caught the imagination of the public from the off, though, with all 20,000 tickets for the Manchester Arena selling out in 20 minutes flat.

Froch was undoubtedly over-confident of his ability to teach the young upstart a boxing lesson. He'd been there, done it and worn the t-shirt, but needed to do more than turn up.

Groves kept his own counsel most of the time, apart from the odd quip, but still had Froch, whose mouth went on and on, claiming he'd been disrespected.

The first fight ended with such a debatable stoppage that a rematch simply had to happen. Froch, who played no part in the decision, went from hero to zero.

The hot favourite, defending his IBF and WBA belts, was down in the first round from an overhand right that dropped him heavily. Undoubtedly hurt, he was saved by the bell.

Groves, who was 11 years younger than Froch, became only the second man to put him on the canvas after Taylor.

But back came Froch and he forced the finish in round nine, with a barrage of right hands to the head and body that left a tiring Groves on unsteady legs.

He went to clinch but fell short, walking on to more punches from Froch. In jumped referee Howard Foster, literally grabbing Groves in a headlock to separate the two.

Groves was incensed, insisting he was fine to continue, and was ahead on all three scorecards. Two judges had him 76-75 up, the other 78-73.

Froch antagonised the critics when he claimed in his post-fight interview that he agreed with the decision. He's never wavered from that opinion.

He said, 'I hadn't trained properly, simple as that. I was dancing on a television show with my other half, Rachel, and that ate into half of my training camp.

'For the rest of it, I stayed at home running on the treadmill and, every now and then, I would go up to Sheffield and hit the pads. He believed he could do the job and he had a very good start. He's a capable fighter, he punches hard and he's fast.

'He was stood in the middle of the ring staring me out, like some sort of Hercules. I just wanted to go out and chin him. My boxing skills were left in the locker room.

'Round one, I got put on the deck for the second time in my pro career, and I could have no excuses. It was heavy, but I walked on to a silly one. He hit me with everything but the kitchen sink to try and build on that, but I knew he had stamina issues from us sparring in the past. I managed to wear him out.

'By round nine, I was catching him with everything. His legs had gone and he was on his way to being knocked out, let's be honest.

'But what a fantastic favour the referee did for both of us, if it was that. He's here for the safety of the fighters and he bailed Groves out of taking some serious punishment.

'I got dog's abuse. On my way backstage, I was getting spat at. I was still the champion – and everyone hated me. It's a fickle sport.'

Groves added, 'As much as time has been a great healer for me and I'm in a happier place now, I know I should have won that first fight.

'I've got punch power. Froch came square but he's got a good chin. That's the only reason he wasn't asleep from that right hand.

'I buzzed around him in the earlier rounds, showing him different things and pegging him back. I told him, "I belong at this level," that's what he called disrespectful, and proved it.

'I knew that I was ahead on points and felt it had been one-sided. We were both tired, I'd thrown a lot of punches and he'd taken them.

'His momentum was knocking me more off balance than his punches, which were flying everywhere. He just wasn't catching me clean.

'For me, Froch hadn't landed when the referee jumped in, so I'd like to think it was a genuine mistake. It cost me a lot of money.

'There would have been a rematch, either way, but the champion's split is always better. That said, the controversy of the stoppage made it worth more to me in the long run.

'There was a bullishness I had to portray just to get my way, because there was no one batting for me. Froch was the champion and he had everyone on his side.

'I was gutted because it was taken away from me unfairly. I should have been a champion that night. The first time around, not the fourth. I can't pretend that it never happened.'

Controversy creates cash and there was a truckload of it to be made from a sequel. Groves, incensed more by the manner of defeat than a desire to cash in, chased it immediately.

He was exchanging texts with the relevant parties on the Christmas morning of 2013, but there was still no guarantee of a rematch.

The IBF, who still considered Groves their mandatory challenger, ordered Froch to fight him again within 90 days or vacate their title, deeming Foster's conduct 'inappropriate'.

Matchroom Boxing had staged the first fight and promoter Eddie Hearn wanted to put on the rematch. Groves, who was self-managed before a deal was struck, wanted his fair share.

He lost an appeal to have the purse split in half, with just 15 per cent going to him and 85 per cent to Froch. He still banked £2 million, with the champion getting £8 million.

A venue still needed to be picked and only a big stadium would hold an attendance large enough to maximise their earnings.

Groves wanted Stamford Bridge, where his beloved Chelsea play, but Arsenal's Emirates and Manchester United's Old Trafford grounds were also under consideration.

In the end, the home of the England national team was selected. Wembley Stadium was set to host boxing on 31 May for the first time since it reopened in 2007.

The contestants could now immerse themselves in fight camp and Froch, who had so nearly been made to look a mug before, wasn't about to make the same mistakes again.

Froch said, 'The preparation between the two fights was like chalk and cheese. The second time, I was under pressure. There were all these question marks over me.

'A world title training camp, for me, would normally last 14 weeks. I'd have a fortnight of prep work, pretty much just ticking over, and then a solid 12 with Rob.

'I'd probably do 120 to 150 rounds of sparring and it's not easy stuff. I used Tony Bellew, for example, when we closed the gym up in Sheffield.

'We shut all of the fire doors, pulled all of the curtains up and we had a 12-round war. We were both wobbled and hanging on at points. That was the week before the Groves rematch. That's the sort of intense training that you have to go through to get yourself ready.'

Groves never skipped a beat in training for either date, but could have been forgiven for thinking he'd already fought Froch at the top of his game and taken his best shots.

The occasion was like nothing either man had ever seen, with four times as many fans than were at the first fight. The rest of the country came to a standstill watching on television.

Groves entered the arena in an open top bus, while Froch strolled into the ring as per usual. When the bell sounded, it was back to business.

The declaration from Groves was that he would prevail in three rounds or less and he certainly did try, landing his jab often and putting together combinations.

Froch was trading with him, though, and the crowd were on their feet in the fifth as several clean punches were exchanged between the two.

It was Froch who led the way in round six, with Groves having to battle back and then land a left hook that led to a stumble in the seventh.

Dramatic probably doesn't do the telling blow in the eighth justice. Froch threw a left, which landed on the gloves, meaning Groves was wide open for a right hand that flattened him.

Froch had put an exclamation mark on their rivalry in a round less than their previous meeting, with 17 seconds left in the eighth. There could be no argument this time.

He was ahead on points on this occasion, too, leading 67-66 with two judges while the other went with Groves, 68-65. The finish was as emphatic as they come.

Groves will never forget the magnitude of the occasion and appreciates, in almost all instances, that someone wins and someone loses. He doesn't harp on about it.

Groves said, 'I stuck my chin out and he knocked me into the middle of next week. He stepped across, poured out the left hand and the right was on the target.

'I only knew that after watching it back. I didn't see it coming, I didn't feel it, it was only when I came to and had no idea how many seconds had been counted. I was finished.

'I tried to get to my feet, but I wouldn't have been able to continue that time. I had to hold my hands up – I made a mistake, he got me and that was the end of the fight.

'I felt I was boxing well, up to that point, but it's boxing and these things can and do happen. I'm over it now, life moves on.'

Froch added, 'I was so focused. I got in the ring and I couldn't look Groves in the eye because he winds me up. I turned my back on him for the whole of the announcements. All I wanted to do was show him my gumshield. I'd had a scientific one made that's supposed to realign your jaw and make you punch harder.

'Groves had asked the same company for one, but a stipulation was that they couldn't do it for him if they were supplying mine.

'We got to the centre of the ring and I smiled at him, so he could see it. It's the little things like that which can psyche you out.

'Round one to the finish, there wasn't much happening, it was tit for tat. I felt I was in control, backing him up and hurting him with the body shots.

'He was fading and he was so naive because he'd told everyone at the press conference he'd knock me out with a left hook.

'I saw him go for it in desperation and he moved on to my right hand, in the corner where I needed him. He's dropped his hand and left the door wide open.

'All I had to do was take the shot and, all in one moment, it was like the weight of the world had been lifted off my shoulders, with Groves a crumpled heap on the floor.

'The first fight was the perfect foil for that rematch at Wembley – you couldn't have written the script any better. Even Groves admitted everything happened for a reason.

'For him, it was to get flattened in front of 80,000 fans. It was very satisfying for me to knock out someone as arrogant and disrespectful as that on such a large platform.'

With that ended one of the greatest rivalries in British boxing history. For Froch, that's where the story finished. Groves, though, would create his own happy ending.

CHAPTER TWELVE

BACK FROM THE BRINK – TYSON FURY

TYSON Fury was almost the orchestrator of his own doom before divine intervention saved his life and put him back on the path to former glories.

Never has the adage 'sometimes life gets in the way of boxing' rung so true as when dark clouds started to gather around a man who seemed to have the world at his feet.

His star had been established when he shocked the sport by dethroning Wladimir Klitschko on a memorable winter's night in Germany.

He became the man of the moment, the conqueror of a force that had gone undefeated for 11 years, during which time he had held all but one of the major titles in his division.

Fury stood tall that night in Dusseldorf, with the belts draped across him, revelling in the highest of highs as a stunned pro-Klitschko crowd wondered how it could have happened.

He burst into song under the lights of the arena, belting out the Aerosmith hit 'I Don't Want to Miss a Thing' romantically to his wife. It's a moment neither will forget.

His other half, Paris, was pregnant with Valencia Amber and their other three children – Prince John James, Venezuela and Prince Tyson Fury II – idolised their parents as heroes.

They've since had a fifth child and a fourth son, but much would happen to Fury in the meantime that changed his perspective. Back then, he was clearly a different man.

He had a happy wife, the kids were content and being the heavyweight champion wasn't bad, either. It felt, to all intents and purposes, like 'the Gypsy King' was on top of the world.

He hadn't banked on it all so nearly coming crashing down. Not at the fists of another fighter, who would take the spoils of war through what is the time-honoured tradition.

Demons were sitting on Fury's shoulder and crept into his psyche, perhaps without him even knowing. The damage they caused was more severe than any physical beating he had taken.

The anguish a deterioration in mental health can cause is understood by some, but not all. There's no user manual to repair a mood so low it could plummet to the point of no return.

Most around him knew something was wrong, as did he, but no one could quite put their finger on what. Fury had always been volatile in temperament, but this was no act.

This was all played out in the public eye, and it heightened after Fury became the new superstar of the heavyweight ranks.

His erratic behaviour was not well received and the words that came out of his mouth were only the half of it. Attempts to put his issues on the back burner and fight fell by the wayside.

Klitschko had a rematch clause and had every intention of triggering it. Fury withdrew twice. The first time he cited an ankle injury, the second time he was deemed 'medically unfit'.

In the meantime, it emerged the UK Anti-Doping agency was planning to pursue Fury over a urine sample, taken nine months before he locked horns with Klitschko.

The banned substance nandrolone was alleged to have been found, but rumours of cocaine abuse were also circling. This was suddenly making Fury the bad boy of British boxing.

He never quite went away from the sport but, at points, the notion of him being in any fit state to compete again seemed far-fetched. To him as much as anyone else.

He looked in the mirror and saw how his physical features had changed through ballooning in weight, caused by a lifestyle that contained alcohol and junk food in spades.

This only added to the feeling of worthlessness that would have been there, even if he'd been ripped to shreds with muscle. His confidence, it appeared, had gone and for no visible reason.

Only the all-clear to resume his boxing career got him back on the path to righteousness, after a bitter legal battle with UKAD finally ended.

After one last session in the pub, he no longer sought solace in voices, but getting back in shape would be an achievement in itself.

He would shed over eight stone in the gruelling process that followed, with 32 months elapsing between the night he faced Klitschko and his next bout.

Fury finally climbed through the ropes again at a boisterous Manchester Arena on 9 June 2018, looking more like his old self than most thought possible.

Opponent Sefer Seferi certainly wasn't Klitschko and was overmatched to the point of a fourth-round retirement. But that barely mattered to Fury, whose life had come full circle.

He talked freely about this and the dark times to guests at Bar Sport, many of whom wanted to hear what really happened to Fury in his own words.

He said, 'Nothing terrible had ever happened to me before. Everything was pretty smooth sailing and I'd complain when, really, I didn't have anything to complain about.

'After the fight in Germany [against Klitschko], I couldn't really be bothered with boxing any more. I was going through a lot of pressure and putting myself through a lot of stress.

'I wasn't mentally or physically ready to box again. I'd put up with a lot of stuff and it just felt like nothing was going right for me.

'I was a newly crowned world champion and I felt like a bum. The biggest bum in the country, actually, at 6ft 9in and 19st!

'I had everything a man could ever want, but I was as low as anyone could ever go. It was so bad that I was seconds away from committing suicide.

'I'd go on drinking and drug binges for weeks on end, hoping to die when I was doing it. Bear in mind, this is a man who has got a wife and kids.

'I'm a husband, a father, a son, a man with responsibilities, but I was taking the pantomime villain I portray in the boxing ring home with me.

'I was acting like the craziest person you could ever meet and that's not really me. I say things, do things and act silly sometimes, but it's all a part of the show.

'I was trying to blank it out. I thought that if I went to the pub and got drunk every day, it would make me feel better. It didn't. I was in a worse state than when I started.

'I had money, cars, a big house and a family, but I was so sad and I didn't know what to do about it. I'd never experienced anything like that and I had no idea where to turn.

'I was 28st at my highest, fat as a pig and grossly obese. I could hardly bend down to tie my shoelaces up. I'd be out of breath trying.

'That made me more depressed. On top of that, I was getting accused of things I hadn't done and I just felt like the whole world was against me.

'Whatever I did, it seemed to be wrong. I couldn't get anything right and I almost lost everything I had. They were difficult times.

'It hit me hard and I don't think I could have went [sic] any lower without killing myself. I sought help, after a long period of trying to do it myself.

'My problem was that, over a period of time, I bottled it up and I did it for so long that I just exploded. No one could stop me. I was nearly at the point of no return.

'There were times when I thought I'd end up in a padded room or something, because I was gone and I didn't know what was going on.

'I still couldn't get my head around what was wrong with me and the doctors and psychiatrists told me not to do anything, boxing wise, while that was still the case.

'I took some time off and I was in a pub, coincidentally, in Blackpool and I got a call from Billy Joe Saunders. He's a good pal of mine, who always checks on me to see if I'm alright.

'He was going over to Spain to train and needed some company. I'd had a few drinks and every time that happened, I fancied coming back to boxing again. The next day, it would wear off.

'I'd train for three days and then think, "I've had enough of this now, I'm going to get back on the drink." I just couldn't get to the next chapter of my career.

'I knew the process, but I just kept going down the same roads. I went over to support Billy, but I was going to have a right party as well. I was planning on training with him during the day and having a good time at night, but I got into the routine of it again. All of a sudden, I didn't feel so depressed.

'I had the bit between my teeth again but, even if I was fit again, I couldn't fight anyway because I didn't have a boxing licence anymore.

'Two or three weeks in, I'd lost 3st. It was a start and the bottom line was it was making me feel better about myself, even if I wasn't going to box.

'When we got home, I got a call from my lawyers about my case and a court date. We got there and it was adjourned until December. This was in June.

'I went off on one and was like, "Right, you've done it to me now, I'm going back to the pub, thank you very much and goodbye." I was being an idiot again.

'Even when the case got done and I got my licence back, I thought I'd go out and celebrate. I'd had such a long time of being persecuted by these people and, finally, victory was mine.

'Ultimately, that meant going out drinking again, but I just couldn't get drunk. I'd probably necked half a pint of vodka, but nothing was working.

'I came home, I got down on my knees and I was crying. I had tears running down my face and was asking, "God, please help me to become a better person."

'I thought I understood the world a little bit, I'd been around and done this and that. I knew how things worked, but I never understood the darkness a man can go to.

'I couldn't live like I was any more and I was never going to be a success in boxing again if I was messing around. I stood up and felt a sense of fulfilment.

'It sounds weird, but a weight had been lifted off my shoulders. I went to the bathroom, washed my face, then went to bed.

'I turned over to my wife and said, "Tomorrow morning, I'm going to start training again and, one day, I'll get my world titles back." This was after telling her this about 500 times before.

'On this occasion, she had this look in her eyes like she knew I was being deadly serious. The next day, I went for a run and ended up walking because I was so unfit.

'From there, I set up a programme and stuck to it. It wasn't easy and there was times I put weight back on but, by the end of it, I was so focused and ready to return.

'When everything was in place and I stepped back through those ropes, it meant more to me than beating Klitschko. Through troubled times, just to be stood there was a blessing.'

All the letters of the world seemed to follow Fury's accomplishments when he had his trinket of titles. He was the IBO, IBF, WBO and WBA 'super' world champion.

To call himself the heavyweight champion of the world just once was his life's mission and, whatever happened from there, it was accomplished. Job done.

Fury insisted only the *Ring* magazine strap and his lineal status, which was also on the line against Klitschko, really mattered to him.

He kept hold of it during his spell on the sidelines. It's a slice of history and was first awarded to Jack Dempsey in 1922. It meant an awful lot to Fury. He revels in his role as the upsetter of Klitschko, too, a man previously unbeaten in 11 years who was making an unprecedented 28th world heavyweight title defence.

Fury was well known for mind games and had employed these to great effect in the build-up to the rescheduled contest, which was originally scheduled for 24 October 2015.

It was postponed with Klitschko citing a calf injury and there was no spring in his step come fight night, where Fury was calling the shots even before they touched gloves.

Klitschko had his hands wrapped twice because no one from Fury's team was there to watch it done the first time. There was another difference in opinion about the gloves used.

The audience also saw padding being removed from the ring before the fight. Conspiracy theorists claim it was made bouncier than usual to protect Klitschko's calf.

A capacity crowd of 55,000 then watched as Fury outjabbed, outworked and outmuscled the champion, with Klitschko's well-known right hand rarely connecting.

Fury actually came on stronger in the later rounds, so knew he was well up at the finish. Klitschko stayed in his face, but looked like he couldn't hang with his younger foe.

All three judges picked Fury at the final bell with scores of 115-112 twice and 116-111 in his favour. He'd even had a point docked for punching behind the head in the tenth.

His 25th victory as a professional boxer, while retaining his '0' and remaining undefeated, was definitely his sweetest.

He was interviewed in the Premier Suite by Richie Woodhall, the one pundit who backed him to beat Klitschko from the get-go. Fury's never forgotten that.

He said, 'I started out in boxing as a little boy to become the heavyweight champion of the world. Had it been anything less, I'd have considered it as "I didn't make it."

'I'd won English, Irish, British, Commonwealth and European titles, which were all very good and hard to do, but nothing less than world belts would have been acceptable.

'Even growing up as an amateur, boxing with a headguard for a plastic cup, Wladimir was one of the top boys and my eyes were always set on him.

'I never forgot that, in the all of the years that it took to get there. It was all about opportunity and being in the right place at the right time.

'I have this gift of being able to figure a boxer out quickly and I've always believed I can beat anybody. I don't think I could have lost that night because it was supposed to happen.

'All I had to do was turn up. I kept telling people that and they thought I was crazy. I'd come across him before, people forget that, as I'd been to one of his training camps in Austria.

'I had this expectation that I was going to see some sort of superhero and it was just a man putting a pair of boxing gloves on. These images that you build up are all in the mind.

'In my mind, I knew I could beat him and whether I got lucky or fluked it, or whatever else has been suggested, it was my time to shine.

'His old trainer, the late, great Emanuel Steward, always told me that I'd be the next golden heavyweight after Wladimir. I reminded him about that.

'I was there with Wladimir and Emanuel was thinking, "Right, this is the man who is going to take over, here we are."

'If someone tells you something so much, over and over again, you end up believing it. If I say I'm the greatest 1,000 times – and I never get proved wrong – you'd agree that I was.

'I've got one of those styles that is awkward and, over 12 rounds, an opponent only has 36 minutes to work it out.

'I'm a tall switch hitter who throws punches from all angles, a lunatic running around the ring and, while I'm doing all that, the clock is ticking.

'The ones who have made the mistake of thinking they'll walk straight through me don't appreciate everything comes off the jab. It's not always pretty, but it's effective.

'To offset someone like Wladimir, you have to use something we call in the sweet science a feint. Most heavyweights around today don't know anything about it or have forgotten.

'I threw so many in the first round that he didn't know whether my punches were coming from New York, Mars or wherever. He just stood there, with a funny look on his face.

'When you get two fighters who stand back, it becomes a chess match. Maybe that's what happened, to a degree, against Wladimir.

'Even though I'd won most of the rounds, I still looked at the sky and thought "Please God, don't let me get robbed here in Germany tonight." All I wanted was for the result to be fair.

'I was waiting for Michael Buffer to say "and the new", and he didn't. He went "from the United Kingdom". I thought he was going to say "from the United Ukraine" or something!

'I'll remember that moment until the day I die. You'd have to go back a long way to see someone go and beat an odds-on favourite and go home with all of his belts.

'Klitschko was my Mount Everest. I did something I wasn't supposed to do and did it pretty easy. He couldn't lay a glove on me.

'I didn't lose the titles because someone was a better boxer than me, I lost them because I lost my mind.

'I've never been bothered about belts, they don't keep me warm at night. The only one that's ever mattered to me was the *Ring* magazine belt, because that's the Holy Grail.

'There was a rematch clause with him, but I didn't think anyone was really that interested in seeing it. A rematch is only an attraction if the first fight was close.

'That chapter is closed now. It's done and I'm not looking back to it. I'm writing new chapters and there's plenty left.'

What Fury may never repair is the offence caused by some of his rants about sexuality, equality and religion, many of which were thought to be ill-advised.

He stands by most of what he said and is of the opinion that it got blown out of all proportion. One MP, Chris Bryant, even accused him of promoting the bullying of homosexuals.

Bryant is a gay man, a fellow Christian and a former vicar. A challenge for a head-to-head exchange of views was wisely refused.

A petition to have Fury removed from the shortlist for the 2015 BBC Sports Personality of the Year award reached 30,000 signatures in just two days.

He caused more uproar with a comment that fellow nominee Jessica Ennis-Hill 'slaps up good', which had the organisers cringing.

Fury attended the ceremony and came fourth behind Andy Murray, rugby ace Kevin Sinfield and, ironically, Ennis-Hill. Fury even finished ahead of Formula One's Lewis Hamilton.

Fury took to the stage during the event and issued a heartfelt speech to all concerned. To this day, there are only elements of the situation he's sorry about.

He said, 'I've come out with a lot of stuff in the past and none of it is with the intention to hurt anybody. It's all a bit tongue in cheek.

'The one regret I did have was I didn't mean anything to one person, like "You're this and you're this", but that might have been how it came across.

'I made general comments about my beliefs and I'm a boxer; I'm not interested in politics or anything else. If you're looking for a "yes man", that's not me.

'I'm a Christian man, not a sexist, racist or bigot, and I would never intentionally hurt someone's feelings. People know now it was years ago and the place I was in then.

'It's not an excuse but it's not the first time heightened media scrutiny has caused me to act out in public and it might not be the last. It all stemmed from me quoting the Bible, which I clearly didn't write. If I'm a devout Christian, I have to believe what the scriptures tell me. Some of the criticism was ridiculous.

'One of the things I got slammed for was saying a woman [Ennis-Hill] looked good in a dress. Why is that bad? Men don't look that good in dresses!

'Are sportswomen not allowed to wear dresses? Do they have to be treated like men? If I'm going to get in trouble for paying women compliments, what has the world come to?

'I wasn't interested in winning BBC Sports Personality of the Year anyway. I've got more personality in the end of my little finger than the rest of the nominations put together.

'What personality does it take to run around the track 100 times? Or hit a ball back and forth? I was the only one with any personality. Those experiences taught me that, when you're on top of the world, everyone wants to bring you down. That's not nice, but it's a fact of life.

'I have my personal beliefs and I should be entitled to them. If anyone wants to dispute that, they should take a look at themselves.'

There was less than a month between his dance with Klitschko and the BBC gong being handed out. Even in that timeframe, he'd been stripped of IBF status.

The rematch clause with Klitschko had prevented Fury from fighting anyone else and the IBF had ordered Vyacheslav Glazkov to challenge for their title.

Glazkov never got to the belt as he was beaten by Charles Martin in just three rounds after suffering a leg injury. That brought in Eddie Hearn and Anthony Joshua.

A deal was struck for Martin to come to England the following April for Joshua's first world title fight. In just his 16th pro outing, 'AJ' flattened Martin in two rounds.

The WBO made noises about wanting their belt back in October. It was then won by Joseph Parker that December. By the time Fury was back boxing, Joshua had it.

Fury was still well over a year away from his comeback and, when that came close, he needed a new team to guide him in and out of the ring.

He'd split with long-term manager Mick Hennessy, along with trainer and uncle Peter Fury. Both were people he relied upon.

There was no one left by his side to guide him back into business, which brought in new coach Ben Davison and an old ally in Frank Warren.

Fury and Warren had had an on-off relationship in the past, but there was still an element of trust there. The same could not be said of Hearn.

There were already pre-disposed views from Fury about Hearn, none of which changed after they started to talk terms about him coming under new management.

The focal point of conversations was to build towards a fight between Fury and Joshua, but Fury was never going to settle for anything less than a 50-50 split of the purse.

Fury revealed that he wasn't exactly blown away by what Hearn had in mind to get him back in the mix, either.

Travis Kauffman was an unheralded but experienced opponent from the US, while Tony Bellew and Dillian Whyte were Hearn's two biggest heavyweight draws behind Joshua.

Fury wanted no part of Bellew, arguing that facing a man who had spent most of his career boxing two divisions below at light-heavyweight served no purpose.

He had more to lose than win had he agreed to go up against Whyte, who wasn't regarded as anywhere near world class at that point.

He was of the opinion that Hearn didn't actually want Fury to fight Joshua, either, and feared he would move the goalposts if he got through the promoter's chosen trio.

Fury has been outspoken in his criticism of Hearn for quite some time, but you never say never in boxing. However, Fury insists it's more than money that talks.

He said: 'Eddie is a good promoter, I'll give him that, and he's made Joshua from the start to becoming a world champion.

'If I'd have joined their team then, they'd have treated me like cannon fodder for him and I don't play second fiddle to anybody. I'm not just an opponent.

'I know what Eddie had in mind for me – Bellew, Whyte and Joshua, hoping one of them would shut me up for good.

'Eddie offered me a three-fight deal. One of them was to fight an American, Travis Kauffman, then Whyte and on to Joshua. We couldn't agree terms on Joshua.

'I'm a straight man, I've never tried to rob or scam anybody, and I don't need to prove myself. All I want is fair play and, if I get that, I'm the easiest person to deal with.

'If me and you went to work, I'd give you a fair share of whatever we made. I could write my contract on the palm of my hand, that's how easy my list of demands are.

'I didn't feel like there was much for me to do after I beat Klitschko. Joshua and Wilder were just hot air at the time.

'Then Joshua and Klitschko ended up boxing for my titles, while I was having problems, and I was watching them on television. They took the IBF title from me seven days after I won it and gave it to some fighter from America [Martin]. It was robbed off me and bought for Joshua.

'He only became the champion because of me. I went to Germany and got those belts off Klitschko. I haven't heard a "thank you" for that.

'Klitschko was a broken man when he fought "AJ". He was trying to come back from a humiliating loss as an old slugger.

'It was an excellent fight, entertaining and enjoyable and, believe it or not, I was screaming for "AJ" to smash him.

'It was exciting for a boxing fan, and it was good for me. Joshua got bounced off the canvas and had a lot of miles put on the clock.

'He got exposed, too, and everybody knew from then that he's not invincible any more. He didn't land a punch for three rounds.

'Klitschko let him off the hook. It was like he didn't want to knock him out. Had Emanuel Steward been in the corner and not his brother, good old Vitali, he'd have finished him off.

'I was one of the first to congratulate Joshua on Twitter, but I had to remind him he had a life-or-death battle with Klitschko and I played with the guy.

'Klitschko detonated right hand after right hand on my jaw and never wobbled me once. You saw what he did to Joshua with the same punch. You could see that Joshua was a pumped-up weightlifter who just looks for one punch. It rarely ever comes when you're looking for it. He's a boxer's dream.'

It's already been quite an existence for Fury and he's been defying the norm since birth. He was born two and a half months premature, weighing next to nothing.

He was named after Mike Tyson, the heavyweight legend who was in his pomp at the time. The Fury name is of Gaelic origin and the family are of Irish traveller heritage.

They are a boxing clan and his father, John Fury, fought bare knuckle and then as a pro in the 1980s. His son would follow suit.

Young Tyson wanted to box at an Olympic Games, but nemesis David Price was ahead of him in the pecking order for England.

He used his roots to try and qualify for Ireland, who didn't select him for the 2008 Olympics. He won the one amateur title he'd always wanted, the senior ABAs, and turned pro that year.

Fury could even look back from troubled points of his time out from boxing and see he'd only ever lost four fights in his life.

The last amateur opponent to have his hand raised at Fury's expense was Russia's Maxim Babanin, who outpointed him in the 2007 European Junior Championships.

In the same year, he'd also been downed by Ivan Bezverkhiy, in his adversary's home country of Ukraine, on his way to becoming a Donbass Junior Cup silver medallist.

His other two defeats came in the 2006 World Junior Championships to Uzbekistan's Sandor Abdullayev and David Price, the latter the only fellow Englishman to do so.

His amateur record finished with 31 wins, 26 by TKO, and four defeats. A decade later, Fury had still to lose another fight.

He boxed for the English title in only his eighth pro contest, in which a points victory over John McDermott could easily have gone the other way.

The 98-92 verdict awarded to Fury by referee Terry O'Connor was borderline ridiculous and the British Boxing Board of Control ordered them to fight again.

Fury silenced McDermott by ninth-round TKO in the rematch and then built towards a feud with Dereck Chisora for the British and Commonwealth titles.

He beat Chisora unanimously on points with resounding scores of 117-112 twice and 118-111. Both were unbeaten, so a first blemish on the ledger of 'Del Boy' went with it.

Winning the Irish title in his 18th pro contest meant something to Fury and halting Martin Rogan in the fifth served as a good result.

Recording a similar victory over Vinny Maddalone in his next outing landed Fury the WBO inter-continental bauble and pushed him towards boxing for their full title.

Fury's US debut in fight 21 was fraught with danger, even though he'd travelled abroad before, scoring an eight-round points success over Zack Page in Quebec, Canada.

Facing Steve Cunningham at Madison Square Garden was another thing entirely, with Fury rebounding from the verge of defeat to win.

He had to climb off the floor in the second round to knock out Cunningham in the seventh when behind on two scorecards.

Fury hadn't tested himself against a big name at that point, but it wasn't for lack of trying. He still holds little regard for David Haye, who twice pulled out of a match against him.

A sequel with Chisora saw his opponent retired on his stool at the start of the tenth as Fury captured the European title. He then called out Klitschko immediately afterwards.

Fury said, 'There's not much about heavyweight boxing that I don't know. I've studied it for the last 15 years. I know every fighter, their stance, their strengths and their weaknesses.

'You have the type that can end your dreams, even if you're rounds and rounds ahead on the scorecards. I just stick my head on their chest.

'I first met Mike Tyson in New York a few years ago. I'd had the chance to meet him before, but it never materialised.

'I told him it was an honour to be named after someone like him and he said he'd always supported me and how proud he was of me.

'A lot of people talk a good fight but when it comes to it, face to face and man to man, it's a different story. To me, it isn't just business.

'If I wanted to fight a man, I wouldn't need a boxing ring. If it meant that much to me, I'd do it in the street if I had to. I know how it would go because I've already seen it in my mind.

'When I go out to the ring, I'll have been on plenty of sunbeds and I'll be in good shape. I'll rub a bit of baby oil over my body, so I glisten under the lights!

'I never lose eye contact with my opponent for one second, from when I see him until the bell goes. If my opponent can't do the same, I know I've got him.

'God's given me the talent, the ability to move, twist, bend, slip and counter. It's unusual. I defy the rules of gravity. Someone my size should not be able to do the things I do.

'I'm one of the hardest punchers in heavyweight boxing, but they don't know it yet. The rest of them are slugfesters, they haven't got a boxing brain cell between them all.

'Someone asked Cunningham what is was like to fight me and he said it was like fighting three men with a fridge freezer stuck on top of you.

'I was behind on the cards against him, having climbed off the canvas, and I knew I needed a knockout to win. I pulled it out of the fire.

'I've got the traveller background, bare knuckle fighting, the guts, bravery and the honour. People say I'm arrogant and I am, because I believe I'm the best.'

Seeing Fury back to himself, with a fresh perspective, allows him to be candid about his struggles and offer advice to those who have been in, or are in, the same boat.

A captivated Bar Sport was both saddened and inspired during his speech. All guests at the Premier Suite agreed they were relieved the story had something close to a happy ending.

Time will tell if Fury can keep up the good work and there's likely to be another transitional period when he hangs up his gloves.

His adage is that you can see the positives in anything if you look hard enough, and Fury will take the brunt of whatever comes his way from here wearing a wry smile.

He said, 'To come from where I'd come from, not knowing if I was going to see the week out, never mind fight again, I'm over the moon.

'Everyone told me it wasn't possible and I had so much against me, but I've turned it around and proved so many people wrong.

'I needed to fight again – for me, to give me that peace of mind. If I can come back from that, it shows that others can do the same.

'I'd been through an horrific experience that I wouldn't wish on my worst enemy. It was worse than 25 training camps back to back!

'There's no shame in depression, it doesn't make you any less of a man, and I want anyone who is going through the same thing to know that.

'The game has changed. You can never look back at the past because nothing is the same. My outlook on life is different now.

'I know what it feels like to be written off, but everyone loves an underdog. I'll find a way to succeed, like I always have done.

'Before, I was just a sportsman but through all the trials and tribulations, I've grown into a real person. I think most people can relate to what I've been through.

'My message is that you can always overcome problems and for me to come back has got to be a statement that you can fight for mental health.

'Boxing is like a marriage – you have to work at it. You do fall in and out of love. We are back at it, better than ever. It's my medicine.

'I'm back with a vengeance and it's almost like I've got a second career. I feel rejuvenated. It's took a lot of sacrifice, will, drive, determination and a little bit of luck, too.

'I've found an inner peace and happiness within. I believe I'm more popular now than when I first became a world champion.

'The appeal is that I'm just a normal person, one of the lads. I've come through the hardest fight of my life and if anyone can do it, the magic man can do it.

'I've started afresh, let go of the past and I'm concentrating on the future. I'm happy. All of the money, fame and glory in the world means nothing if you're not happy.'

So that's the new and improved Tyson Fury. He's been to hell and back and it's a journey he only plans on doing once.

It would only take two fights before he was back in the world title picture, with a ten-round points whitewash over Francesco Pianeta proving to be his last warm-up.

He would establish himself in the US, most probably once and for all, even if he failed to rip the WBC belt from Deontay Wilder.

Fury put in a performance that was boxing brilliance, at times, but also found himself on the floor twice against the most dangerous puncher in the division.

The second knockdown, which looked crucial in the 12th round, looked to have rendered him unconscious, but he stunned all that were watching when he rose to beat the count.

Scores of 115-111 for Wilder, which most onlookers disputed, 114-112 for Fury and a 113-113 draw made it a split decision stalemate. A rematch would not be forthcoming.

Fury has boxed Stateside again since and this time lit up Las Vegas, donning the full Apollo Creed garb before he wiped out Tom Schwarz in two.

More singing in the ring followed, as 'the Gypsy King' further became the people's champion. Coming back from the brink has never looked sweeter.

This does not appear to be the end of the road. What appears certain is that Fury has and will continue to inspire people fighting their own personal demons. Long may he reign.